FURTHER UP AND FURTHER IN

Orthodox Conversations with C. S. Lewis
on Scripture and Theology

Further Up
and
Further In

Orthodox Conversations with C. S. Lewis
on Scripture and Theology

E D I T H M. H U M P H R E Y

ST VLADIMIR'S SEMINARY PRESS
YONKERS, NY 10707
2017

Library of Congress Cataloging-in-Publication Data

Names: Humphrey, Edith Mary, author.

Title: Further up and further in : Orthodox conversations with C. S. Lewis on scripture and theology / Edith M. Humphrey.

Description: Yonkers, NY : St Vladimir's Seminary Press, 2017.

Identifiers: LCCN 2017023521 (print) | LCCN 2017024941 (ebook) | ISBN 9780881415988 | ISBN 9780881415971 (print)

Subjects: LCSH: Lewis, C. S. (Clive Staples), 1898–1963—Religion. | Religion and literature. | Orthodox Eastern Church—Doctrines.

Classification: LCC PR6023.E926 (ebook) | LCC PR6023.E926 Z695 2017 (print) | DDC 823/.912—dc23

LC record available at https://lccn.loc.gov/2017023521

Drawing of Reepicheep the mouse on the half title page by Joëlle Alice Sykes, the author's daughter.

COPYRIGHT © 2017

ST VLADIMIR'S SEMINARY PRESS

575 Scarsdale Rd, Yonkers, NY 10707

1–800–204–2665

www.svspress.com

ISBN 978–0-88141–597–1 (paper)

ISBN 978–0-88141–598–8 (electronic)

PRINTED IN THE UNITED STATES OF AMERICA

For the twelve (and any more whom the Lord may add):

Madeleine, Katherine, Rachael, Naomi, James, Isaiah,

William, Gideon, Sophia, Susanna, Andrew, and Julianna

Table of Contents

Preface

I finish this manuscript on the hopeful feast of the Conception of the Forerunner John. This seems particularly apt, because the entire book is, in a sense, about one who can run before *us,* helping us to see things that we may not have seen, or to see them in a new light so that they come alive.

I regularly suggest two small books to friends who are inquiring about spiritual matters. One I offer to those who are preparing for ministry: Fr Alexander Schmemann's luminous *For the Life of the World.* That book was instrumental in bringing me to the Orthodox faith, with my many questions and difficulties about what it had to say about the nature of the holy mysteries and the Church. The other book has long been a travelling companion since my late teens, and I give it to anyone who is not yet convinced that Jesus is the Lord: C. S. Lewis's *Mere Christianity.*

But I loved Lewis long before reading that book. Indeed, as an ill child in the earliest levels of school, I spent many delightful hours, though resting, with the *Chronicles of Narnia.* I even wrote to C. S. Lewis in February of 1964 asking if he could please write some more; I was devastated to receive a letter from Walter Hooper informing me that my favorite author had passed away the same day as John F. Kennedy's assassination, a few months earlier. Fortunately, these novels are of the sort that they can be reread with great enjoyment, and I have done this, first as a child, then as a mother, and now as a grandmother of twelve. Within a few years after my disappointment that there were no more books on Narnia forthcoming, I was old enough to enjoy his Space (or Cosmic) Trilogy and *The Screwtape Letters*; I tried to read *The Great Divorce* and *Till We Have Faces* long before I was ready to do so.

As an adolescent I was all too eager to climb with him, both up to the cliffs and down to the valleys and caves. But I was unprepared. In teaching a course on C. S. Lewis and the Bible at Pittsburgh Theological Seminary, I have discovered that many otherwise keen adults are similarly unprepared. We live in an age when logic and rhetoric are not taught in schools, let alone classical texts. For many, Lewis may be a reader's very first introduction not only to Greek mythology, but also Platonic philosophy, and the Church fathers. To read him with full profit, one needs a classical education—something that is a rare commodity today!

Many of the best books can be read on different levels. When my two oldest girls were listening to the books of Lewis at bedtime, they both loved the stories, despite their gap of three years. The oldest caught the biblical allusions; the youngest tracked with the story and the humor. And their mother enjoyed the books the best, I think, because she appreciated the full scope and the artistry. (Besides, I have never really grown up!) Some treks, however, are simply too difficult, though we may gaze at the snow-covered mountaintops, or long to go spelunking. For this reason, I write this book as a guide to help us follow Lewis, our guide, as he leads us into difficult territory. His more neglected books— *The Silver Chair, The Pilgrim's Regress, The Great Divorce, Till We Have Faces*, and *That Hideous Strength*—tackle less well-known philosophical and theological matters, and lead us to portions of the Scripture that have been debated by many. We will read these books, along with others (consider the Table of Contents for an inventory) that help us to trace the path, comparing what Lewis says alongside Scripture, the Church fathers, and more contemporary authors, both faithful and problematic.

I do not assume, then, that any of my readers will have an exhaustive knowledge of any of these matters—for neither do I. Instead, I write as one who has come on a long journey, from a childhood in the Salvation Army, then into the Anglican Communion (interrupted by a brief sojourn in a nondenominational Church), and finally embracing the Orthodox faith. I hope that my familiarity with different worshipping communities and my love for Christian brothers and sisters of various communities have made my writing welcoming to friends beyond the Orthodox Church. Many of the difficulties that evangelicals face with some of Lewis's books spring from his concern to tell the *whole* of the faith that we have received, including those teachings (like purification after death and *theōsis*) that seem to have been jettisoned in the Protestant Reformation.

Other pious readers continue to worry, especially in this day when the fantasy genre has been revived, that Lewis's imaginative flair is not an apt vehicle for godly theology: what have witches, wizards, and pagan mythology to do with Christ? And more progressive readers may be tempted to dismiss him as a relic of the past for his steady concentration upon miracles, atonement, and the justice of God. My prayer is that this study will make such matters clearer. Readers can decide for themselves whether Lewis has sometimes crossed a line or become a dinosaur, or whether he is instead recovering shining strands in the fabric of the Christian faith that have been forgotten in some quarters. That his work has fascinated such a varied audience—irreligious, evangelical, mainline Protestant, Catholic, and Orthodox—should be a clue that he has better spiritual eyesight than most!

In my final preparation of this study, I have been helped by many friends from various Christian traditions, all of whom have made valuable suggestions and urged me to further clarify complex matters. Thanks are especially due to to the sensitive and incisive work of Fr Ignatius Green at St Vladimir's Press, to enthusiastic students at Pittsburgh Theological Seminary who studied Lewis with me in several classes, to my Orthodox brother Curtis Magnuson and my fellow Orthodox New Testament colleague Leslie Baynes (with whom I have had absorbing discussions on Lewis and other subjects), to Sean and

Andrea Hall, who read the entire manuscript and commented from a Reformed perspective, to Richard and Faye D'Ippolito, who met with me monthly and offered their encouragement from yet another Protestant stance, and to the inimitable Fr Sean Taylor, without whose probing guidance this book would have missed the mark in innumerable ways. To these friends, along with my older grandchildren who indulge me as I read Narnia aloud with them, I am deeply grateful.

My advice is that the reader *not* use this book like a set of *Cliffs* (or in Canada, *Coles*) *Notes*. That will kill the books and make a drudgery out of something that should bring joy. Besides, the three sections, with their three subsections, are meant to build upon each other, introducing the theological themes that Lewis touches upon in *various* books, not just the one being highlighted in each particular discussion. So then, it is best to read Lewis's books *first,* if at all possible—though I will try not to put too many spoilers in. Then, engage with me in discussion as I read them with you. If you like (and I am sure you will want to), then return to his books and see what emerges!

Even in rereading these pieces, with which I have lived for close to half a century, I have learned things I did not see before. Why? Because these are not Lewis's novel ideas, but windows and doors onto ancient vistas. Lewis was motivated by a joyful longing, and throughout his life he was intent to learn as much of the faith given to us by Christ, the apostles, and the Church fathers as he could. It is the richness of his subject matter and his desire not to overshadow this by artistic arrogance, that give his guidance its worth. All the while we travel with him to heights and depths, further up and further into the Faith, we only rarely think of *him* and his abilities, but instead concentrate upon what we are seeing. (Yet, as my recent trip to Ireland taught me, a guide with wit and knowledge makes a bracing travelling companion.) When all is said and done, a good mentor points the way without calling attention to himself. I have tried to do the same.

The Conception of the Forerunner John, 2016

Part I

MAPPING THE TERRAIN

"Creatures, I give you yourselves. . . .
I give you the woods, the fruits, the rivers. I give you the stars
and I give you myself."
(Aslan to the Narnians)

CHAPTER I

Lewis and Reepicheep: Reality and Mythology, Writing and Reading

("An Experiment in Criticism" and other essays)

Any child who reaches the end of the *Chronicles of Narnia* is delighted to be met, along with the Pevensie children, by Reepicheep. That dauntless mouse, in an earlier adventure aboard the *Dawn Treader*, had found the sweet waters of the "utter east," had drunk deeply of them, and sailed off ahead into Aslan's country, safe and "alive there,"[1] waiting for them (and us). As the children in *The Last Battle* enter the huge country beyond the stable door, they are led by Jewel, the unicorn, until finally they come to a walled garden. As the gates open, they are greeted by Reepicheep, who welcomes them "in the Lion's name," and urges them "further up and further in."[2] The mouse invites them to enter a place that is (to borrow a saying from that hipster-series *Doctor Who*) "bigger on the inside than the outside." This small creature, their forerunner into that wondrous land, leads them onwards. Reepicheep is a living gift from Aslan for the final leg of their final journey.

Since childhood, I have claimed Reepicheep's creator, C. S. Lewis, as my mentor, fondly imagining in Anne-of-Green-Gables style, that he is a "kindred spirit." On November 29, 1898, Clive Staples Lewis

[1] *The Voyage of the Dawn Treader* in *The Chronicles of Narnia* (1952; repr., New York: HarperEntertainment, 2005), 540.
[2] *The Last Battle* in *Chronicles* (1956; 2005), 763.

was born, like my grandmother's people, in Belfast; he died the same day as President John Kennedy—November 22, 1963. His life of nearly sixty-five years, less than the biblical "three score and ten" (seventy), was astonishingly fruitful. Lewis has been taken as a guide not only by me, but by young and old, as well as by Christians (and even non-Christians) from decidedly different communities. Even though he was a life-long Anglican, some have wondered if Lewis might not be an "anonymous Eastern Orthodox"; indeed, leaders as honored as Metropolitan Kallistos (Ware) have documented many places where he is in harmony with an Orthodox theology and approach. The knightly mouse Reepicheep, with all his idiosyncrasies, is the exploring pilgrim who compels the children "further up and further in." Similarly, for many Lewis has become an unexpected guide to adventure, excellence in writing, careful thought about the faith, and exuberant celebration of Christ and the world (or worlds) created through that One who took on everything that it is to be human.

Unusually for one with a Protestant background, Lewis himself was well aware of the importance of closely following those with more experience in the fraught issues of life. As a professor of literature, he used the model of Dante (who had his mentors Virgil and Beatrice), or of Bunyan, who offered to the reader the guide aptly named "Christian." There were, of course, such *psychopomps* ("guides of souls") in literature before the Christian era. In the classical precedents, these were invariably gods, goddesses, or other supernatural beings who led the living or the dead into unseen realms. However, essential to the life of the Church, as Lewis points out in numerous ways, is the interdependence of Christians upon each other: to be fully alive and human in Christ is to depend upon others and to be depended upon. Left to ourselves, and to our own devices and desires, our "arrows" of prayer, which Lewis pictures in a sonnet, may well shoot wide of the mark. We tend to imagine God other than He is: we "dream of fancies" that are not God Himself.[3] Indeed, we also imagine reality other than it is, preferring our own easy version, or blinkering our eyes, so that we cannot see God's creation in all its complexity:

> He whom I bow to only knows to whom I bow
> When I attempt the ineffable Name, murmuring Thou,
> And dream of Pheidian fancies and embrace in heart
> Symbols (I know) which cannot be the thing Thou art.
> Thus always, taken at their word, all prayers blaspheme . . .
> . . . . Unless
> Thou in magnetic mercy to Thyself divert
> Our arrows, aimed unskillfully, beyond desert. . . .[4]

In order to see Him more and more clearly, and to glimpse where we stand in this huge cosmos, we need the Lord to redirect our prayers, drawing them magnetically to Himself, rather than towards idols who cannot hear. Seemingly, God's most characteristic way of correcting our path is through other pilgrims who have been where we now stand.

In fact, this is the argument of the New Testament book of Hebrews, which reveals Jesus to us as the eldest brother (though he is also the Almighty God) who has gone ahead by the way of the cross, blazing the trail for us. Curiously, though, his role as the great forerunner does not render all other guides insignificant, just as his role as the great

---

[3]In following the Bible, tradition, and Lewis himself, I will not avoid the masculine pronoun for God. Instead, by using the capital letter I will register that this is a special use, not intended to suggest that God is a human "male." I hope that my feminist and pro-feminist friends will not be distracted by this move, but will understand it as a recovery of Jesus' own prayer-language for "Abba." It is difficult to evaluate what has been lost in the habits of this "gender-inclusive" era. Further to this discussion is Lewis's own consideration of gendered language and metaphor, seen in the final section of this book.

[4]"Footnote to All Prayers" in C. S. Lewis, *Poems* (London: Geoffrey Bles, 1964; rpt. New York: Harcourt Brace Jovanovich, 1977). Pheidias was a fifth century B. C. sculptor, who represented the gods, using himself or other renowned people as his models. His statue of Zeus at Olympia was one of the Seven Wonders of the Ancient World. Each of us is prone to "create God in our own image," however cunning our image-making!

high Priest does not nullify the priesthood of believers, nor the bridge-making work of those set apart as pastors in the Church. Rather, as the blessed Augustine points out in his preface to *On Doctrine*, we see God's *modus operandi* everywhere: He commits Saul into the very hands of those Christians whom that zealot was intending to persecute; during his ministry, Jesus appoints apostles; they appoint elders and deacons; St Philip is whisked to the chariot of the Ethiopian; we are told to pray for one other. The "communion of saints," then, involves interdependence, which requires both mutuality and due respect for those more experienced in godly matters.

Unsurprisingly, guides to help the pilgrim characters (and the readers) pop up everywhere in Lewis's writings. From the simplest *Chronicles of Narnia* (where we encounter Reepicheep and Puddleglum) to complex works such as *Pilgrim's Regress* (where we meet Vertue and Mother Kirk) and *The Great Divorce* (where the narrator has his George MacDonald), we are not alone. Indeed, in the *Great Divorce,* every soul not yet at home in paradise is greeted by a personal guide. We have need of those who lead, because of the challenging "topography"—shining high cliffs that beckon *and* threaten, deep waters to cross, seemingly impenetrable swamps, caves where the light is hardly seen, and gates or doors to pass through.

Back in the mid-twentieth century when contemporary English versions of the Bible were not so plentiful, the noted English author J. B. Phillips composed a vivid (if slightly loose) translation of the New Testament, which has helped many, including me. Once, when stalled in the project at a difficult point in his life, he reveals that he was encouraged to finish the translation during two visions of C. S. Lewis, whom he had barely met while Lewis was living, and who had already fallen asleep in the Lord not long before. Lewis spoke just one short sentence to Phillips: "J. B., it's not as hard as you think, you know!"[5]

[5]Details of Phillip's twin experience are given in Marie A. Conn, *C. S. Lewis and Human Suffering: Light Among the Shadows* (Mahwah, NJ: Hidden Spring, 2008), 1.

Some have, of course, looked askance at Phillips's story, especially those whose understanding of the Church does not include a living communion of saints whereby such communication is possible—or even lawful! However, prayer and encouragement between the living and the dead who are in Christ is no novel idea, nor should it be feared as an attempt to manipulate God or to be involved in necromancy. Rather, both in the East and in the West, intercommunion between the living and those unseen who are "in the Lord" has for almost twenty centuries been understood as a mystery that expresses the unified nature of the Church. Indeed, it need not alarm even Protestants if they see it as an extension of the mediating prayer that they now exercise for the living. After all, Jesus said, regarding Abraham, Isaac, and Jacob and the resurrection: God "is not the God of the dead, but the living" (Mt 22.32).

Lewis had his own mentors—men as varied as St Athanasius and Scottish author George MacDonald. In our turn, Lewis may serve as a helpful guide for us in many matters, for he has imbibed deeply of the waters of the Scriptures and the Church fathers. Though Lewis is much beloved, some can be left cold or confused by his more obscure or complex books. Certainly, he does not avoid engaging with various difficult doctrines in the biblical and patristic Tradition: these more demanding books and teachings are the main focus of this book.

I suspect that had Lewis written in an Eastern Christian context, those very books that have caused concern, such as *The Great Divorce,* or *The Last Battle,* would have been received enthusiastically. It is frequently just where he has jostled Protestant sensibilities that he is most misunderstood—for example, where his plots suggest that there may be opportunity, for those who have not explicitly rejected Christ in this life, to turn to the truth after death. This is not to say that Orthodox will agree with everything that Lewis has written: for example, one cannot expect to hear an Orthodox account of ecclesiology from an Anglican. But there are many places where the teachings of the Fathers—those very teachings left behind in the Reformation or by the contemporary world—shine forth in his works. For Orthodox in their current Western contexts, he is likely to be an invaluable guide, with whom we may have a deep and fruitful conversation while we trek homewards. For Catholics and Protestants, there is no need to plead his relevance: many have fruitfully taken him as a guide and travelling companion and learned much, even when they may, in some details, disagree.

Before we begin, we may ask: What kind of a man was C. S. Lewis, who led and inspired so many? As was common for British boys in his day, he was educated both by his tutor and in a private school. This formation left both positive and negative marks upon him, providing much material for his writing. Particularly he was indebted to the hard-nosed but brilliant atheist W. T. Kirkpatrick (whom he called "The Knock"), whose tutoring helped to shape Lewis into the formidable apologist he finally became. However, his "day job" was teaching literature, first in Magdalen College, Oxford, and in later years, at Cambridge University. His speciality in medieval literature is not nearly as known or celebrated as his radio talks, Christian apologetics, and fantasy novels—especially the children's series *The Chronicles of Narnia*. But his work as a professor clearly informed those endeavors, too.

Most know that Lewis ran in a circle of friends known as the Inklings, which included J. R. R. Tolkien (*The Hobbit, The Lord of the Rings*), the whimsical Charles Williams (*The Place of the Lion,* among other fabulous novels), and others. Tolkien, indeed, was a major influence in Lewis's conversion from atheism to "theism" (the belief that there is a personal God), and finally to Christianity. He did not join Tolkien in the Roman Catholic Church, but remained, like Williams, "a very ordinary layman of the Church of England."[6] In his later years, this confirmed bachelor married the American writer Joy Davidman, who died four years after their marriage, at the age of forty-five. Prior to his marriage, he did not live alone, but in a curiously composed

[6]Preface to *Mere Christianity* (Glasgow: Collins Fount Paperbacks, 1984), 6. *Mere Christianity* was first published in three parts over 1942–44.

household at "the Kilns" (near Oxford) with his brother "Warnie," and the mother of a friend who had died in the war, and for whom he had promised to care. Perhaps the unusual nature of his domestic arrangement influenced the memorable household that he creates in his novel *That Hideous Strength*. Undoubtedly, his time with Joy Davidman moved him from the earlier brilliant (but analytical) treatment of the fallen world in *The Problem of Pain* to his more trenchant and personally vulnerable *A Grief Observed*.

At this point I can almost hear Lewis spinning in his grave—if that is, indeed, where he is, which I doubt! For Lewis would wonder why I should begin a book on his works and the Bible with a biographical note, and be concerned that I was explaining away his work through false psychologizing. He believed strongly in the following precept of the school of literature that has been called "The New Literary Criticism": a work of art is *not* to be approached by trying to understand its author's subjective experience! Lewis and the major proponent of this movement, T. S. Eliot, differed greatly over what constituted good poetry—and they admitted to this disagreement. But both insisted that to know an author's personal life is not the same as understanding his or her work. They resisted any whiff of psychologizing a writer's works: the idea that by probing a writer's psyche one could claim to have truly interpreted and mastered that author's writings.[7] It was an example of "the personal heresy" if any student or critic exclaimed, "Obviously, he wrote that *because* he was brought up in a terrible family or a repressive school environment." With Eliot, Lewis was appalled at the presumption that a poem or work of art deals mainly with what is going on inside the author's head, or, even worse, his feelings. Even an introspective piece has an outside focus, and should not be summed up by subjective explanation.

---

[7]Intrigued readers may compare T. S. Eliot's essay "Tradition and the Individual Talent" (1919) with what Lewis says in "The Personal Heresy in Criticism" (1934).

Why was this war on "subjectivism" so very important to Lewis? Simply because, independent of our feelings and limitations, he recognized a reality outside our heads—or perhaps we should say a Truth, by which we are governed, with all our opinions and misapprehensions. This repudiation of the modern tendency to dismiss all opinions as Freudian projections of the speaker, and this cleaving to an objective reality, formed a fundamental bond between Eliot and Lewis. That bond was enough, it seems, to heal the personal breaches between them. And so, despite his inability to appreciate the strange poem, *The Love Song of J. Alfred Prufrock,* with its "patient aetherized upon a table," Lewis declared, "I agree with Eliot on matters of such great importance that all literary questions are trivial in comparison."[8] Later, he even said that he loved Eliot. Eliot returned the compliment when Joy died, by influencing Faber and Faber to publish Lewis's poignant *A Grief Observed* in 1961.

With this caution against thinking one can primarily understand a work of art or writing by recourse to the author's life, it is nevertheless worthwhile to know something about the person who will be our guide. I have focused first on Lewis's life, not to "explain away" his writings, but as a Christian introducing some of the personal aspects of our older brother to other Christians. For I believe that we should not simply meet these wonderful works in isolation, detached from the mind and heart and life from which they sprang. The umbilical cord between author and brainchild may be cut—and of course it is—so that anyone can simply read the pieces and enjoy them. But there is even more joy when we know something of the person who has given us these great riches, particularly when that one belongs to the household of faith.[9] With this brief introduction in place, let us turn to the subject

[8]*A Preface to Paradise Lost* (1942; repr. New York, NY: Oxford University Press/Galaxy Books, 1961), 9.

[9]With this description of Lewis, I open the door to a debated matter—one that we will not deal with explicitly in this study. This is the historic claim of Orthodox to be *the* Church in continuity with the apostles, a claim that I embrace. It is possible

that Lewis considered to be of primary importance—God Himself as the foundation of reality.

The Foundational God

When those who have not been formally educated in philosophy or theology think about "reality," they quite naturally begin by considering "everything that is" as a whole, and class God as one of those "things" that happen to be real (or not). Those who have been influenced in any way by what has been called the "turn to the subject," that is, the idea that we should measure all things against the one who is thinking about them, take another route. They make the individual, or his or her thought processes, foundational.

The sixteenth-century philosopher Descartes' *Cogito ergo sum* may be cashed out in English, stressing "*I* think, therefore I am," or "I *think*, therefore I am." It is, of course, true that if someone thinks they must exist! Building upon that practical insight, later thinkers, especially those indebted to Immanuel Kant, unfortunately exaggerated the situation and made the thinker, the subject, wholly foundational. This has affected the views of almost everyone in the western world today. This is true even for those who have not heard of Descartes, Kant, or the more recent "post-structuralists," who have intensified these earlier ideas. "Reality" is considered by many to be a construct of my own thought processes, something that proceeds from me. I can really only ever know my perception, not things in themselves. Thus, the whole

to hold this conviction alongside an eagerness to engage in discussion and friendship with others who name Christ: consider especially the late Father Georges Florovsky and the Orthodox members of the St Alban's Institute. Orthodox do not subscribe to a "branch" theory of the Church (as Lewis, with many Anglicans, appears to have done), nor do they accept Protestant notions of an invisible Church. On the other hand, they recognize that God wills all to be in the household, and humbly admit that we do not yet see everything that the Church will be in its fullness. In this book, I will use the name "Christian" for anyone who names Jesus as the Christ and who believes in the ecumenical creeds, without thereby implying that membership in the visible Orthodox Church is unimportant.

concept of "reality" is totally redefined. If all that is cannot be known even in part as it truly is, then how do I then know that anything exists outside of my own imagination? Everything becomes a matter of "my reality" or "what is real to me."

The starting point of the Bible, indeed, that of the Christian tradition in general, has been very different from either of these "default" modes of thinking. The earlier idea, that Reality is a "set" or "classification" in which everything (including God) exists, doesn't match the Christian story. Equally inapplicable is the idea that everything turns upon the perceptions of the thinker, the subject. Instead, God is seen uniquely existing unto or within Himself. Thus the foundation and origin of all, including the human thinker and human thought, and the cosmos, is revealed and declared to be God: "in the beginning, *God.*" Jesus Himself said, "I am the Way and the Truth and the Life," expanding upon the mysterious and holy Name YHWH, a Hebrew verb associated with *being* ("I am that I am"), and translated in Orthodox liturgy and iconography by the Greek title, *Ho Ōn*—"the Existing One."

This understanding leads us beyond our experience to acknowledge a world bigger than ourselves. In practical terms, a person begins with his or her own conscious life and experience. However, if a baby were able to reflect on such matters, she would of course be wrong to think that her own thought processes or her own identity preceded or even generated reality. She existed as a fetus, and before that an embryo, and before that a zygote, alive even before any brain waves or awareness started, and before she had much data (or anything outside the womb) to ponder. Indeed, before her, and before her parents and ancestors— before creation itself—was (we are told) the Existing One.

In Scripture, Jeremiah 2.11–13 speaks of this utterly foundational LORD: "Has a nation changed its gods, even though they are no gods? But my people have changed their glory for that which does not profit. Be appalled, O heavens, at this, be shocked, be utterly desolate, says the LORD, for my people have committed two evils: they have forsaken me, the fountain of living waters, and hewed out cisterns for themselves, broken cisterns, that can hold no water" (Jer 2.11–13). Similarly, the prophet Isaiah declares,

> Thus says the LORD, the King of Israel and his Redeemer, the LORD of hosts: "I am the first and I am the last; besides me there is no god. Who is like me? Let him proclaim it, let him declare and set it forth before me. Who has announced from of old the things to come? Let them tell us what is yet to be. Fear not, nor be afraid; have I not told you from of old and declared it? And you are my witnesses! Is there a God besides me? There is no [other] Rock; I know not any" (Is 44.6–8).

God, then, reveals Himself to be the sole fountain, when all else cannot hold water. He is the First and the Last, the One who cannot be set in a class. He is both real and Reality itself—and any reality that other things or beings or persons have is entirely derivative.

We know from experience: there are not only real things, there are also approximations of the Real, shadows of reality. When my husband and I were young graduate students, and raising a young family, things were tough financially. We ate a lot of Kraft Mac 'n Cheese, and thus unwittingly prejudiced our toddlers' palettes against the *real* cheese macaroni scrumptiously made with cream and cheddar cheese by their grandmother. A similar situation is described by C. S. Lewis with regards to music. He relates that as a young child he was incredibly disappointed by his first experience hearing a symphony orchestra, because he could hear each instrument separately, and longed for the homogenized sound that had emitted from the primitive gramophone upon which he had first listened to classical music. The real thing seemed a poor substitute for the badly reproduced music to which he had become accustomed![10]

[10] "Religion: Reality or Substitute," in Walter Hooper, ed., *Christian Reflections* (Grand Rapids, MI: Eerdmans, 1967), 39.

We hear a good deal about contrast between the "real thing" and shadows in the New Testament Epistle to the Hebrews, especially in chapters ten and twelve:

> For since the law has but a shadow of the good things to come instead of the true form of these realities, it can never, by the same sacrifices which are continually offered year after year, make perfect those who draw near. . . . But you have come to Mount Zion and to the city of the living God, the heavenly Jerusalem, and to innumerable angels in festal gathering, and to the assembly of the first-born who are enrolled in heaven, and to a judge who is God of all, and to the spirits of just men made perfect, and to Jesus, the mediator of a new covenant, and to the sprinkled blood that speaks more graciously than the blood of Abel. . . . Therefore let us be grateful for receiving a kingdom that cannot be shaken, and thus let us offer to God acceptable worship, with reverence and awe. (Heb 10.1; 12.22–24, 28)

The Jews who revered the Torah (the Law) in the first century would have been astonished to hear that the Torah was only a shadow of the reality, intended always to bear witness to the LORD, who would come among humanity in person. As a result, Christians, the apostle tells us, have come to the real thing—to God the Son Himself, to all those centered around him, and to a solid, unshakeable kingdom. The fact that God is in a class by Himself, as the Foundation of all, means that human beings must be modest when they talk about Him, knowing that even prayers "taken at their word" may misconstrue the Lord of all things. Yet, that very inimitable quality of the Lord Almighty gives the faithful confidence that God will divert their mistaken ideas and prayers in a merciful gravitation towards Him: "unless Thou in magnetic mercy to Thyself divert our arrows." We hope ultimately to see Him as He is, and meanwhile to learn to see the world that He has created more and more clearly by His light.

When Lewis puts forth the solidity and reality of God and the created world—especially the blessed world to come—he stands in stark contrast with his generation, and with ours, as well. The common belief today that "everything is perception" is given shape by the first *Matrix* film, in which a reality created by the subject is coupled with a technological horror story. Morpheus, in illumining the protagonist Neo, takes him inside a computerized "virtual reality." Asked by Neo if a chair is real, Morpheus responds, "What is real? How do you define 'real'? If you're talking about what you can feel, what you can smell, what you can taste and see, then 'real' is simply electrical signals interpreted by your brain." Some minutes later, he shows Neo a picture of the late-twentieth-century world that Neo believes he has been inhabiting, and then contrasts that with a video of a desolate, destroyed world, which, he declares, is "really" what is out there. Quoting a famous post-structuralist philosopher, Baudrillard, he intones, "Welcome to the desert of the real." And in case the audience hasn't grasped the point fully, later in the film Neo comments, "I thought it wasn't real," only to be told, "Your mind makes it real."

Of course, the philosophical conundrums posed by the film are enormous, for on what ground can Morpheus claim that he knows *anything* to be real, since his thought processes, too, are "simply" made up of the movement of electrons? His explanation of the *real* world is equally as suspect as the fantasy in which Neo and others have been living. In the end, we are directed to one firm conclusion: distrust any claim to Reality, any story that claims to encompass a larger truth, because everything we know is projected by each one of us.

The contrast between *The Matrix*'s hollow skepticism and relativism and Lewis's Christian worldview is stark. We grasp this in two scenes from *The Lion, the Witch, and the Wardrobe*. In the first scene (Chapter 5), the two older children, Peter and Susan, speak with the wise old Professor about the problem that they are having arbitrating between Lucy and Edmund over the truth about Narnia. In the second scene (Chapter

15), our drive to find out "what will happen next" is diverted to the delighted response of Susan and Lucy when Aslan comes alive after being sacrificed by the White Witch on the Stone Table. Both episodes suggest that the world is a more complex place than we might normally think. Faced with a mystery, we must sometimes question our presuppositions, pause, and go more deeply into the matter to understand it.

The older children Susan and Peter, even though they know that Lucy is normally the more truthful child, are stymied by her story of a world that they have never seen, a world into which she had been unable to bring them by means of the wardrobe that had been *her* portal. The Professor points out to them that there are only three possibilities: young Lucy is lying, or mad, or telling the truth. There is no compelling evidence for the first two options, except for the children's reluctance to accept an unlikely story. The Professor helps the children both to open their minds to the possibility of unseen and unusual things, and to be practical—to mind their own business and leave Lucy to hers!

The second scene between the girls and the great lion Aslan occurs at the turning point of the entire book. The children have hidden themselves at the margins of the scene, horrified by Aslan's ordeal, and then lamenting his death. As the morning dawns golden, they hear the Stone Table crack, and rush to find it empty—suddenly to be jolted into a new reality by a "great voice behind their backs."[11] On turning, they see the newly risen Lion, his corona of a mane grown back from the ugly shearing of the Witch, and his breath warm upon their foreheads. He is no ghost, but "real," and he proves it by leading in a playful "mad chase" in which they romp, are caught up in his paws, and roll over together on the grass: he shows himself to be variously but truly real, first like a "thunderstorm" and then as a "kitten." In explaining what has happened, the Lion speaks to Susan and Lucy about "the Deep Magic," "deeper" even than the Witch's occult knowledge. Aslan reveals how "Death itself would start working backwards" if One like

[11] *The Lion, the Witch and the Wardrobe,* in *Chronicles* (1950; 2005), 184–85.

him were willing to be sacrificed. The resurrected Aslan then leads the children to victory over the Witch and her minions, bringing back to life everyone that she has petrified, and leading those who are following him to victory. His very appearance in the battle strikes the Witch with "terror and amazement,"[12] for she cannot, as a usurper, face the true and rightful King of Narnia. Faced with the reality of Aslan, she is vanquished, along with her cruel and evil powers.

Reality and Mimesis

The Matrix, then, tells its story in order to question whether there is any difference between what is real and what is unreal—in the end, we are left with no assurances, only skepticism and various perceptions. Lewis, in contrast, tells his fictive stories in order to describe a world in which there is Reality, and in which there are various distortions and true copies of that Reality. Aslan is no ghost, but real and fully alive; the White Witch is not pure white, but deadly pale and destined for death. Winter, in which Narnia is locked, is only the absence of warmth, which Aslan, on returning, provides by a new springtime. At his return, streams gush, trees bloom, and animals rejoice. On feeling his breath, frozen statues return to life. Reality, according to the perspective of the Matrix, is brutish and ugly; in Lewis's hands, reality includes harsh details (such as the treachery of Edmund and the death of Aslan) but undergirding it is a "deeper" reality where evil cannot stand firm. We are not contrasting a "pessimistic" over against "optimistic" worldview, but an understanding of reality as something humanly or divinely constructed. If God is the ground of reality, then all things in that reality must depend on the One Who Is.

These first principles, intimated in his stories, are explored in the essay "Religion: Reality or Substitute."[13] There Lewis speaks about the

---

[12] *Lion*, 191.
[13] "Religion: Reality or Substitute," 37–43 in *Christian Reflections*.

mode by which human beings judge what is "real," in *any* domain, not simply matters of faith. He insists that we do not really make such judgments based on instinct, or gut feeling alone. Rather, on the trio "[a]uthority, reason, experience . . . mixed in varying proportions, all our knowledge depends."[14]

This brings us back to the children's conversation with the professor as they puzzle through their conundrum about Narnia's possible existence. He is Authority personified, illuminating for them the various options in seeking an answer. The professor encourages them to look to reason, as well as their own experience, as they weigh the conflicting details in their minds: is Lucy usually deceptive? Is she mad? Have they any evidence of unseen worlds? In speaking specifically about matters of belief, Lewis advises: "Faith [is] the power of continuing to believe what we honestly thought to be true until cogent reasons for honestly changing our minds are brought before us."[15] The children's presuppositions—that reality is simple, that reality is always just as it appears—are challenged by Lucy's report of Narnia. Later, their own experience bears out the advice offered by the authoritative professor, so that they must honestly change their minds about what is real. Similarly, Lucy and Susan must come to a new understanding concerning the limits to the White Witch's power, and concerning life and death when they are confronted by the risen Aslan.

Foundational, then, is an understanding of the Creator in personal relation to His creation. This is for Lewis a seminal idea that becomes his warrant for writing, and indeed for writing about other worlds. Implanted within creation, and especially within human beings, are the prints of the Creator Himself. So it is that we hear echoes of the Maker in what is made, and especially in the human work of "mimesis" or imitation of the Real in art or literature—or, indeed, in other aspects of life. This goes far beyond a mere statement that there *is* a Creator.

[14]"Religion," 41.
[15]"Religion," 42.

It describes this Creator as one who cares deeply about what has been created, who has made humanity after His image, and against whom all reality must be measured. If these things are so, then human beings can and will engage in the work and play that Lewis calls "sub-creative." (We pause to notice that this differs from an arrogant claim that human beings are "co-creators," and upholds what Orthodox describe as the *monarchy* of God: He alone is the source and head of everything.) The Puritan austerity that forbids such playfulness, though pious, is deeply mistaken, for it has confused what it is to tell the truth, and what it is to be human. In the heyday of English and American Puritanism, even wholesome novels were considered by many serious Christians to be either sheer deceit, and therefore immoral, or subversive of a pious life, and therefore not worthy of Christian interest. Yet truth need not be confined to "fact," and make-believe and the use of imagination—sub-creation—is not mere lying.[16] Rather, the creation is full of echoes of the true God, and reflections of His story in dealing with and redeeming humankind. Thus, we can see hints and glimmerings of truth in many stories—including, surprisingly, even the garbled versions of the story told in pagan mythology. Some early Christian philosophers, such as Justin Martyr, put forward the idea of *logoi spermatikoi,* reasonable ideas scattered even upon the pagans, to which Christian missionaries could appeal. In a similar vein, some[17] have suggested that Lewis posits a doctrine of *mythoi spermatikoi, stories* of reality and of God, though incomplete and distorted, spread among human cultures, and responding to the deepest longings and yearnings of our hearts. Human beings, by virtue of being created in the divine image, instinctively engage in *mimesis,* the imitation of their Creator. As

[16]For a brilliant and helpful guide to the different modes in which the Bible itself expresses truth, see G. B. Caird's *The Language and Imagery of the Bible* (London: Duckworth and Co., 1980).

[17]The term appears to be coined first by Fabienne Claire Caland, "Le mythos spermatikos," in *Horizons du mythe,* eds. Denise Brassard and Fabienne Claire Calend (Montreal: Cahiers du CELAT, 2007), 7–32.

sub-creators, they have all the material (physical and ideological) that the Creator Himself has placed within their reach.

This vision of God as the foundation for all genuine human insight issues a challenge to brittle and insular forms of Christianity that see no truth or beauty or goodness outside an explicitly Christian culture. The Puritan who spurns fantasy and imagined stories has too narrow a view of reality, humanity, and God. But Lewis offers a challenge, too, to the radical relativist, who thinks that each individual creates his or her own truth and reality. For the stories passed on by human beings stand in varying degrees of proximity to the True Story: not all commend themselves equally to our reason, nor are they proven by experience to be equally useful. Relativity as a basis for thinking is self-defeating nonsense to Lewis, as we shall see when we consider the question of "worldviews" in a later chapter.

Mimesis and Literature

How, then, does Lewis understand mimesis and its role in art or literature? First, it means that that "sub-creation" is not constrained by the quest to do something "fresh" or "novel," as many might assume. This endless and elusive search for all that is new is understood by many to be the primary virtue of good art or literature. However, novelty alone does not express adequately the principle of mimesis embedded in our sub-creative humanity, and indeed, in the created order as a whole. Indeed, many of us in the disciplines of the humanities have struggled with this criterion of novelty[18] for exemplary scholarship. For example,

[18]Lewis spoke of how the criterion of novelty pervades modern culture, in contrast to the ancient and medieval world: "For the aim is not self-expression or 'creation'; it is to hand on the 'historial' matter worthily; not worthily of your own genius or of the poetic art but of the matter itself. I doubt if they would have understood our demand for originality or valued those works in their own age which were original any more on that account. If you had asked Layamon or Chaucer 'Why do you not make up a brand-new story of your own?' I think they might have replied (in effect) 'Surely we are not yet reduced to that?' " C. S. Lewis, *The Discarded Image: An Introduction to Medieval and Renaissance Literature* (1964; repr. Cambridge: Cambridge University Press, 2002), 211.

academics are routinely asked, when applying for a grant, how our research will bring a new source of aid or a significantly novel insight to society.

Let us look to our guide for insight. In his remarkable essay "Christianity and Literature" (also published as "Rehabilitations"), Lewis muses along the following lines:

> What are the key-words of modern criticism? *Creative,* with its opposite *derivative; spontaneity,* with its opposite *convention; freedom,* contrasted with *rules.* Great authors are innovators, pioneers, explorers; bad authors bunch in schools and follow models. Or again, great authors are always 'breaking fetters' and 'bursting bonds'. They have personality, they 'are themselves'. . . . [W]e certainly have a general picture of bad work flowing from conformity and discipleship, and of good work bursting out from certain centres of explosive force—apparently self-originating force—which we call men of genius.[19]

Lewis then warns us against over-emphasizing the poetical nature of Jesus' words, and highlights instead Christ's shrewd manner of speaking. More generally, he remarks that the New Testament is not a primer on literature. Moreover, the Scriptures put forward a worldview that radically questions the contemporary author's simplistic love affair with novelty. Moving into the description of interrelationships pictured by the apostle Paul in 1 Corinthians 11, he points out that we are faced with a "whole series of Head relations running from God to woman" in which "one glorifies by copying or imitating."[20] Paul does not give us this picture as a controlling system, Lewis admits, and describes relationships in other ways, such as the symbiosis of a "body."

---

[19]"Christianity and Literature," 1–11 in *Christian Reflections.* For this citation, see page 3.

[20]"Christianity and Literature," 4.

But here, at least, we receive a clear picture of "imitation" as part of the stuff of life.

We will return to Lewis's exegesis of this passage and how he construes male and female (perhaps not quite in as nuanced a way as St Paul), in our final chapter of this study. At this point we want only to notice the importance of the concept of mimesis, or imitation, not only in the created order and in human life, but also within the life of the Holy Trinity: for the Son says that He does what He sees the Father doing! Lewis may well be right in arguing that "the art of life itself is an art of imitation" and that true "[o]riginality . . . is quite plainly the prerogative of God alone. . . ." Applying this to the author, he ends with this maxim: "an author should never conceive himself as bringing into existence beauty or wisdom which did not exist before, but simply and solely as trying to embody in terms of his own art some reflection of eternal Beauty and Wisdom."[21] This perspective sets the Christian artist free from taking his art too seriously, and from seeking only endless novelty. It also makes room for humility and playfulness.

The Power of Myth

The human delight in sub-creation entailed, for Lewis, being caught up in the luminous quality of "myth," as he plied his craft. He does not seek, in the first place, to be unique or creative. In his own day, he brought to life such mythological narratives and enabled these poignant stories to strike the deeper chords of the human mind and imagination. One enthusiast of Lewis rightly states that it is "impossible fully to understand these novels and his fictional work as a whole, apart from this subject [of myth]."[22] Lewis recounts how as a child he was fascinated by the fairy tales and ancient legends recounted to him by his Irish nurse. Indeed, the image of a faun carrying parcels and an

---

[21]"Christianity and Literature," 6–7.

[22]Clyde S. Kilby, *The Christian World of C. S. Lewis* (Grand Rapids, MI, Eerdmans, 1964), 80.

umbrella in a snowy wood came to him when he was a young man of sixteen.[23] This was the "seed" of the Narnia stories, the mythological image from which his *Chronicles* would grow and flower. Arguably, the Narnian *Chronicles* are good literature precisely because they engage adults as well as children, and were written by someone who knew and loved literature of many sorts—Lewis had a full repertoire, so to speak. But Lewis himself would say that what gives the *Chronicles* their depth is not primarily his expertise, but their mythic quality, that central core of Reality that they evoke among various readers.

In distinguishing myth from good literature, Lewis points to its folk quality. A myth is a story that has virtue and power in itself, regardless of how well the artist tells the tale. This particular and simple quality commends *itself* on levels deeper than cognition to a number of different hearers. Myths have "a satisfactory and inevitable shape, like a good vase or a tulip."[24] In a myth, he says, we see the following characteristics:

- It is, in its essence, extra-literary. That is, it can live on in oral and variable forms, for its essence is in the overall shape, not the artistic rendition.

- It does not depend on suspense or surprise, but has throughout a sense of inevitability, a "flavor," or quality like a particular chord of music. By this quality, we are introduced to a deep thought, idea, or image, and are compelled to contemplate it.

- Its story does not work on our emotions, and we do not immediately place ourselves within the story, in sympathy with the characters. That is, the myth is not psychological, "not leading us to sympathize with Sally," but to be sorry for all human beings.

[23]"It All Began With A Picture ... ," pages 78–79 in *Of This and Other Worlds* (London: Collins, 1982).
[24]C. S. Lewis, *An Experiment in Criticism* (1961; repr. Cambridge: Cambridge University Press, 1988), 42. The characteristics I list below are drawn from pp. 43–44.

- Myth deals with fantastic worlds or situations.

- There is a sobriety or seriousness to the story, whether it is joyful or sorrowful.

- Mythical story inspires awe at the deepest level.

All of these elements taken together show us that a myth is similar to a classical religious icon in the impact that it makes upon us. As with the icon, which is not primarily a work of art, but a means of devotion, we are led outside of ourselves to contemplate something (or Some*one*) that *draws* us. Hearing a myth will not direct us inward to our own notions; it will not lead us to psychologize the characters of the story, and compare them to ourselves; it will not cause us to think mostly about the artful telling of the myth. Rather, it will intimate something bigger than ourselves, deeper than our experience, and greater even than the story itself. As Lewis puts it, "Myth is a real though unfocused gleam of divine truth falling on human imagination."[25] It reflects the greater reality for which we yearn, and for some is a compelling call from that greatest Reality: the personal God, who entreats us to be reconciled with Him. If myth is the sort of thing that communicates awe, and points to something greater than we might otherwise imagine, then the writer who uses myth becomes for those who hear a guide or mentor to worlds as yet unseen. In all play, there is a serious element, as well. This is something that even a toddler knows, as he or she repeats over and over a "pretend," or insists upon hearing a favorite story retold, with the devotion that an adult gives to liturgy or other "serious business."

Logos and Poiēma in Literature

In going beyond myth to speak about literature, Lewis explains how the elements of *Logos* (something said) and *Poiēma* (something made)

---

[25] *Miracles: A Preliminary Study* (London: Macmillan, 1947; London: Collins / Fontana, 1974), 138, footnote beginning on p. 137.

depend upon each other. By means of *Logos,* the writer tells the story, instructs, or communicates emotion. This helps us to grow, as we see things from another's point of view: what is said gives the *Poiēma* direction, or intent. *Poiēma,* the thing made, is the delightful factor that absorbs our attention, causing us to rest within the writing. A world is created as the artist engages in *mimēsis;* in this world we are struck by the beauty and the balance, the "fearful symmetry" (as William Blake called it) of what is created. "It is only by being also a Poiema that a Logos becomes a work of literary art at all,"[26] Lewis tells us. Some critics assert that poetry only *is* and does not *mean.* Lewis would understand the sentiment, but also insists that without *Logos,* there is nothing for the *Poiēma* to build upon or direct itself towards. A literary work engages us in both dimensions.

From Lewis's perspective, when myth is incorporated, we are far more deeply engaged with a written work. Myth fosters within us a longing, a yearning for "an enlargement of our being" that will "heal [our] loneliness."[27] We see further and deeper if we see through the eyes of others who have spied, with delight (or perhaps horror!) other worlds. There is so much to see: reality is much more solid than we could imagine and the extent of this cosmos so vast. We need every possible window to reveal the new landscape, and every possible guide to tour its terrain. We must be prodded "out" of ourselves and "into" something we barely thought possible. In our best moments, we have surely echoed his yearning words:

> Reality, even seen through the eyes of many, is not enough. . . . Even the eyes of all humanity are not enough. I regret that the brutes cannot write books. Very gladly would I learn what face things present to a mouse or a bee; more gladly still would I perceive the olfactory world charged with all the information and emotion it carries for a

[26]*Experiment,* 135–36.
[27]*Experiment,* 137–38.

dog. . . . [I]n reading great literature I become a thousand men and yet remain myself. . . . I see with a myriad eyes, but it is still I who see. Here, as in worship, in love, in moral action, and in knowing, I transcend myself; and am never more myself than when I do.[28]

With Lewis as our wide-eyed guide, we learn to receive what we read as a gift and not pragmatically to use or exploit it.[29] To delight in these glimpses of myth, these trenchant words, these luminous fictions is to befriend Lewis, and then to gaze, wonderstruck, at those things about the world and about its Creator that he sees and, in his own turn, has seen through the eyes of others. Like Reepicheep, he calls us "further up and further in."

Perspective and Reality

There is a final element of human experience illumined by Lewis's writings: humor. Though he insists that myth, whether joyful or sad, is solemn, myth does not set the tone entirely in his writings. Lewis obstinately refuses to take himself (or his art) too seriously. As human beings, we notice when something surprises or jars us. If we know ourselves well, we understand that our perceptions only partially correspond to reality, and smile at our former self when we are enlightened. It is suitable, then, for even serious literature to include an element of fun. Such comedy is not simply "a spoonful of sugar to help the medicine go down." It is an acknowledgement that some things don't quite "fit" in our world. Indeed, there is something not quite fitting about our feeble human minds dallying in great matters! Such an admission is a necessary part of perceiving reality and our humble place in the great scheme of things. Even children can understand this.

[28] *Experiment*, 140–141.
[29] "Receivers" and "users" are the categories that Lewis uses in *Experiment* to describe two kinds of readers.

In the solemn and engrossing chapter in which Narnia is created, there is a moment of self-consciousness for one of the talking creatures, who does not tell, but *becomes* "the first joke"—and the entire kingdom laughs. Likewise, at the height of the battle, when Aslan is about to rout the White Witch, another lion (who recently has been unfrozen by Aslan) prances around, ridiculously pleased that Aslan has included *him* in the phrase "us lions"—much to the reader's delight.

Any good artist, then, reveals how a full human life is a balancing act. There are serious words (the *Logos*) to hear; there are delightful and fearful images to discern (the mythological); there are intricate artistic moves (the *Poiēma*) to appreciate: and there is sheer play in all of this. For as Lewis warns us, "the Christian knows from the outset that the salvation of a single soul is more important than the production or preservation of all the epics and tragedies in the world. . . . We can play, as we can eat, to the glory of God."[30] It is the seriousness of the subject matter that lends sublimity to a story, not the artistry of the writer. And so, through humor itself, Lewis throws open a window to air out our stuffy self-importance, and to help us get beyond ourselves! Indeed, the picture of Reepicheep guiding us is an apt emblem: this proud little creature, initially preoccupied with his own integrity, grows in humility as he serves. In this way, the Knightly Mouse reminds us that all our human interactions, whether we are followers or leaders, are not the be-all-and-end-all. After all, there is only One who is the true Human Being and the perfect leader.

As an antidote to self-absorption, and to the temptation even to make Lewis the final focus of our attention, let us recall the story of the Sorcerer's Apprentice, especially that delightful version of the story in Disney's *Fantasia*. The apprentice, played by the inimitable Mickey Mouse, engages in mimesis—the mimesis of magic-making. He takes up his mentor's tools (hat and wand) and uses his master's moves, but only for his own benefit, to avoid the drudgery of his tasks. He is

---

[30]"Christianity and Literature" in *Reflections,* 10.

exploiting magic for a mundane rather than exalted purpose. As he naps, the magic runs amok. Umpteen walking broomsticks carry his water, but pour a deluge that threatens to wash the wayward apprentice away. Finally, he is saved by his master—a salvation that comes with a well-deserved spank. This story is found famously in various forms, from the Greek author Lucian (second c. AD) to the eighteenth-century Goethe, and beyond, and is told for various purposes. For Lucian, it was a tale of ridicule, but in Goethe's poem it carried the "message" that only the strong can summon the spirits with impunity.

It is the image of the overcome apprentice that sticks in the imagination. It has that compelling quality of a myth whose images abide in the mind and the imagination. Of course, the collaborators for *Fantasia* supplemented the myth with music and animated pictures, and so the film becomes an object which we view, evaluate, and approve for its entertainment value, rather than a transparent and revealing window through which we glimpse wonderful and truthful things. Yet even in the film two key elements emerge: the sheer fun of making and the danger of distortion in mimesis. That sub-creative drive, of both the Apprentice and of the artists who frame his tale, leads us on to our next topic—that of Creation and Sub-Creation, as seen in two of Lewis's lesser known children's stories.

CHAPTER 2

Creation, "Sub-Creation," and Thanksgiving

(The Magician's Nephew, The Silver Chair and
Fr Schmemann's *For the Life of the World)*

Almighty and Everlasting God, who hatest nothing that thou hast made, and dost forgive the sins of all them that are penitent: Create and make in us new and contrite hearts, that we worthily lamenting our sins, and acknowledging our wretchedness, may obtain of thee, the God of all mercy, perfect remission and forgiveness; through Jesus Christ our Lord, Amen.[1]

*Christ creating the cosmos
(contemporary icon)*

A s we move into a discussion of Lewis and creation, some Christians may recall the "Song of the Three" (known in the West as *Benedictus es,* "Blessed art Thou"). This has been a beloved hymn for millennia among Christians, both in the East and West, and given various musical arrangements or simply recited. Unfortunately, it is not well known in Protestant circles today, aside from some Lutheran and Anglican congregations. This is because it comes from the "additions to Daniel,"

[1]Collect for Ash Wednesday, Anglican Book of Common Prayer.

which are found in the ancient Greek translation of Daniel (called the Septuagint, or LXX). For Protestants, it is mainly available in the Apocrypha, as the second half of *The Prayer of Azariah*. Roman Catholics and Orthodox, however, have an extended third chapter for the book of Daniel that includes this sequence, which is not separated out as something "extra."

Here, in this Song of the Three Young Men (or Children), we linger in a dramatic cosmic litany of praise. Indeed, the hymn is still celebrated in the Orthodox Matins (i.e., "morning") service, as well as in Lauds and Feast Days for Roman Catholics. Though lengthy, it was known by heart in ancient days, due to its frequent use in worship: we know this because there are prayer books which simply indicate where it should be sung, without the words! In this mighty hymn, our human exaltation of God is folded into that of the entire cosmos, beginning with the winds and rains, moving to the angels, and finishing with the persecuted faithful (personified by the three in the furnace). It is a fulsome song for God's people, placing us within a lively universe of praise and thanksgiving, regardless of our circumstances. Here are some excerpts, though a complete singing of the psalm is always better:[2]

> Blessed art thou, O Lord, God of our fathers,
> and to be praised and highly exalted for ever . . .
>
> Bless the Lord, all works of the Lord,
> sing praise to him and highly exalt him for ever.
> Bless the Lord, you heavens,
> sing praise to him and highly exalt him for ever.
> Bless the Lord, you angels of the Lord,
> sing praise to him and highly exalt him for ever.
> Bless the Lord, all waters above the heaven,

[2]Here are two examples, a western setting in chant and the classical Byzantine version: https://www.youtube.com/watch?v=AU3sQGotstg and https://www.youtube.com/watch?v=Gf_IGU7PnTo.

sing praise to him and highly exalt him for ever.
Bless the Lord, all powers,
sing praise to him and highly exalt him for ever.
Bless the Lord, sun and moon,
sing praise to him and highly exalt him for ever.
Bless the Lord, stars of heaven,
sing praise to him and highly exalt him for ever.
Bless the Lord, all rain and dew,
sing praise to him and highly exalt him for ever.
Bless the Lord, all winds,
sing praise to him and highly exalt him for ever....

Bless the Lord, you sons of men,
sing praise to him and highly exalt him for ever.
Bless the Lord, O Israel,
sing praise to him and highly exalt him for ever.
Bless the Lord, you priests of the Lord,
sing praise to him and highly exalt him for ever.
Bless the Lord, you servants of the Lord,
sing praise to him and highly exalt him for ever.
Bless the Lord, spirits and souls of the righteous,
sing praise to him and highly exalt him for ever.
Bless the Lord, you who are holy and humble in heart,
sing praise to him and highly exalt him for ever.

Bless the Lord, Hananiah, Azariah, and Mishael,
sing praise to him and highly exalt him for ever;
for he has rescued us from Hades and saved us from the
  hand of death,
and delivered us from the midst of the burning fiery
  furnace;
from the midst of the fire he has delivered us.
Give thanks to the Lord, for he is good,

for his mercy endures for ever.

Bless him, all who worship the Lord, the God of gods,
sing praise to him and give thanks to him,
for his mercy endures for ever.

Is this not an astonishing song of praise?

The three friends of Daniel—Hananiah, Mishael, and Azariah
(commonly known by their Chaldean names in English: Shadrach,
Meschach, and Abednego)—have been thrown into the furnace because
they refuse to be idolaters. As they walk around in the flames, Azariah
confesses that the Hebrew people are in exile, and oppressed by unbelievers, because of God's righteous judgment. He then prays concerning his would-be executioners: "Let them know that you alone are the
Lord God, glorious over the whole world" (*Prayer of Azariah* 1.22; Dan
3.45 LXX). Then the angel of the Lord drives out the burning flame,
and makes the interior of the furnace moist, like a humid wind, so that
the three are preserved. (Later hymnody saw this humid environment as
a kind of womb, or crucible, from which the faithful emerge newborn.)
Walking in the fire with them is one like a "Son of Man," whom the
ancient Church fathers understood as an appearance of the Son prior
to the incarnation. He is the very personification of God's great Mercy,
of which the three are singing! With one voice they praise God the
Creator, calling upon every element of the cosmos to bless and praise
God—angels, waters, heavenly bodies, earthly elements of water, wind,
heat and cold, temporal elements, dark and light, geographical elements,
all creatures of the earth, all the peoples of earth, especially the chosen
people, both those living on earth and those asleep awaiting the resurrection. Finally, they admonish themselves to praise the Lord who has
rescued them from hell and death. Throughout these encouragements
for creation to give its praise, they cry out, "Give thanks to the Lord, for
he is good, for his mercy endures for ever."

As the three men call on the elements, they celebrate the creative power of God, who "alone is glorious over the whole world." Overcome by the great goodness and bounty of the Creating Lord, they themselves enter into the activity which Lewis and his Inkling friends called "sub-creation": they represent and give voice to the whole creation, in all its teeming splendor. Humankind, made in the image of God, is most fully human when spontaneously echoing the mercy, fullness, and joy of the Creator. Even in the fiery furnace, in the sub-regions of the cosmos, where life is at the margins, these three are not beyond God's reach. They sing praise to Him, re-calling the wide world from which they are physically cut off while they are in the furnace.

As they remember, they bless the Lord and set forth for those who hear their psalm a vivid picture. The vast cosmos is as high as the cherubim and the firmament of heavens, as deep as the rivers and the strange creatures in the sea, as wild as the forest beasts, and as civilized (perhaps) as the nations. It is full of things seen and unseen, energies gentle and fierce. Indeed, the Three instruct all the works of the Lord to praise and bless Him, because that is what God's creation is meant to do, by its very living and being. Acting as priests between creation and God, they give voice to those elements of the cosmos that have no voice; they also draw us, the hearers, into thanksgiving. (It may be helpful to remember that the Latin word for priest, *pontifex,* means quite literally "bridge-builder.") When we use a psalm like this in worship, we also become "sub-creators," creators *under* the great Creator, corporately painting a picture of God's world, encouraging others to worship, and also bringing ourselves and our artistry before the great Creator in adoration.

These themes of creation, sub-creation, and thanksgiving command our attention as we consider Lewis's children's novels. Since he was a Christian writer, we expect that he made theological sense of his own occupation. For him, the reason for his writing arose from the concept of "sub-creation." However, it is not only writers or artists who create "under" God. Just as the Three in the furnace celebrated God's creation as all-encompassing, so Lewis adores the LORD and gives thanks in his writings, showing that sub-creation is the human way to do this. The themes of creation, sub-creation, and thanksgiving are particularly strong in two of his less well-known children's books, *The Magician's Nephew* and *The Silver Chair.*

The Magician's Nephew

This novel takes logical priority in the *Chronicles of Narnia*, though it was not written first. It relates to his best-known children's book, *The Lion, the Witch and the Wardrobe,* in the same way that Genesis relates to the Gospels. Here we learn the "backstory" for the exploits of the Pevensie children, and find out how and why a magic wardrobe came to be in Professor Kirke's house, providing a portal into another world. Here, too, we meet Aslan, the Witch, and the primordial Narnia, uncannily interconnected with our own human realm.

THE CREATION AND ASLAN

Since this is a story of creation, it provides ample scope for Lewis's artistic desire to engage in sub-creative art. Of course, always prior to human sub-creation must be God's own original activity of creation and re-creation, echoed poignantly in *The Magician's Nephew.* Where better to go than that unforgettable passage where Lewis's creating Lion "sings" Narnia into existence?[3] The young character who witnesses that first wondrous dawn over Narnia strains his eyes in the pitch black; then he hears a voice singing, at first far away, but seemingly coming from every direction, including low notes from the earth beneath his feet: "It was so beautiful he could hardly bear it." After this, we are told, "two wonders happen at the same moment." Joining the first voice, other myriad higher voices join, in harmony, and the blackness

---

[3]C. S. Lewis, *The Magician's Nephew* in *Chronicles* (1955; 2005) 58–63. All the following quotations come from these pages.

is pierced by countless stars. Those listening have a sense that the stars themselves are singing, and that the first Voice had made them come to light and join his song. Their awe (and ours!) is comically interrupted by one of the onlooking characters in the novel: "Glory be! . . . I'd ha' been a better man all my life if I'd known there were things like this. . . ."

Readers who know the Scriptures will ask, what are the similarities and difference between this story and the story of creation in Genesis? Yes, the sounds and sights come out of nothing, in response to a divine voice. However, into the Narnian scene have come characters from an earlier world (indeed, from several different worlds), who witness the creation. There are the two children from earth; there are the comic Cab-driver and his wife; and there is a wicked sorceress-Queen from another darker, defunct world. (Perhaps, in Lewis's imagination, these elements from outside of primordial Narnia correspond to unexplained details in the Biblical story. Eden suffered the inexplicable appearance of a "serpent" who subverts God's order, and thus the garden was not, in that sense, entirely pristine).

The commanding Creator and the sub-ordered response of the stars recall the awe-inspiring majesty of Genesis 1. Then the wonder is broken by the Cabby's outburst about being "a better man!" This comic touch domesticates the Narnian story, and highlights the human agents present at its birth. The solemn narrative of Genesis 1, however, has no human spectators, and thus stays wholly in the realm of liturgy and divine myth. (I use the word "myth" as a technical label of genre that narrates a story about the divine, and *not* to suggest falsehood or unreliability). However, even Genesis 1.1–2.4 clearly is told with a view to the *human* story. Especially, it foreshadows Israel and the Torah, since it highlights the seven-day pattern that the Hebrews are later instructed to follow. And, of course, it comes to a climax on the sixth day, with the creation of humanity, male and female. Similarly, Lewis's "beginning" includes elements that will figure strongly in Narnia's future: the seemingly random detail of a broken lamp-pole, snatched in a brief rampage of the Witch through a London street, will have a very important role in the comings and goings of the Pevensie children.

There is, of course, one great difference between the biblical narrative and this compelling story: the Lion sings and does not simply speak. In Genesis, God is the great Alpha, the great initiator, and the creation is called to answer to God. There God speaks and it is done. Response is proper to Creation, who, according to human tradition, sings her song in the angelic "music of the spheres." But *God* has no need of incantations, nor must he need to coax his creatures by singing: the divine words in the biblical story of creation are solemnly spoken. The Creator gives His word, and it is so.

Some might worry that the imaginary creation of Lewis in *The Magician's Nephew* is therefore not quite consonant with the Christian one. Some might wonder if creative singing comes rather from Scandinavian ancient stories, and consider that Lewis thus added a foreign romantic element to the Genesis story. I am not so sure. After all, the seven-day sequence in Genesis points to the liturgical life of the Hebrews that ended on the Sabbath: and their liturgy was always *sung*. In Christian understanding, creation is the work of Father, Son, and Holy Spirit, who, by the patristic reckoning of Genesis, will and work and speak together, "let *us* make Adam." As taught by Christ and the apostles, we read Genesis in the light of the gospel. Christ our God is One who, in the fullness of time, comes to dwell with those created ones who are made after His image, and in doing so, He thus glorifies the Father. Lewis knows all this, and so his Aslan is conceived after God the Son, who responds as well as initiates. Through Lewis's artistry, we are led to think differently about the primordial time when the first created light emerged, as the Logos responded to this divine deliberation, and honored the divine handiwork with song. The Creation is God's idea—so is the singing and the celebration of it!

The Lion's "new song" accompanies those elements of danger and beauty brought into the newly-created Narnia from our world, including humor and a sense of perspective. Even when he engages in the serious work of sub-creation, and so mirrors God's unique activity of creation, Lewis is not somber. He knows that he is giving a human representation, a story that tells of another creation in light of the world that we know, with some fancy and complication added. By deft touches of perspective and humor, he stands firmly against contemporary proponents of "co-creation" who arrogantly blur the distinction between the Creator and creation, and take the human role far too seriously. Yet, in his tenderness and attention to the details of his own creation, Lewis also corrects those who might denigrate the material world: for God "hates nothing that He has made," as the Anglican prayer for Lent puts it.

Lewis will not stand, either, with those who consider human creativity a trivial activity. Just as God has made the material universe, He also created humanity, and the whole gamut of human actions for his greater glory and our blessing. God therefore delights in all human pursuits that are undertaken to praise Him, not simply in our intellectual and "spiritual" practices. The very choice of a Cab-driver and his country wife as the equivalent of Lord Adam and Lady Eve in the new world of Narnia is telling! The diligence, honesty, humility, fidelity, and love shown by this ordinary couple are all that the Lion requires in transforming them for their new role. (This is quite reminiscent of how God "made the fishermen most wise" on Pentecost.)[4] Similarly, in the other books about Narnia, mere school-children, the four Pevensies, play their unlikely parts as heroes and monarchs, helping to redeem this new world that has, from its dawn, been infected with evil.

[4]Here I quote the Orthodox hymn for Pentecost, which itself reflects the surprise that bystanders express in the book of Acts as they note the wisdom of the unlearned apostles.

DELIGHTING IN SUB-CREATION

In *The Magician's Nephew,* as we survey the newly created Narnia, we will notice details that mirror our own world. The narrator gives us opportunity for this contemplation by drawing implicit or explicit contrasts with the human realm that we know, and by signaling to us obvious parallels. Narnia is linked, from its inception, with England: there is the Cabby, his wife, and the lamp-post, and there is Aslan's warning that Earth may destroy herself, just as Charn did (102). This connection is sustained right up to the final novel (*The Last Battle),* where England and Narnia are together comprehended in the limitless new realm of Aslan. In this way, the sub-creation renews and transforms our vision of the primary creation.

This is not the only world Lewis "created," of course. As a child, he and his brother Warnie imagined the land of Boxham with its talking animals, and wrote stories about it; in his second adult science fiction novel, *Perelandra (Voyage to Venus),* he creates a world not marred by evil or death, which yet stands new, vulnerable, and at the precipice of a possible Fall. *Perelandra* demonstrates that Lewis did not simply conjure his alternate realities as a thin pretext for disseminating ideas or teaching theology. He retained, in his adult writing, his childhood delight in the making up and the "peopling" of his sub-created world. In a leisurely way, he adds compelling detail to the scenes, as well as to the characters and backstory, and so defies any impatient reader's drive to find out "what is going to happen." We must dwell in the land, as do his characters. Consider, for example, the amazement of Lewis's character Ransom, on surveying the lush and watery vistas of Perelandra:

> There was no land in sight. The sky was pure, flat gold, like the background of a medieval picture. . . . The nearer waves, though golden where their summits caught the light, were green on their slopes: first emerald, and lower down a lustrous bottle green, deepening to blue where they passed beneath the shadow of other waves. . . . The

water gleamed, the sky burned with gold, but all was rich and dim, and his eyes fed upon it undazzled and unaching. . . . He sighed."[5]

With Ransom, we forget, for a moment, the uncertainty of events, and the suspense of the story. Instead, we pause with Ransom to relish God's handiwork—and the handiwork of the author, the sub-creator of this unknown world.

For the grown-up imagination, then, Lewis offers us the strange land of Perelandra (Venus). We discover it to be intricately connected with our earth by mythology, astronomy, and the amazing flight of Ransom (the main character) in his space-capsule from earth to Venus. But the connections go deeper than space and time. Ransom is surprised that the sentient beings on this planet are humanoid rather than eccentric in form, as were the inhabitants of Malacandra, or Mars, in Ransom's previous journey (*Out of the Silent Planet*). He learns that, since the incarnation of "Maleldil" on earth, every reasonable being in the cosmos is now made to honor that One by means of his or her appearance. Presumably this is a reference not simply to the outward body, but to all that it means to be human. The three species on Mars were unlike human beings in their physical features and their psychologies; the Lord and Lady of Venus (Perelandra) are like human beings not simply in their bodies, but in their capacity for both weakness and greatness. But let us return to Narnia and its talking animals, which, in their parallel existence, highlight what it is to be fully human.

THE NATURE OF NARNIANS

In *The Magician's Nephew*, we come to see our own created natures—not only how we are, but also how we are meant to be. As the first animate beings come to life, Aslan looks upon each, choosing and then speaking specifically to some of them. Before he speaks, the eyes of

---

[5]C. S. Lewis, *Perelandra* in *The Cosmic Trilogy* (1943; repr., London: Pan/Bodley Head, 1999), 174.

every chosen beast are fixed on him. He breathes upon the chosen, there is a numinous flash of fire, and he calls Narnia by name, commanding his creatures: "Awake. Love. Think. Speak." And the animals respond, "Hail, Aslan. We hear and obey."[6] Aslan turns his face upon them, speaks, and calls; they respond. Notice that the emphasis is upon God's sovereign choice (only some of the creation becomes sentient), but that listening and responding also have their place. Lewis will not choose between election and freedom, but holds them both together in a mystery. In this he follows the great Church fathers of the past, who rejected both systematic predestination (as in Calvinism) and the fancy of utter human autonomy—the mistaken idea that human beings are in a position to rule themselves.

Despite the elevation of the creatures above the others, there is no sense that those not so honored are to be despised. Indeed, Aslan explicitly hands over the rest of the Narnians into the care of the chosen, and admonishes the reasoning beasts to "treat them gently and cherish them" without taking on their bestial ways, since "out of them you were taken and into them you can return."[7] Without devolving into a shallow allegory (*this* stands for *that*)—for Narnia has a logic all of its own—the story speaks to our own situation. Adam was taken from the earth (Hebrew: *adama*), as the Hebrew name for humankind signifies. Without constant dependence upon our Creator, and without regard for humankind's final destiny (to be "perfect" as the Father is perfect), we are liable to become worse than beasts, even demonic! This fragility comes through in the offhand but sharp rebuke that the child Digory levels at his despicable Uncle Andrew for experimenting on guinea-pigs: "It was a jolly cruel thing to do!"[8] Andrew remains oblivious; from his perspective, the animals are raw material, possessions that he has bought for the very purpose of risking their lives. For Andrew, every-

[6] *Magician's*, 70–71.
[7] *Magician's*, 71.
[8] *Magician's*, 21.

thing and everyone are fodder for his work, and the ends always justify the means, even if the means are inhumane. Brutish action, indeed, eats away at Uncle Andrew's personhood until eventually he is little better than one of the Narnian insentient beasts. He has *used* creation, rather than protecting it, and so dehumanizes himself.

Aslan gives over his new world to the Cabby and his wife, who are decidedly more suitable to rule, though not formally educated like Andrew. We get some of the backstory of the Cabby's kindness to his horse, and his sense of teamwork with the brute beast, "Strawberry," in the cruel streets of England. At first only the Cabby is present in the story, "long known"[9] by Aslan, who intends to make him custodian. Then the divine Lion summons the Cabby's wife to his side, and the two are told to "rule and name," "do justice," and "protect"[10] the Narnians from harm—especially the harm of the Witch, who has already infiltrated the paradise. Indeed, the *mode* by which they will do this is made explicit. Aslan reminds them that these are *free* talking animals, and that the couple has a duty not only to rule wisely, but to pass on a tradition of compassion, justice, defense, and humility to their children who will rule after them. In all this, we imbibe Lewis's remarkable vision of the created order. It is replete with glory and freedom, but requires humility and deference from the guardians as well as from the ordinary inhabitants of this world. Some will find it "archaic," while others will see elements that may be called "progressive": it defies classification.

Though Narnia is new and mostly unspoiled, there already are dangers. The ridiculous presence of terrified but greedy Uncle Andrew, unrecognizable to the inhabitants of Narnia as either a human or an animal, makes this clear. The children, despite what the old man has done, are moved by his plight, and ask Aslan both to remove the man's fear, and curb his greed to exploit the new world. Yet all that Andrew is able to receive from the Great Lion is the rest of sleep: "Oh, Adam's

[9] *Magician's*, 80.
[10] *Magician's*, 81.

sons, how cleverly you defend yourselves against all that might do you good!"[11] We are reminded of Jesus' lament over Jerusalem. In Andrew's case, the mercy of sleep is temporary, buying a space of time until his evil has been reversed, or at least contained. Indeed, he is reformed at the end of the story to become a less selfish person.

Yet another danger lurks in Narnia, and with the Witch, the condition is terminal. Though immortal, she is in a situation of immortal decay, with every day a drawn-out life of misery that will never bring her joy. Her fate brings to life Lewis's comment elsewhere that human death, though tragic, may be viewed as "a severe mercy."[12] Human mortality, inflicted upon us in Eden, is not merely a consequence of sin, but the means by which God prevents eternal misery and evil in our world.[13] *The Magician's Nephew* subtly instructs us, as we consider the fates of Andrew, the Witch, and others, on a level just below that of conscious reflection: the novel is no allegory, with each character corresponding one-to-one with elements in our own world. Rather, we learn *deeply* from the whole assemblage and plot, even while enjoying the story for its own sake.

SALUTARY COMEDY AND SENSIBLE PERSPECTIVE

Alongside the potential grandeur and folly of creation, we are also warned of the potential terrifying link between creatures and the demonic. Digory has his own sadness to bring before Aslan, and his hopes that Aslan can bring this to a happy resolution; but he has also been complicit in the marring of Narnia. Before Aslan will consider his plea for his own

---

[11] *Magician's*, 98.

[12] The term comes from a series of letters between Lewis and a friend, and has been enshrined in Sheldon Vanauken's book, *A Severe Mercy*.

[13] This notion is taught by the Church fathers and Orthodox Tradition; see Theophilus of Antioch (*To Autolycus* 2.25–26), St Irenaeus (*Against Heresies* 3.23.6), St Gregory of Nyssa (*Oration of Consolation for Pulcheria*, PG 46:877), St Gregory of Nazianzus (*Oration* 45.8), St John Climacus (*Ladder* 15, foreword). We should not be surprised to discover that the Church's liturgical services also contain the idea (e.g. first prayer of absolution read by a bishop at the funeral of a layman, in the Greek tradition).

mother, Digory must confess to his act of *un*-creation, the evil that he has brought into this primordial world. The Witch, of course, is responsible for her actions, but Digory is guilty, too. By his arrogance and feebleness, and because of his desire to lord it over his friend Polly, he has done more damage than he could imagine: unwittingly, his ringing of a bell has brought vital power back into this evil figure.

The details make us ponder the complexities of sin and responsibility, about which the Christian tradition has always spoken carefully. Despite the shadowy presence of the Enemy, who "because of envy" (Wis 2.28) brought death into the world, human beings cannot excuse themselves with the declaration, "The devil made me do it," or "God made me this way." There are certainly powers that would seduce us away from the right path, induce us to turn away from God, and suggest that we might profitably (mis)use the creation to our own ends. In a fallen world, it seems all too human to desire the status of an autonomous "creator" rather than a joyful sub-creator. But the fault is not with how God has made us. The letter of James is very clear about the operative factor:

> Let no one say when he is tempted, 'I am tempted by God'; for God cannot be tempted with evil and he himself tempts no one; but each person is tempted when he is lured and enticed by his own desire. Then desire when it has conceived gives birth to sin; and sin when it is full-grown brings forth death. (James 3.15)

We may, when put to the test, want to think that it is impossible to resist the allure, as Digory almost convinces himself, when tempted to ring the forbidden bell in the dead world. But Digory's actions and choices, both in the dead halls of Charn (where he awakens the Witch) and in the delights of Aslan's garden (where he resists her wiles), remind us that such pretexts are merely "making excuses in sin."[14]

[14]This is a quotation from the Old Greek version of Psalm 141, LXX Psalm 140.4, traditional in Eastern Orthodox Vespers.

Our creaturely potential for good and evil is a serious matter. Yet, the story-spinning Lewis, ever aware of the incongruities of life, does not deaden his world with heavy philosophy. Delights are spotted here and there, as moments of lightheartedness aptly adorn his sub-creation. For example, just as the Narnians are told to come alive, and respond with solemnity: "Hail, Aslan, We hear and obey.... We speak. We know," Strawberry's horsey voice pipes up, "But please, we don't know very much yet."[15] There is also humor in the scene where Uncle Andrew meets his match in the evil Witch, and responds to her like a dog with its tail between its legs; he is no great Magician, and also no Casanova to attract such a proud woman. At the end of the story, we also smile to hear him reminisce about her: "A devilish temper she had . . . but she was a dem fine woman, sir."[16] (No doubt, the words "devilish" and "dem" are the author's subtle nod to the more mature reader, who will recognize the ironic humor.) As we remember from the last chapter, Lewis put much stock in this humorous perspective, highlighting the "first joke" in Narnia, and even entitling an entire chapter of his children's novel "The First Joke." Comedy is a sign of health in creatures (and writers), who must not take their activities, or themselves, in a deadly serious manner. We are fallen beings in a fallen world, and therefore it is appropriate to notice incongruity here, rather than simply life and death. Lewis, unlike the character Uncle Andrew, is well aware of his own limitations, and indeed the feebleness of all human pursuits.

Comparing Lewis's perspective over against that of another author, Michael O'Brien, is salutary. Recently, I thoroughly enjoyed Michael O'Brien's *The Island of the World*, with its powerful narrative and nuanced presentation of Serbia/Bosnia/the former Yugoslavia. However, this author—no doubt reacting to the decline of the "arts" in North America—throughout the novel persists in an overblown and romanticized

---

[15]*Magician's*, 71.
[16]*Magician's*, 105.

understanding of culture as salvific in an absolute sense. In stark contrast
to this exaltation of the human stands the humility of Lewis:

> If . . . cultural activities are innocent and even useful, then they
> also . . . can be done to the Lord. The work of a charwoman and
> the work of a poet become spiritual in the same way and on the
> same condition . . . [T]here are two kinds of good and bad . . . [I]n
> literature, in addition to the spiritual good and evil which it carries,
> there is also a good and evil of the second class, a properly cultural
> or literary good and evil, which must not be allowed to masquer-
> ade as good and evil of the first class. . . . I enjoyed my breakfast
> this morning, and I think that was a good thing and do not think
> it was condemned by God. But I do not think myself a good man
> for enjoying it.[17]

On a brief personal note, I might add that it is even more tempting for
theologians than novelists to share O'Brien's grandiosity and apply it to
their own discipline. One infamous example is Elisabeth Schüssler Fiorenza's astonishing claim about biblical scholarship in her book *Rhetoric
and Ethic*. She seems to believe that the contemporary discipline of
biblical studies can actually reform the world! I would counter that
theologians, biblical scholars, Christian artists, and even pastors should
be under no illusions that our work has (or should ever be afforded)
such power. Formal theologizing is an activity that should always be
at the service of—and subject to the correction of—the Church. If its
object is not to glorify God, the only Creator and Savior, then we have
strayed off the path. Humility and prayer provide the necessary suste-
nance for any faithful theological inquiry, "professional" or otherwise.
It is salutary to keep in our minds, as we think and work, the words of
Evagrius, "If you are a theologian, you will pray truly; and if you pray
truly, you are a theologian."

---

[17]"Christianity and Culture," pp. 12–26 in *Christian Reflections*, 35–36.

There are simple believers who have seen more of the Lord than I ever will, despite my academic training—I know this, for I have met them! It is the ordinary workhorse Strawberry whom Aslan chooses to become "Fledge," a transformed flying warhorse, who shows the necessary courage for an epic adventure. It is Digory, a simple boy with all the foibles of the young, who in the end brings good, not evil, to Narnia. Perspective, preserved for us in this real world by means of humor, keeps us real. The Narnians, then, display fragility and courage, freedom and obedience, potential for good and evil, and a healthy ability not to take themselves so very seriously. In them we see mirrored our own situation; yet they live as themselves, frolicking like Leviathan in their own setting (Psalm LXX 103/104.26).[18] Sheer delight in even the lowliest denizens of the created world is something that Lewis shares with Orthodox: we remind ourselves of these joys every time we contemplate God's world at the beginning of vespers, in which Orthodox worshippers recite this very psalm.

THE GREAT ACTOR AND OUR ROLE IN THE STORY

When Lewis pictures Aslan as creator and contrasts him with his creatures, *The Magician's Nephew* fosters an awe of God as the only Holy One. Young Digory finds out that there is no bargaining with Aslan, yet Aslan is endlessly more loving than he could ever have imagined. The story behind the story discloses Digory's great sorrow over his ill mother; the story moves on to his discovery of a chance for new life for her, found in the pure regions of Aslan's country; and the climax shows us his struggle to be obedient, without succumbing to his fears, forbidden shortcuts, or easy answers. So it is that Digory and Polly are sent, riding on the now-pegasus Fledge, to bring back the apple of life for the healing of Narnia, which Digory has compromised by his dalliance

---

[18]Throughout this book, I will provide both sets of numbers for the Psalms, from the Septuagint (LXX) version used by Orthodox, and from the Masoretic text, followed by most English translations.

with the Witch. In a heart-wrenching scene between Digory and the
Witch at the base of the tree, he learns how to recognize and stand up
to temptation, even when what is offered to him appears as a "good."
Aslan's enemy seduces the boy to seize the fruit for himself—actually, for the healing of his bedridden mother. Her ploy misfires when
she goes too far, suggesting that he need not tell anyone what he has
done, and could even leave his friend Polly behind as he travels home
to deliver the medicine. It is at that point that Digory realizes that the
Witch has no interest in his mother (or him), but seeks only to play
upon his fears to distract him from his greater quest.

On his sad but victorious return to Aslan, Digory is told about what
happens when someone "mis-plucks" the fruit, willfully, in the wrong
time and the wrong way—that it will do its job, but that it will bring
no joy. "The fruit is good, but they loathe it ever after."[19] There are,
Digory discovers, things "more terrible" than death. Aslan tells the boy,
"Well done!" and invites him to cast the apple deep into the earth. That
planted apple, the fruit of Digory's labor, produces a tree that protects
Narnia, at its borders, from the Witch, for many years. The son of Adam,
through his testing, and through his humble obedience to Aslan's plan,
takes a part in the undoing (or at least partial undoing) of the curse on
Narnia, and so becomes a miniature Christ-figure.

In the final analysis, it is the shape of the story, its tragicomic shape
of something good gone wrong and then restored, that is so satisfying.
The birth and healing of Narnia parallel the birth of a moral young man
(Digory) and the resuscitation of his mother. Digory acts out Paul's word
concerning the first and second Adam: "As by man came death, so by
man has come also the resurrection of the dead" (1 Cor 15.21). On the
level of the story, of course, Digory's mother does not enter the general
resurrection at the end of time. But Aslan's power to bring about new
life in her gives the reader hope for something even more wonderful.

[19]*Magician's,* 162.

As for the main story of the newly created world, readers hope that in Narnia the full power of the Witch will one day be broken.

Indeed, the story sets up themes that will be pursued in the other six books. The apple core that remains from the apple eaten by Digory's mother becomes a tree in tune with the winds of Narnia. When it is eventually uprooted in a storm, its Narnian wood is used for the marvelous wardrobe that will bring the four promised children, destined to be Kings and Queens, into the besieged world. Thus, the apple given by Aslan becomes the "way" between the two worlds, and the means by which Narnia is finally rescued. Moreover, even the top of a London lamp-post, wrested by the Witch from its position, is planted in that magical country, and becomes a light to guide Lucy and the children to their great adventure. Even from violence and evil, good is conjured. The positive role of the Witch's makeshift weapon (the lamp-post) is similar to Moses' use of the bronze serpent, fixed atop of the pole, which brought life to the transgressing Hebrews, when they gazed upon it (Num 21.9; Jn 3.14). In contrast to the Witch's self-will, Lewis exalts Aslan's generosity and strength, as the Lion fruitfully uses things that seem inconsequential, and brings life out of death. Aslan's character and face shine over the pages of the book, far outstripping both the Witch's magic and the power of Uncle Andrew's rings. His character is not bounded by human (or demonic) self-will and manipulation, but expressed in generosity and self-sacrifice.

As we read through the books, we are bound to wonder about the final shape of the entire Narnian collection. Will the conclusion to the stories show that the *Chronicles* are like our Christian story of resurrection and ascension? That is, will they go beyond the mere "v" shape of a restoration (down, and then up), as seen in the first book? Will we at the last find a story patterned along a check mark of triumph (down, then up *beyond* the original starting point)? Those who read the whole series and who persist to the final book, *The Last Battle,* will not be disappointed.

The Silver Chair

The intriguingly titled book, *The Silver Chair,* from the middle of the series, contains many of the same themes as *The Magician's Nephew,* including creation and sub-creation, but also introduces some new ones. Of all the children's stories, this volume clearly shows the importance of stories and storytelling. We are treated to several subplots, including backstories and narratives that are tangential to the main story. On top of this, the main plot depends upon the power of writing, and the power of images evoked by the written or spoken word. In all this writerly concern, both the playfulness and the potency of words come to light.

SUBPLOTS WITHIN THE STORY

Let us see how these subplots fit into the main story, a story that concerns the young duo Eustace (who has already been transformed by a visit to Narnia) and his school friend Jill. The story begins with Eustace shyly explaining his changed state to his friend, by divulging his remarkable experiences in Narnia (found in more detail in the previous novel, *The Voyage of the Dawn Treader*). As a consummate artist, Lewis does not reveal "spoilers" of that earlier story. Instead, Eustace tempts Jill (and those of us who have skipped this book) by referring generally to a wondrous story of enchantments, dragons, magic, and the power of Aslan. Because Eustace understands that a character like Aslan cannot be manipulated, the two children do not engage in any incantations or "magic" in their desire to visit this strange world. They simply ask Aslan to bring them to Narnia, only to find that Aslan has something for them to do there: "You would not have called to me unless I had been calling you."[20]

They are whisked off to Narnia, then, and given a quest to recover the lost son of the good but elderly King Caspian—a quest complicated

[20] *The Silver Chair* in *Chronicles* (1953; 2005), 558 (cf. Jn 6.44).

by Jill's careless actions and various evil forces set against them. Shortly after they arrive in Narnia, they enjoy a sumptuous meal in the castle, during which a blind poet rehearses before the company "the grand old tale"[21] of *The Horse and His Boy* (another of Lewis's Narnian novels). The narrator teases us with a quick reference to this subplot, referring to its main characters and their "adventure" in the time of Peter the King. Yet there is no time to tell this story, which is "well worth hearing." Here is a kind of reverse irony, for Jill and Eustace, in hearing the tale, know more than the readers—unless, of course, we have read the stories in sequence and already have enjoyed the story of Prince Cor, Aravis, and the horse Bree. If so, then the reader may enjoy a delightful "aha!" moment, and briefly recall the twists and turns of that earlier yarn.

The sung story-within-the-story reminds us that a good tale, like the meal that it accompanies, is a wholesome thing. Stories are not elevated to some ethereal, spiritual level, but live on the same level as food, drink, and company: they are human fare. The art of storytelling is not only a legitimate and good thing, but is to be thoroughly enjoyed. Lewis neither exalts his craft nor denigrates it, but considers it as part of our shared humanity. As he remarks in *Mere Christianity*,

> There is no good trying to be more spiritual than God. God never meant man to be a purely spiritual creature. That is why He uses material things like bread and wine to put the new life into us. We may think this rather crude and unspiritual. God does not: He invented eating. He likes matter. He invented it.[22]

Storytelling, too, requires matter—mouths and ears, paper and pen, and the stuff of the stories themselves. Lewis's earthiness comes to the fore here, as it does also in *The Lion, the Witch and the Wardrobe*, where the campaign against the White Witch is interrupted by a delicious Christ-

[21] *Silver*, 569.
[22] *Mere Christianity*, 62.

mas dinner and the appearance of Father Christmas, or where Mrs Badger takes her time packing delicious rations for the trek that she and the children must make in haste. Stories, like meals, are wholesome things.

We return to *The Silver Chair* and its subplots. Though Eustace and Jill are well fed at the feast, they do not sleep soundly that night, but are whisked, flying bird-back, to a "conference of the owls." Here, too, a story intrudes. They hear, amidst plans for the campaign, the backstory of Prince Rilian, son of Caspian, and the circumstances of his disappearance. The story, which is quite involved, takes about a page and a half.[23] By the second paragraph, we are so caught up in the lush green and merriment of the Narnian courtiers that we forget we are hearing a story-within-a-story. The appearance of the evil green serpent, the death of Caspian's lovely wife, the quest of Prince Rilian to find her, the appearance of a breathtaking Green Lady, and the final solitary ride of the lost Prince whisk *us* away. We are entranced by the mythic details of the story, and it abides in our imagination. Like the children, we long to discover if our warning instincts about the Green Lady are correct. Even more, we long for the valiant Prince Rilian to return.

Besides the sub-stories, *The Silver Chair* includes fragments of stories—oracles, written encoded symbols—that serve as clues for the children, and tease the reader. A strange series of walls and troughs interrupts the children's path. Later, as they look down from a castle where they are imprisoned, they see that these "walls" and "troughs" were actually huge stone letters spelling the cryptic message "Under me." This they take to be a sign directing them to find Rilian, but later are told that the "message" is really part of a longer inscription from a giant-king's tombstone: "Though under Earth and throneless now I be / Yet, while I lived, all Earth was under me."[24]

Here Lewis plays with what writers call "polyvalence"—that something written can evoke multiple meanings, and have more than one

[23] *Silver,* 575–76.
[24] *Silver,* 620.

purpose. The children are initially disheartened by this historicizing (and debunking) explanation for the huge letters. Soon, though, they are reinvigorated by their guide Puddleglum, who insists that there are no mere "accidents," if Aslan is the guide. The ancient giant king may have intended the letters as a celebration of his prowess, but Aslan was using the king's epitaph to guide the children in their present quest. This speaks, of course, to the question of intentionality and inspiration in the Old Testament Scriptures. It reminds the attuned reader that though the older sacred books had their own historical context, they also rightly serve as signposts to Christ. This way of reading, taught by Christ himself to the apostles on the road to Emmaus (Lk 24.27) and in the Upper Room (Lk 24.44), is no mere imposition. The stories of the Old Testament do "double duty." They speak of their own ancient times, of the patriarchs, prophets, kings, and priests; at the same time, all the Hebrew Scriptures truly "speak of Him." (In the second century, St Irenaeus explained that this second way of reading the ancient writings, as pointing forward to Jesus, was part of what the Church called the apostolic "rule of faith" or of "truth.") The cryptic messages in *The Silver Chair,* which had an original context, but also refer beyond themselves to the children's context, work in the same way. Lewis, or the narrator, does not need to give children heavy instruction about this way of understanding old writings. Rather, the characters and their conversation about the messages plant this seed in our imaginations.

THE POWER OF WRITING, IMAGES, AND WORDS

Words are agile things, and especially potent in the hands of a skilled and enthusiastic writer like Lewis. Towards the end of the story, when the quest has been fulfilled, Jill asks Aslan if they can go home now. By the deft turn of a phrase and the use of a capital, Lewis suggests a different meaning to "Home": Aslan responds, "Yes, I have come to bring you Home."[25] Then, as at the beginning of the story, he breathes

[25] *Silver,* 660.

upon the two children. We are surprised to discover that they do not immediately return to what they call home, but have a brief dramatic sojourn in yet another realm that is infinitely more real than England and even Narnia. Indeed, as the divine Lion blows, they do not themselves move, but everything around them is blown away by the breath of Aslan. I leave it to you, my friends, to read and discover the wonders that they find there.

Suffice it to say that Lewis uses words and the power of description in order to show the difference between shadows and reality. Time is not meaningless, nor are the events of the world futile: they find their fulfillment and purpose in that other, normally unseen realm. Lewis has frequently been accused of "Neo-Platonism," that is, of reviving the Platonic teaching of celestial "forms," and confusing this philosophic schema with Christian doctrine. Certainly, there are in this novel (and other of Lewis's books) traces of Plato's teaching: he taught, in his idea of "forms," that all appearances of things in this world correspond to eternal realities. Plato has been a force to contend with for centuries. But, like the book of Hebrews, Lewis has thoroughly adapted the Platonic concept that the phenomena of this world are mere shadows in comparison to the eternal "forms" that we do not presently see. For example, Lewis's Form of forms, Aslan, the *real* Lion, intrudes into the shadow world of Narnia, rather than staying in an unseen celestial world. He even is mysteriously present with the children (though not bodily) as they enter the underworld. His guiding presence ensures that what happens *in time* has a purpose. Indeed, their quest has been his idea.

Plato's well-known "allegory of the cave," with its flickering shadows of reality on the wall, is mimicked in the children's descent to the unlit caverns. Indeed, their conversation with the evil Green Lady about what is real also recalls Plato's parable: she seeks to enchant them so that they forget everything about the real "overworld" of light. Like the chained and blinkered denizens of Plato's cave, those so enchanted by

her settle placidly in the shadows, and forget the real world. They come
to believe that there is no sun, and that they have projected their idea
of a "lamp" into an imaginary upper world; there is no great Lion, they
agree, but this myth is simply an extrapolation from their idea of a cat.

Up to this point we might think that Lewis is simply remixing
Plato. Yet it is not the refusal of the evil Lady to acknowledge *forms* that
proves to be the last final straw, but her denial of *Aslan* Himself. Nor
is it philosophy that breaks the Lady's spell, but a jarring dose of self-
inflicted pain, by the guide of their company. Then Puddleglum, the
unphilosophical marshwiggle, points out the obvious problem: exactly
how could mere children *make up* something that was better than the
Green Lady's dark underground "real world"? There must be something to the idea of an upper world that is not dependent upon them;
and if *not,* then everything is futile, anyway! With this, the Lady's spell
on the children—to disbelieve in anything more than the cavern walls
they see around them—is dispelled, and the real battle begins.

Lewis engages well-known philosophical ideas and images, putting them to a higher use for his own sub-creative story. For as truly
as there is an Overworld (Narnia) above the Lady's dungeon-like caverns, there is an England beyond that, and—greater still—Aslan's own
unseen world and Kingdom even further beyond. In the intersection
of these worlds, temporal (yet eternally significant) suffering promises
to establish a secure reality, and the great battle, joined by those seen
and unseen, is rumored to bring deliverance. Words, pictures, and events
figure in this story, and all take their proper place. Lewis does not reca-
pitulate Plato's dualistic picture of reality, but using that philosopher's
initial ideas, reclaims and exalts the power of earthly words and stories.

The poignant and saving words of Scripture echo throughout the
book. Especially, these allusions are clustered in the dénouement of *The
Silver Chair.* I will only mention a few of these generally, in case a few of
my readers have not heeded my advice to read the actual books before
joining our conversations with Lewis: I do not want to spoil the fresh

impact of the images beforehand! Towards the end of the book there is a marvelous sequence in which we see both a funeral and a resurrection of a king; by it, we are reminded of the great story of Life through Death. Lewis paints a haunting picture incorporating the Lion's tears, the prick of a thorn (imposed by a son of Adam), and a revitalizing drop of blood mixed with water. This is followed by a great manifestation of Aslan's turned "back" to the children's own English world, a surprising turn of events recalling the fear of the Hebrews at the foot of Mount Sinai, and Moses' vision of God's "back" from the cleft of the rock. In Narnia, these majestic images are incomparably more powerful than the incantations of the usurping Green Lady, or the sword of the soldier. Lewis saves these most potent pictures until the last: Aslan's breath, Aslan's tears, Aslan's command, Aslan's shining appearance, make their greatest and lasting impression on our imaginations.

SACRAMENTAL REALITY AND HOMO ADORANS

The beauty of creation in *The Magician's Nephew* and Lewis's luminous use of words and images in *The Silver Chair* show that he understands God's creation as *sacramental*—a theme to which we will return in the final chapter of this study. Aslan's song at the beginning of the first book is matched by the mythical quality of the garden-story at its end. Again, the signs given at the beginning of *Silver Chair* are far more than mere mechanical cues for the children's quest. They are part and parcel of the worlds that the children visit, and, as deep symbols, are caught up in the larger reality of Aslan's Realm, glimpsed at the end of the story.

Even the Narnian landscape provides hints of Aslan's will and presence. Indeed, some of the more curious features of Narnia are suggested in the hints given ahead of time by Aslan on the mountain: but Jill finds them hard both to remember and to recognize during her quest in the realms below. Meeting and knowing Aslan is the key that brings these signs into focus. As Lewis will put it more prosaically in his allegory, *Pilgrim's Regress,* human reason can level the playing field, but only the sight of God can teach the difference between the copy and the reality.

This teaching that nature reveals aspects of God's nature is not unique to Lewis, of course. Throughout St Paul's letter to the Romans (1.18–2.1; 5.6; 8.27; 8.37–39), we hear about deception, unreality, reality, truth, creation, reflections, distortions, and release from an imperfect understanding of the world. Everything in creation has been given that we might know God better, but the most direct sign is in Jesus himself:

> O the depth of the riches and wisdom and knowledge of God!
> How unsearchable are his judgments and how inscrutable his ways!
> For who has known the mind of the Lord, or who has been his
> counselor? Or who has given a gift to him that he might be repaid?
> For from him and through him and to him are all things. To him be
> glory for ever. Amen. (Rom 11.33–36)

Our deepest desires can, if pursued with the clues, gifts, words, story, and signs that God has given us, lead us to Him. According to an early hymn of the Church (Col 1.15–20), Jesus is the Head over everything in Creation and over the Church. He is thus both the cosmic and the personal God, whose love for us may lead us finally to our place under the sun, and under the Son, as sub-creators. Almost certainly Lewis would have warmed to the words of Fr Alexander Schmemann, who speaks of our human calling to be *homo adorans* ("humanity that worships"), and how the created order encourages us in this:

> Man is a hungry being. But he is hungry for God. All desire is
> finally a need for Him. . . . The whole creation depends upon food.
> But the unique position of man in the universe is that he alone is
> to *bless* God for the food and the life he receives from Him. He
> alone is to respond to God's blessing with his blessing. The signifi-
> cant fact about the life in the garden is that man is to *name* things.

...To name a thing ... is to bless God for it and in it. ...The first, the basic definition of man is that he is *the priest*. He stands in the center of the world and unifies it with his act of blessing God, of both receiving the world from God and offering it to God.[26]

Humankind, then, is called to recognize our dependence upon God, and our role in receiving and offering up the rest of the cosmos *with thanks*—literally, "eucharistically"—to Him. To give thanks to the Lord is our calling and primary activity, like the three youths in the furnace, who give voice to the rest of Creation, and like Digory, who offers an apple that is mysteriously used by God in ways that he could never have imagined. St Paul teaches in Romans 1.21 that the refusal to give thanks to God is connected with the refusal to worship Him. Our misuse of the created order, and desire to be creators in our own right, is at the root of our great illness, our fallen condition. Yet, for those with eyes to see the images, and ears to hear the sounds, "[t]he world ... becomes an *epiphany* of God, a means of his revelation, presence, and power."[27] Fr Alexander Schmemann concludes that, over against religions that downplay or vilify created things, our faith speaks of a God who gives all things to us for our sanctification, and us to *them* that we might bless them: "We *need* water and oil, bread and wine, in order to be in communion with God and to know him."[28] The whole world is overflowing with the glory of God, pointing to Him—including writings that are the fruit of thankful and worshipping minds.

Lewis would agree. His understanding of the sacramental nature of the cosmos is shown even as Jill begins her adventure in *The Silver Chair*. There a very thirsty Jill is confronted by an imposing Lion, who lies by the side of the stream. "Are you not thirsty?" asks Aslan, and the girl responds that she is *"dying* of thirst." To this, the Lion responds,

[26]*For the Life of the World*, 2nd rev. ed. (Crestwood, NY: St.Vladimir's Press, 1973), 14–15.
[27]*For the Life*, 120.
[28]*For the Life*, 120.

"Then drink," but she fearfully refuses until she is told, "There is no other stream."[29] Just a few sips quench her thirst immediately, and she realizes that there is no escaping the Lion at this point. The invitation and the slaking of thirst have led to communion with the One who gives the water.

And that is the beginning of the story for Jill and Eustace. Next, Jill stands on the high land with Aslan, and surveys the realm of Narnia, mapping the terrain just as Moses did with the Lord from Mount Pisgah. Unlike Moses, however, she also enters the Land, with Eustace, as they are sent on a quest by the Lion to plumb the depths of the unseen caves. In their adventure they learn not only more about that land but also more about themselves. It is not enough to see and hear the Lion, but Jill must taste the water that he offers her. It is not enough to view Narnia from a distance, but they must go deeper into it before they can go further up, finally catching a glimpse of Aslan's own country, which few have ever seen.

This is a story told by a humble sub-creator who delights in the water, in the images, and in the words, because they mirror the living water and larger story that is given to us by the One who is the Living Water, the Word, and the Creator of all. As Aslan issues a challenging invitation to Jill, so we too receive a call to "Come and see."[30]

---

[29] Silver, 557.
[30] Jn 1.39, 46.

CHAPTER 3

"Worldview," Miracles, and Magic

("Modern Theology and Biblical Criticism" and *Miracles*)

The world picture of the NT is a mythical world picture. The world is a three-story structure, with earth in the middle, heaven above it, and hell below it. Heaven is the dwelling place of God and of heavenly figures, the angels; the world below is hell, the place of torment. But even the earth is not simply the scene of natural day-to-day occurrences . . . rather it, too, is a theater for the working of supernatural powers, God and his angels, Satan and his demons. . . . History does not run its own steady, lawful course, but is moved and guided by supernatural powers. This age stands under the power of Satan, sin, and death. . . . It is hastening towards its imminent end, which will take place in a cosmic catastrophe. . . . All of this mythological talk . . . may be easily traced to the contemporary mythology of Jewish apocalypticism and of the Gnostic myth of redemption. . . . Can Christian proclamation today expect men and women to acknowledge the mythical world picture as true? To do so would be . . . pointless. . . . It would be pointless because there is nothing specifically Christian about the mythical world picture, which is simply the world picture of a time now past that was not yet formed by scientific thinking. . . . We cannot use electric lights and radios, and, in the event of illness, avail ourselves of modern medical and clinical means and at the same time believe in the spirit and wonder world of the NT.[1]

[1] Rudolf Bultmann, *The New Testament and Mythology and Other Basic Writings*, trans. and ed. Schubert M. Ogden (Philadelphia, PA: Fortress, 1984), 1–4.

S o wrote Rudolf Bultmann in 1941. It should be apparent that such words did not impress C. S. Lewis, his younger contemporary. Lewis, as we have seen, gave his fullest approval to the power of myth. He aimed in *his* writing to lead others to see what might happen if they submitted their imaginations to the One who is the source of all luminous stories. We might note that Bultmann and Lewis did not use the word "myth" in precisely the same way, and certainly not with the same connotative value. For Lewis, the word conjured nymphs, green hills, and animism, whereas Bultmann was more intent upon the time-line of ancient biblical mythology, and its fixation upon the end of the age. Sometimes, then, they may talk past each other. However, there is enough overlap to bring the two into conflict concerning the ongo-ing power (Lewis would say, necessity) of myth and picture language in every age. According to Bultmann, mythology was most at home in the infancy of humanity; Lewis insisted that it is a natural habit of the human mind in every day and age. Lewis's essay "Modern Theology and Biblical Criticism" (also called "Fern-seed and Elephants") tackles Bultmann's assumptions and conclusions head-on. His longer study, *Miracles,* is wide-ranging, but amidst its various arguments probes the influence of what Bultmann calls "world pictures," and what Lewis refers to as "the kind of philosophy we bring to experience."

If the terrain that we mapped in the children's novels was imme-diately delightful, the landscape that we survey at this point may prove less engaging for readers of a less philosophical bent. We are no longer well trained, as were the educated of past generations, to work hard at logic. For at least two generations, students have been swept up in sound bites, pictures, and impressions. It is less natural to consider presupposi-tions, the relationship between rhetoric and honesty, and how to mount a cogent argument that goes beyond a sales pitch. The question of worldview may be intriguing, so long as we don't have to delve into the deeper realms of ontology (the study of being), epistemology (the study of how we know), argumentation, and coherence. These matters are, for the classical debater, serious business, and require hard work. Indeed, it is interesting to hear the saga of Lewis's ongoing debate with the brilliant Elizabeth Anscombe, who, Lewis admitted, roundly defeated him in a famous 1948 debate about reason and reality. He took her criticisms to heart, and thoroughly revised the third chapter of his 1947 original version of *Miracles,* reshaping his argument so as to answer her critique: the new version was published in 1960, which she acknowledged to be a much better presentation. Neither interlocutor reversed his or her position, for their premises did not match: but they took the discussion seriously enough to persist in the debate, and to improve the expression of their basic differences.[2]

Few of us engage in such involved debate, nor have most of us been shaped by an education that values rhetoric and logic so highly, as was the case in their day. As a lure for our balky minds, we can turn to the work of Richard Middleton and Brian Walsh, *Truth Is Stranger Than It Used to Be.* They suggest that a "worldview" in society works by offering "faith answers to a set of ultimate and grounding questions." According to them, a worldview attempts to answer the following basic questions:

- "Where am I?"

- "Who am I?"

- "What's wrong?"

- "What's the remedy?"[3]

---

[2] A cogent account of the intricacies of their arguments, the changes made by Lewis, and Anscombe's final response has been written by Arend Smilde, in "What Lewis Really Did to *Miracles,*" *Journal of Inklings Studies* 1, no. 2 (October 2011): 9–24. It is available online at http://www.lewisiana.nl/anscombe/ (accessed September 2016).

[3] J. Richard Middleton and Brian J. Walsh, *Truth Is Stranger Than It Used to Be* (Downer's Grove, IL, InterVarsity Press, 1995), 11–12.

Actually, I have slightly reshaped their guiding questions. My friends framed them in the first person plural ("we"), not the first person singular ("I"). But I believe that we are now seeing the demise even of a common modernist story about "us" that might hold Americans together. According to Walsh and Middleton, this narrative pictures us as inhabitants of "the New World": we are conquerors whose progress was held back by medieval European society, but who are freeing ourselves from all limits. Even that American story, they admit, is now being challenged by "postmodern" insistence upon hearing "alternative voices":

> [D]ebates about college curricula have been dominated by the question of the voice of "other cultures." Although this might at first appear to be a healthy opening up of our culture in such a way that the voiceless are finally heard, this opening up is something of a double-edged sword. . . . [T]he result is a bewildering cacophony.[4]

In fact, the postmodern chatter accentuates one aspect of modernism that accompanied the national story—the value of the individual. Alongside a turn from the supernatural to the natural world, a belief in a progressive future rather than the past, and confidence in experimental study, came a turn from external authorities *to the individual*. Americans may have been brought together by the national story of their escape from European oppression into a brave new world. Along with that common heritage came the seeds of disintegration, for the individual took pride of place. Modernism, despite its individualistic tone, retained a corporate edge in the desire to improve the lot of modern "man." However, emphasis on autonomy ("self-rule") meant that this desire for improvement was framed in terms of *contracts between individuals*. Human progress as a whole was important because it benefited the individual. The questions were, and still are, fundamentally about "me" and not really "us." As Walsh and Middleton put it, this emphasis has

---

[4] *Truth*, 13.

increased to the point that the current generation sees itself as *homo autonomous,* trying to build a tower "built on a foundation of radical, self-determining freedom."[5]

Yet this Babel tower of modern progress is collapsing under its own weight. Many of the younger generation disbelieve the story and have been left only with disorientation, fragmentation, and chaos. They have no single guiding narrative—not even the initial American myth of escape and hope for the future—to answer the four questions. In place of the American dream, limited though it was, there remains only the barren conviction that there *is* no one story. Yes, we still have those among us who could be termed "hypermodern," and who continue to believe without doubt in the potential of science, progress, and technology. There remains among some the dream that we can build our own version of an intelligent universe, as seen in the monuments to this faith. Disneyworld, other theme parks, and "climate controlled malls that attempt to look like old-fashioned shopping neighborhoods,"[6] are an emblem to some of a new world to come. At any rate, virtual worlds distract the disillusioned. However, modernism's common project of progress has cracked from within, compromised by its shaky foundation of individualism. Why should I care about where humanity as a whole is headed if the main measure of success is my own private happiness? Modernism and what has emerged afterwards ("postmodernism") jostle in our day for attention; without a common story, humanity seems lost.

There are those who make a virtue out of necessity, and celebrate the confusion. On the popular level, we see beer commercials exhorting us to "celebrate the diversity." On the academic level, there are not only universities, but also seminaries that embrace diversity in their self-descriptions, seeking to highlight it in their vision statements and foster it in their strategies. This has affected the Church as well. Translations

---

[5] *Truth,* 20–21.
[6] *Truth,* 39.

of the Scripture soft-pedal the apostle Paul's desire that the Corinthians "say the same thing" (1 Cor 1.10) and rephrase his actual words to be more palatable for today—that we should "live in harmony" (NLV) or "be in agreement" (NRSV). In a world where individualism is the touchstone, a bewildering "variety" in matters of faith is espoused as easily as variety in cultural expression or personal taste. This would have been incomprehensible to the apostles. In an irreverent moment, Lewis might have called this "damned nonsense."

For Lewis had an uncanny prescience, by which he saw half a century or so ahead to our time, even while he commented astutely on his own. Let's turn to Lewis's trenchant critique of modernism in his essay "Modern Theology and Biblical Criticism," then to his proposed picture of reality in *Miracles*. We will not consider every aspect of these dense pieces, but highlight those passages that illuminate questions having to do with worldview, miracles, and magic—themes found throughout Lewis's fictional writing. Our study here, though brief, is like an arduous training ground or in-depth mapping of the terrain, so that we can follow Lewis with more agility as he leads us to heights and depths, further up and further in.

"Modern Theology and Biblical Criticism" ("Fern-seed and Elephants")

The foundational questions of Walsh and Middleton help us in our reading of Lewis's short essay. The first question, "Where am I?" is suggested by the way that Lewis addressed the theological students to whom this paper was originally presented. His location is in the Church of England, whose leaders are compromised by the spirit of the times. His answer to the second question, "Who am I?", is intended to defuse the awkwardness of the situation, but also to jolt them into listening, for as those who are training to be clergy, they should care about their people. Professor Lewis's answer is *not* that he is an expert among pastors or biblical scholars: he is "a sheep," not a shepherd. His lowly position, however, gives him an advantage, for he is "[a] sheep, telling shepherds what only a sheep can tell them." Obviously Lewis is having a bit of fun here, since he is a well-educated person, and not truly naïve. Yet he is not educated in the manner of Bultmann and other biblical scholars. Indeed, some have pointed out passages in his writings where he seems to have mistaken the aims of biblical critics, and even where he may display naiveté and generalizations concerning the texts of the Bible.[7] Be this as it may, his sheepy "bleats" remain instructive, as he indicates another of the worldview-questions: "What's wrong?" His answer is that the shepherds (mistaught, confused, or faithless themselves) are misleading the flock. Too many of them doubt the historical reliability of much of the Gospels, and so are undermining, perhaps unwittingly, the very foundations of the faith. Lewis explains:

> A theology which denies the historicity of nearly everything in the Gospels to which Christian life and affections and thought have been fastened for nearly two millennia—which either denies the miraculous altogether or, more strangely, after swallowing the camel of the Resurrection strains at such gnats as the feeding of the multitudes—if offered to the uneducated man can produce only one or other of two effects. It will make him a Roman Catholic or an atheist.[8]

Frequently, of course, Anglican priests in Lewis's time did not readily preach a "progressive" message from the pulpit or admit publicly to the kind of skepticism displayed on their shelves, and inculcated in

---

[7] Leslie Baynes, in "C. S. Lewis's Use of Scripture in the Liar, Lunatic, or Lord Argument," *Journal for Inklings Studies* 4, no. 2 (2014): 27–66, argues that Lewis's argument is flawed because he lacks knowledge of the historical-critical method. For example, he uses a passage not found in the best Johannine manuscripts (the woman caught in adultery) in order to argue for historical veracity. I do not agree with my friend concerning the seriousness of these problems for Lewis's major arguments, but acknowledge (as would Lewis) that he was no expert in our field.

[8] "Modern Theology and Biblical Criticism," in *Christian Reflections*, 153.

their theological education. Their sermons continued to make pious noises and use "picture-truth," without coming clean on their more "advanced" way of approaching the Bible. But, in confrontation with a parishioner who stumbles across the new ways of thinking, there is likely to be fallout. That is, any honest layperson will not be satisfied with the explanation that we cannot know what Jesus did or said, but yet somehow the stories still make an existential or moral impact on us, and so historicity simply does not matter. The wise sheep, says Lewis, will either accept the critical verdict, but decline to stay in the Church, or will find a place where the "old orthodoxy" is still taught, and food is to be found. In Lewis's day, that would have been the Roman Catholic Church in England, since Alfred Loisy (mentioned by Lewis in this essay), a major proponent of the modernist biblical critical methods, had been excommunicated.

Lewis's concern is not only for historicity, but for the impact that a hospitable reading of Bultmann and others like him must inevitably have upon the reader's assessment of Jesus. Lewis insists upon the luminosity of Jesus in the pages of the Gospels, where a living personality emerges as we read: everywhere we encounter his "peasant shrewdness, intolerable severity, and irresistible tenderness."[9] This picture is so vivid that the "sheep hear his voice" and distinguish falsely attributed sayings from true when they hear them. Lewis is interested in the theory of this debate, but far more engrossed by the reality of our Lord. It appalls Lewis that scholars claim to be able to see the intricacies of historical development in the early Church, and yet such experts mistakenly classify the Gospels as "spiritual romance" or even "legend." As he observes, "They claim to see fern-seed and can't see an elephant ten yards away in broad daylight."[10] His first bleat, then, is that skeptical biblical scholars make great claims to precision even as they are missing the obvi-

---

[9]"Modern Theology," 156.
[10]"Modern Theology," 157.

ous—the glory of Jesus, a personality shining from the pages of the Bible, compelling to many for nearly twenty centuries.

The second bleat matches Lewis's entire approach to writing and reading: the danger of what he calls elsewhere "chronological snobbery." This is the assumption that ancient people were hopelessly naïve. In this account, the apostles (and those who followed) misunderstood Jesus' teaching, whereas advanced modern historians can recover what he actually said, why he said it, and what he "really" meant. Against these ideas, Lewis musters his expert knowledge of bizarre theories among scholars of English literature, who refashioned Plato or Shakespeare so that their writing was more palatable to their own day. Here Lewis cheerfully points out the obvious. It is ridiculous to think that those who live twenty centuries later are in a better position to understand someone than those—some eyewitnesses!—who lived in the same culture. The historical arrogance of some advocates of the historical-critical method is a huge red flag. Such critics are largely blinded by their own philosophical, cultural, and religious presuppositions, while not acknowledging the limitations of their own perspective.

Thirdly, Lewis questions the precept that many of the critics seem to follow: "if miraculous, unhistorical."[11] He points out that this is a philosophical assumption, not a matter of biblical criticism. We began this discussion of worldview with Bultmann, who presumed that it was impossible to use electric lightbulbs and believe in unseen beings. Such critics, concludes Lewis, are "obviously influenced by, and perhaps insufficiently critical of, the spirit of the age they grew up in."[12]

These three bleats lead up to his "loudest and longest": the unreliability of a historical reconstruction of an author's circumstances and intent based only on the study of that person's writing. Lewis does not fill out what this might mean in biblical studies. In fact, intentionality *is* sought on various levels as Biblical scholars tackle the texts. Frequently,

[11]"Modern Theology," 158.
[12]"Modern Theology," 158.

scholars and critics who engage in what is called "form" criticism aim to find the original setting, and possible intent, of a word of Jesus, or of the community who either passed on or (according to many) *created* this saying. Then there are those who engage in "redaction" criticism in order to recover the motivation, or theological tendency, of the gospel writers. These studies produce ingenious, and sometimes contradictory, results.

Lewis's own experience as an author taught him that those trying to read between the lines in this way are on shaky ground. Even those who review writings from their own culture and time make obvious and glaring mistakes when they try to determine what the author meant to say. Tolkien's *Lord of the Rings* was *not* influenced by or "really about" twentieth-century fear of the atom bomb; Roger Lancelyn Green's tiger (in *The Land of the Lord High Tiger*) was not modelled on Aslan. Such reconstructions, then, "are more unlikely to be anything but sheer illusions,"[13] especially when they deal with ancient writings. The general difficulty in knowing another person's inner motivation, any critic's distance in time from the text, and the academic habit of piling hypothesis upon hypothesis in forging reconstructions all militate against any solid results. Lewis's advice to these would-be shepherds is "Try doubting something"[14] besides the historical connections implied in the Gospels. His challenge is redoubled by the inimitable biblical scholar, Morna Hooker, who laments over form critics and theories about Jesus run amok: "If only they would say they don't know!"[15]

Lewis wraps up his bleats with a major argument against all who assume the impossibility of miracles. We need first of all to acknowledge that we have limited experience of any world but our own. We are, in Lewis's imagination, like the imaginary rational dog who reverences human beings and is trying to understand human daily life: he is

[13]"Modern Theoogy," 161.
[14]"Modern Theology," 164.
[15]"On Using the Wrong Tool," *Theology* 75 (1972): 570–81.

shocked to discover that human beings actually eat or engage in bodily functions.[16] But the dog fails to realize that only some of the language that he would use to explain human activity must be analogical. He rightly assumes that human beings do research *as* dogs look for rats in the garden: this is only an analogy. But at other points, there is a real and non-analogical connection between the dog and the human world: human beings really must eat and sleep, as their pets do. If human beings are distinct from God because of their animal nature, but also made in the image of God, then a similar situation may well apply: much of our language about God may be mere analogy, but we cannot be certain that all of it is. As he reminds us, "You cannot know if the representation of a thing is symbolical unless you have independent access to the thing and can compare it with the representation."[17]

We hear the story of Jesus' ascension, and as moderns may assume that the direction "up" is simply unhistorical picture language: the symbolically minded may read this as a mere legend that is intended to show forth the "high and lifted up" majesty of Jesus. But attention to the type of writing we see in Luke-Acts shows that this double book is written not in the same vein as the "hills clapping their hands" in the Psalms. Surely Luke, a fairly literary author, intended to describe, even allowing for the conventions of the times, an event that the apostolic witnesses claimed to have seen. (Consider his own stated intent in the first pages of his Gospel and his Acts.)

We come, at last, to Lewis's answer to the fourth question, "What's the solution?" His response is that those teaching, preaching, and reading the Bible must resist the temptation to think of the ancient writers as simpletons. Further, we ourselves should pay attention to differences in genre—that is, in the different *kinds* of writings—found in the pages of Scripture. And how, in fact, do we know that "up" is irrelevant to the ascension, questions Lewis, having not undergone an

[16]"Modern Theology," 165.
[17]"Modern Theology," 166.

ascension ourselves? What *is* the relationship of this space-time world to the heavenly unseen one? Only the Pioneer of our faith knows, for He has the vantage point. Finally then, Lewis pleads that biblical scholars—indeed, all who think about the things of God—should exhibit humility regarding the limits of reason and experience. We find ourselves back in Professor Kirke's study, listening to his reasoning with the Pevensie children about Lucy's visit to Narnia. Lewis's essay is neither anti-rationalistic nor disdainful of experience: but above reason and personal experience he places the importance of authority and humility, at least in the face of something we are not adequately prepared to understand. For Christians, this means specifically to acknowledge the authority of the holy apostolic community, who passed on the traditions given by Jesus, and concerning Him. To "map the terrain" is to know our own limitations and also where we can get help in seeing the whole picture in proper perspective.

Miracles

The phenomenon of miracles is one of those matters that rest upon acceptance of authority for most Christians: "blessed are those who have not seen, but believe." Lewis's subtitle to *Miracles* ("A Preliminary Study") indicates its purpose as a first step in thinking about signs and wonders in the Bible. That is, the book operates as a philosophical clearinghouse, answering big "worldview" questions. (As such, it is not intended as an historical inquiry about whether the Christian story actually happened as presented.) Our brief sketch of its major points is even more preliminary, and cannot replace a leisurely walk with Lewis himself, who, we have seen, thought deeply about these questions, and rephrased them when writing his book, in order to answer the misgivings of the philosopher whom he had debated. I urge my readers to spend much time in this book: it does not have the same initial allure as his novels, but it is well worth the time and effort.

Here are the main threads of his argument. First, Lewis presents two contrasting views for understanding reality, the "naturalist" and "supernaturalist" perspectives. Is the universe a closed box (naturalism), or an open system, with which sometimes another super-"nature" (or other natures) can intersect? The problem with naturalism is that it cannot be argued robustly without undermining the very argument and logic upon which it stands. Quoting the biologist J. B. S. Haldane (who himself was a critic of Lewis), Lewis agrees: if I am sure that my mental processes are simply random accidents caused by moving matter (electrons), then I have no grounds for thinking so! "Our whole idea of Nature depends on the thinking that we are actually doing."[18] Lewis's subtle arguments at this point address the astute critique of Elizabeth Anscombe, whom Lewis deeply admired as an interlocutor. We can better grasp the interchange between Lewis (L) and the naturalist Anscombe (A) by means of the brief summary produced by Arend Smilde, below (with my supplemental explanations in brackets):

L. *If thoughts have only natural causes, then all thought must be irrational.* [But we do not really think that thought is irrational, or we would not be having this discussion.]

A. *But there is nothing irrational about causation.* [What I mean is, it may be non-rational, but it is not *against* reason, and there may be non-rational causes of reason.]

L. *Ah, you're right there—but I'm afraid there is nothing rational to it either.* [Okay, I will call causation non-rational, but my argument still holds, so long as you mean cause-and-effect, and not logical consequence. And you will find it difficult to give an explanation for how reason arose from non-rational causes!]

A. *Don't be afraid: rationality has no causes, and needs no causes.*

---

[18] *Miracles*, 28.

[Evolutionary selection, experience, and the practice of making inferences are part of the natural world, and so we don't have to explain rationality].

L. *I daresay it doesn't. It's very special indeed. It's not caused by other things, nor causing them, but "about" them. Nor would we humans have ever begun to distinguish reason from the rest* [of the world we experience] *if reason had not been there in the first place. Apparently causes are not everything: which is what I was saying.* [The best way of looking at Reason, the one that we assume whenever we "reason" something out, is that it comes first as an axiom, or first principle, not that it emerges out of Nature.][19]

The debate that Lewis lays out, without mentioning Anscombe, hinges on the trickiness of the word "because." We use that word both to describe:

(a) cause and effect ("the apple fell *because* the branch broke"),

and also in logical argument to describe:

(b) ground and consequence ("I say that *because* I have evidence").

Sometimes, in argument, we switch from one to the other sense of "because" without noticing it. Mixing meanings confuses any argument, including this one. So, then, when the naturalist claims that rational thought is the product of natural selection, experience, or daily practice in making inferences, he or she uses *because* in terms of (a), cause and effect, but lets the use slide into (b), ground and consequence. That a human being has evolved so that he or she makes inferences about reality does not, argues Lewis, give us grounds for thinking that such reasonings actually correspond to reality!

[19]Smilde, "What Lewis Really Did."

In the end, anyone arguing this way *about* Reason must admit that he or she *assumes* that Reason is either chronologically or logically *prior* to whatever events or facts have been used by the human mind as it considers these things: otherwise even arguments about Reason itself are absurd. We simply assume, as we think about Reality, that there is a correlation between what is being reasoned in the human mind and actual reality. The best possible explanation that corresponds to how we think and argue is that Reason is *outside* of causation, and that Reason itself is the firm ground for our thinking about Reality in the first place. "Reason is not related to Nature as Nature is related to Reason."[20] We may indeed find Reason *in* nature and in our human minds; but for our thought to work at all, in practical terms, we must admit that Reason is independent of nature, and not conditioned wholly by cause and effect. The human capacity to think about both Nature and Reason is in itself an indication that more exists than what we call Nature. Lewis's argument here is complex, because it calls us to think about our foundational assumptions, those very means by which we think.

Lewis's second plank in the argument for miracles is our moral sense. We cannot move directly from knowing "what I want" or "what is real" to explain the compelling thought that every human experiences at one time or another: "I ought/ought not to do this." That is, material urges and physical observation cannot produce or explain our conscience or sense of right and wrong. There are, then, two arguments:

1. The best way to explain rational thought in humanity is to see Reason as ultimately *outside* of what is being considered.

2. The universal human sense of "ought" (even granted differences in moral standards) cannot come from what exists or from what we want.

[20] *Miracles,* 30.

These two precepts come into focus if one tries, for example, to explain, on natural grounds alone, why sexual assault is inherently wrong for human beings, if we see them as simply more intelligent animals. No real argument can be made for this moral judgment on the basis of what we observe in nature and on the basis of human power and desire. Yet in no culture have humans accepted the idea of untrammeled sexual expression. Lewis suggests, then, that both with the reasonable human mind, and with the strange existence of human conscience, we have evidence for "supernature" operating within nature. Both rationality and ethics, exhibited in our physical selves, appear to be at the "frontier" of the natural world, examples of "supernature" working within nature. In this sense, they are miracles, outside the normal bounds of cause and effect.

Along the way, Lewis does damage control on sloppy misconceptions. First is the red herring we have already encountered: "chronological snobbery," whereby the modern person discounts reports of the unusual from the first century, on the grounds that they were gullible and had a different worldview. (To this sneer, he responds that Joseph didn't need a contemporary degree in embryology to know that babies aren't normally conceived without a male sperm.) Part of rightly mapping the terrain is to recognize what we have *in common* with ancient writers, as well as differences from culture to culture.

In another chapter, entitled "Horrid Red Things," Lewis acknowledges that some faithful Christians may hold naïve and childish ideas of God. However, the childishness does not consist in using picture language to talk about God the Father—the old man with the grey beard, for example. That picture may be inadequate, and (say the Orthodox) heretical: indeed, it is not according to Orthodox practice even to make an icon of the Father. However, we can't get rid of pictures, when we think of spiritual things. "Father" comes with an image attached, even if it is a mental one: so, too, does "force" or "substance."

Even *if* early Christians were literalists, this doesn't mean that their doctrines are not true in a larger sense. Indeed, when we say that something spiritual is being expressed metaphorically, we should not assume that this spiritual reality is *less* true than the material. It is *more* solid, *more* real, and *more* true: "They rightly think that Christ spoke metaphorically when he told us to carry the cross: they wrongly conclude that carrying the cross means nothing more than leading a respectable life and subscribing moderately to charities."[21] Given the way that the miracles are presented in the New Testament, and their centrality to the story, it is simply dishonest to suggest that they are intended "symbolically." We require symbolism to speak adequately about some of the aspects of God's character and action among us, but the feeding of the five thousand is not a moral story to encourage us to share our food with others! It is about God's meeting our need in surprising—even miraculous—yet physical ways, as He does when we ingest the holy mysteries in bread and wine.

So, then, Lewis sweeps away unexamined assumptions and misconceptions about his topic. Next, he turns to the hard work of examining biblical miracles. They have been challenged on three grounds: miracles are impossible, improbable, or inappropriate. On the charge of impossibility, we may suspect rightly (from our eavesdropping on Professor Kirke and the children) that Lewis will warn us about assumptions and reality. We are not to be like indoor cats who believe that the natural universe is always constant in temperature between 65 and 75 degrees Fahrenheit. If we do not think that the space-time universe is a closed system, then we must allow the possibility that it may be acted upon by Another, by Someone who is not confined to it. Lewis argues, then, that a miracle does not actually "break" the law of nature. It may not be linked backwards in time with material cause and effect, because it is an exceptional act of God: but it *is* linked forwards. The wine Jesus

---

[21] *Miracles*, 82.

created from water at Cana could slake thirst, or make someone drunk, even if it was not made by the ordinary means.

Nature, then, assimilates these unexpected events, even though the miracle has an ultimate Author and Cause who has bypassed the usual chain of cause and effect. In the midst of this discussion, we delightedly note Lewis's tender awe towards Nature: "this astonishing cataract of bears, babies, and bananas" who is "herself" "our old enemy, friend, playfellow, and foster-mother."[22] She is our companion, neither to be worshiped nor misused! God deigns to work with matter and time; Nature is not herself an invincible deity, not pantheistically "all that there is." Part of our scouting the territory, then, is to understand our natural context, and our relationship with it, because "the theologians" tell us that Nature, too, "is to be redeemed"[23]—as, of course, does the Apostle in his eighth chapter of Romans. Nature is neither unreachable to God's touch nor divine in herself. Thus, miracles—direct acts of the Creator within her—are not impossible.

But are they improbable? Scottish philosopher David Hume thought so (reports Lewis), because they go against the majority vote of our past experiences. In response, urges Lewis, consider the complexity and improbability of our experience. Nature is full of surprises. Our ability as animals to reason should be a first sign that this visible world is not all that there is. Once we admit the possibility of a creating God, then we must admit the possibility of miracles. We cannot, of course, show that they are *probable*, but with the hypothesis of God there comes "the risk of a few miracles."[24]

We move on to judge the probable historicity of specific alleged miracles. We judge these by our "innate sense of the fitness of things." With this in mind, Lewis moves to counter the charge that miracles are inappropriate. He argues that Christianity is centered around "the

---

[22] *Miracles,* 70–71.
[23] *Miracles,* 70.
[24] *Miracles,* 110.

Grand Miracle" (the incarnation of God the Son) and that other biblical miracles may be seen as aptly connected with this central miracle, so that some are associated with the Old Creation, while others anticipate the New Creation. It is true that the credibility of particular miracles depends upon the soundness of the witness to them. But it also depends upon their suitability in relation to the Grand Miracle—does the miracle, like a spoke, fit rightly into that central hub or not? In mapping the terrain, it is as though he takes us to the center of the map, then moves back and forth from East to West, showing us how the wild terrain on each side fits with the better known area in the middle.

Western Christians may be surprised to discover that the great miracle for Lewis is not the passion and resurrection, but the entire incarnation of Christ. In this, he clearly takes a page from the Church fathers, who influenced him deeply, such as St Athanasius. In his chapter on the "Grand Miracle," (i.e., the incarnation) Lewis stresses: the composite nature of humanity; the pattern that we see in nature itself of "descent and re-ascent"; the "selectiveness" that we see all around us; "vicariousness" as a principle with which we live daily; and the need for humility in the face of a clearly hierarchical reality.

The astonishing ability of human beings as rational animals, which he has established already, makes a good starting point for his argument. So he declares, "we cannot conceive how the Divine Spirit dwelled within the created and human spirit of Jesus: but neither can we conceive how His human spirit, or that of any man, dwells within his natural organism."[25] In this subtle comparison we may perceive that Lewis sees things in a way more consonant with Eastern than Western theology: it is the eastern fathers who emphasized the miraculous microcosm of human nature, and it is Eastern piety that routinely calls upon the immanent "Spirit of truth."[26] Nonetheless, Lewis is also influenced by

[25]*Miracles*, 115.
[26]Most Orthodox services, as well as private prayers, begin with the prayer *O Heavenly King*, which begins, "O Heavenly King, the Comforter, the Spirit of truth, who art everywhere present and fillest all things . . ." (cf. Jn 14.16, 26; 16.7, 13).

his Western surroundings, and sometimes depicts "miracle" as a kind
of "invasion" of Nature by Supernature. We may justly criticize this
particular choice of words, since it suggests that God is not at home
in the creation that He has made. Eastern Orthodox frequently note
that the West, so preoccupied with the Fall, seems to have forgotten
that God judged His creation to be "very good." Similarly, there is, in
this creation, a being who bears God's very image, and with whom, in
primordial times, He walked! Further, the Holy Spirit is "everywhere
present," and the Apostle assures us that in Him "we live and move and
have our being" (Acts 17.28).

Getting the balance right in these matters is not easy. How do we
account fully for the difference between Creator and creation while
acknowledging their interrelationship? How do we hold to a normative mode of life for that creation while also reckoning with a sovereign
God who may, at His will, work upon it directly? It seems that Lewis
here is walking on a razor's edge. He must acknowledge the unusual
nature of a "miracle"—otherwise, it would not be a cause of wonder
that points to the divine will at work in a direct way in our world. Yet
he is well aware of the right of the Creator to make himself at home
with us. A clue to this mystery is seen, in fact, in the nature of the
human being, as God created us. Lewis suggests that it is in the iconic,
or "image-bearing," nature of humanity that we see a faint glimpse of
God's greatest action on our behalf: the incarnation. God, as enlivening
us and giving us reason, dwells with us. To speak of this is to sing the
song of God dwelling in us "in a minor key," and to anticipate the great
symphony of the incarnation. Already, the Fall notwithstanding, God
has created humanity as suitable for His companionship. God walked
with Adam and Eve in the garden, and so, His coming to dwell among
and within us permanently by means of the incarnation "is not a cat-
egory-error"—as my mentor and colleague N.T. Wright used to say in
our graduate classes. The incarnation is a surprise, but it is also the cli-

max to which the story was always leading. God condescends to dwell with us, in our rationality, and in our consciences, for starters.

This descending to re-ascend is a principle that we see everywhere imprinted in nature, in fact. The higher and greater is able to enter the lower and smaller. Thus, "in the Christian story God descends to re-ascend."[27] Lewis sketches the magnetic picture of a man who must stoop to lift a great burden, or a diver who descends into the depths to rescue a treasure, bring it to light, and show its true color. Everywhere, in the animal world, in the vegetable world, in mythology, we see hints of this great story of death and rebirth. The difference with the Christian story is that eyewitnesses say that it happened, at a particular time and place, when God the Son came to reclaim His creation, beginning with Lord Adam and Lady Eve. Jesus, the only righteous One, came down even lower than the point of death, in order to reverse death. As the Orthodox sing, He trampled down death by death.[28]

The story is grand, but contains two essential elements that are difficult for some to accept—first, the selectivity of God working in Israel, then in Judah, then in Mary the Theotokos ("God-bearer") herself; and secondly, the *vicariousness* of life, whereby we are dependent upon others, and especially on this greatest Other. These themes of *descent and ascent*, *selectivity*, and *vicariousness* are key in Lewis's fiction, and so worth highlighting out of the many other jewels in Lewis's important chapter. (We will return to this chapter itself in more detail in our next section, where we will see its links with his master novel, *Till We Have Faces*.)

In the light of this Grand Miracle all the others are to be understood and gathered around it, as the two parts of the Bible, Old and New Testament, gather around God's climactic coming in the flesh. In what Lewis classes "miracles of the Old Creation," we see God doing suddenly something in a particular place that corresponds to His general work

---

[27] *Miracles*, 115.

[28] "Christ is risen from the dead, trampling down death by death, and upon those in the tombs bestowing life" (the paschal troparion).

in creation. So, for example, the God-Man turns water into wine—something that ordinarily happens over time, with the mediation of human vine dressers and winemakers. He multiplies bread and fish for the crowds, just as the natural world that He made supplies creatures with their food. He uses water or the natural elements to heal, just as these things can be used by doctors to heighten the body's innate self-reparative facility, a facility given by God. "The Divine Man [is] focusing for us what the God of Nature has done already on a larger scale."[29] We get a sense of what life *might* have been like if humankind had not fallen, and nature and mankind had not devolved into a kind of civil war.

What is the difference between these God-given signs and magic? Why do they appear suitable, in a way that Mickey's waving of the Sorcerer's wand does not? Two passages of Scripture help us grasp Lewis's presentation of these miracles. The first is Luke 10.1–24, where the Seventy are sent around Galilee to present the good news to the towns, by the authority of Jesus, who sends by authority of the Father. They come back, elated at the success that they have had, only to be redirected by Jesus towards first things—worship, and not pride; their inclusion in the household of faith, and not their own prowess. Jesus tells them that there has been a cosmic shift so that Satan no longer has authority, and He Himself rejoices that God is now working in "infants." In this knowledge, He calls upon the Seventy to rejoice with Him at God's new presence and rule in the world. This means that they are to exhibit humility, not power, as they represent the Almighty One. Though they are able to cast out demons, heal, and do wonders, the greatest wonder is

---

[29]*Miracles,* 145. Lewis owes this insight to St Athanasius: "His [St Athanasius'] approach to the Miracles is badly needed today, for it is the final answer to those who object to them as 'arbitrary and meaningless violations of the laws of Nature.' They are here shown to be rather the re-telling in capital letters of the same message which Nature writes in her crabbed cursive hand." From Lewis's preface to *On the Incarnation,* by Athanasius of Alexandria, trans. John Behr, Popular Patristics Series 44a (Yonkers, NY: St Vladimir's Seminary Press, 2011), 16–17. (The preface was first published in Sr Penelope's 1944 translation.)

that God is among them, calling them and others to worship. The very signature of God, the "One who does great things," is His humility in revealing wonders to the simple. Miracles of healing, feeding, winemaking, and even destruction (as the fig tree was made a warning) are to bless those who receive them (and Him!), not for the demonstration of raw power or overwhelming glory. God's glory is the cross.

Similarly, in Acts 10.11–20, we read the strange story of the Apostle Paul, and the miracles done through him—even in his absence, when articles of his clothing are brought to those who were ill. Such use of material means for divine healing may be immediately off-putting to those not comfortable with the idea of relics. To some it may smack of magic, as well. But, in fact, the story itself forbids us from taking a mechanistic view of these events. It is not that the articles possessed power in and of themselves, but that they were connected with the apostle, who was intimately connected with the Lord. Later, in the saga of Paul's journeys, we hear about the seven sons of Sceva (Acts 19.11–20), who thought that they could use magical incantation—the name of Jesus— in order to receive similar results to the apostle. They were rudely corrected when the demons said, "we have heard of Paul and of Jesus, but who are *you?*" It is neither a magical object nor a magical name that heals and saves the ailing, but Jesus himself, the Only Holy One—the incarnate and embodied Lord—who delegates authority over disease and evil to his faith-filled and humble apostles. He works, astonishingly, among physical men and even by means of their clothing, and so cares for flesh-and-blood people in a material world. Acts done for show, and disconnected from Him, are not miracles, but mere willful magic, and will misfire. For the hallmark of God the Son is sacrificial compassion and humility: the Greatest coming among those in need, going deeper than even they have had to go.

Next are the miracles of the New Creation that show forth reversal and glorification. The centerpiece of Lewis's discussion here is that great miracle that informs all of Orthodox worship—the Transfiguration.

Here Lewis discerns an "anticipatory glimpse"[30] of the glory to come, when Old (Moses and Elijah) and New (the three apostles) are united in the shining Christ, and where worshippers "fear" as they enter His glory. Lewis focusses upon the splendor of Jesus, as do the Gospel narratives: the episode clearly reveals something of the glory of God the Son, and His radiance as the true Human Being. Furthermore (and Lewis is suitably cautious), it may well also reveal the glory that redeemed humanity will inherit in the New Creation.

His focus and reserve here are compatible with the wonder expressed by both the Apostles Paul and Peter. In 2 Corinthians 4.6–5.5, St Paul fastens our eyes upon "the light of the knowledge of the glory" of Jesus, the marvel that God can shine out of our earthen vessels, and the hope of what is to come when we are newly clothed with our resurrection bodies. In 2 Peter 1, the apostle teaches about the apostolic enlightening lamp that helps believers to interpret the Scriptures rightly. The apostles have seen the luminous Jesus on Tabor, and have heard God's voice say that they should listen to Him. In this glorious first coming of Jesus, testified to by Peter and the others, Christians have what they need to enter "into the eternal kingdom of our Lord and Savior Jesus Christ (1.11) and to "participate in the divine nature" (1.4). Lewis, with the apostles, strikes just the right balance between astonishment at the future resurrected and glorified life, and maintaining that it is in continuity with our present embodied state. He also echoes that well-known statement attributed to St Basil by St Gregory the Theologian: "Man is a creature who has received the command to become god."[31] These wonders will be revisited in the novels that we will tackle in the next two sections of this study.

The presence of miracles in the New Testament raises a crucial question: do miracles compel belief? Clearly not—even in Jesus' day, when miracles abounded because God, like Aslan, was "on the move."

[30]*Miracles*, 156.
[31]*Funeral Oration for Basil* 48 (PG 36:560A).

John 12.35–50 tells of that poignant turning point in Jesus' ministry when many refused to believe, despite the evidence all around them, for their eyes were blinkered and their hearts hardened. We may see the same pathology today, though the impediments to belief take a different shape. Today, as we move away from the "modernist" paradigm of a closed universe, more people seem prepared to accept strange and bizarre things as a possibility. Yet the turn from materialism and the acceptance of mystery alone do not open a person's eyes to Jesus as the only Holy One. Nor does such a change in worldview guarantee the embrace of that great and overarching true Story for every creature under heaven, for all the sons of Adam and daughters of Eve.

Instead, many doubting post-moderns now wonder if we can really ask intelligent questions about reality at all. Alternately, they may refuse to see the explicit hand of the Creator in what we would call the "miraculous," and speak instead about innate human powers. The scandal for this younger generation is no longer the possibility of miracle, but the unique status of the God-Man, from whose hand we receive all blessings. If everything depends upon one's perspective, and we "create" our own (countless) "realities" in our minds, in virtual worlds, and by contract with one another, then the reception of a *gift* may be too hard to stomach.

Thus, miracles cannot, in themselves, compel belief. That is clear from the Gospels and from our own experience. But the miracles of the Scriptures point to the nature of God in Jesus, showing forth God's plan for the world that He created, loves, and shall redeem. The point of the miracles, as John's term for miracle, *sēmeion* ("a sign"), signifies, is that they fit within the whole structure of the good-news story, showcasing the Grand Miracle—or rather, the Subject of the Grand Miracle, the divine Human Being. So it is that those who beheld the wonders of Pentecost were redirected by the apostle Peter (Acts 2.14–36) to grasp their *significance.* The Spirit had been poured upon humanity because of Jesus' death, resurrection, and ascension. What matters now, as then, is not the phenomena, but Jesus Christ, and his invitation to be baptized and begin a new life in Him. The pattern of God's saving action, descending to re-ascend, was embracing the pilgrims in Jerusalem that day, but also the entire cosmos for all time!

Just as Peter redirected the crowd on Pentecost, Lewis reframes the worldview questions: Where am I? Who am I? What's wrong? And what's the remedy? The governing questions now become: Who is God? Who are we meant to be? Where is God in this fallen and dying world? And who is our fulfillment? The answer to all these questions is singular: "One is holy! One is Lord, Jesus Christ!" In antiphonal echo, we hear the blessed corollary: "The holy things are for the holy!"[32] Our completed map, now sketched in, fills us with wonder and adoration, for Lewis has shown how the Father has "freely given us all things in the Beloved One" (Eph 1.6). Having scouted this vast terrain, and heard the call to go higher up and deeper in, we can begin our travel in more arduous highland places.

---

[32]Of course, in the Divine Liturgy, the statements are reversed. The priest invites the congregation to the Eucharist, soon to come, by saying, "The holy things are for the holy!" The congregation, in humility, responds, "One is holy!" not daring to take that adjective as a descriptor for humanity. But God the Son, in speaking to us, reverses the pattern. For as we acknowledge His unique holiness, yet He is "not ashamed to call us brothers" (Heb 2.11)—even friends (Jn 5.15)—and invites us, startlingly, to partake of his holiness.

Part II

TRAVELLING IN ARDUOUS PLACES

Now calmly through the world I wend my way:
That which I crave may everywhere be had,
With me I bring the one thing needful—love.[1]

[1]Johann Wolfgang von Goethe, "Food in Travel" (1807), in *The Poems of Goethe, Translated in the Original Metres,* trans. E. A. Bowring. (London: Parker and Sons, 1853), 281.

CHAPTER 4

Thinking Carefully and Acting Ethically

(*The Abolition of Man* and *The Pilgrim's Regress*)

T eachers of the New Testament frequently uphold the Epistle to the Romans as a clear example of St Paul's typical manner of constructing letters: he begins with theology, then unfolds the practical outcomes. The first eleven chapters of Romans set forth numerous and weighty theological themes: the beginning of the world and its fall, the division between male and female or Jew and Gentile, the conundrum of human beings who are all apt to sin, the work of Jesus Christ in restoring us and the world in which we live, the importance of faith in the faithful actions of Jesus, God's continued care for Jew and Gentile, and the hope for unimaginable glory. Then, in chapter twelve, comes the great "therefore." In light of all these theological mysteries, the apostle urges us to break with the spirit of the age, and offer up ourselves—body and soul—so that God can do His transforming work:

> Therefore, brothers (and sisters), I appeal to you by the mercies of God, to present your bodies as a living sacrifice, holy and well-pleasing to God, which is your spiritual (or reasonable) worship. Do not be conformed to this world but be transformed by the renewal of your mind, that you may prove by testing what is the will of God, that which is good and well-pleasing and perfect. (Rom 12.1–2, my translation)

Effectively, the apostle says, "You have fed upon these theological and historical lessons; now do something about what you've learned, and you shall see God's promises fulfilled in you." By speaking of our lives as *sacrifice*, St Paul introduces the remaining, practical chapters of Romans. There he deals with life in the Church, life in society, obedience to authorities, payment of taxes, and the nitty-gritty discipline of cultivating Christian behavior.

Like the apostle, Lewis also forged (and urged) a strong link between belief and practice. We see this in two of his most demanding pieces, *The Abolition of Man* and *The Pilgrim's Regress,* which are both philosophical and practical. These are written for educated readers—indeed, the first is written for educators. Beyond that, they are written for those who have been classically taught, and who therefore possess a literary and historical storehouse from which to dig deeply as they read. Most of us will need some help in identifying and understanding the Greek and Latin terms, as well as the echoes and allusions that once would have been obvious to such readers.[2] (I will not deal with these matters here, but highlight helpful general themes and concepts in our quest for careful thought and Christian ethics.) Besides such technical obstacles, Lewis's closely argued points demand our full attention.

The Abolition of Man is a sequence of three dense lectures, written without a whiff of fantasy, though with some engaging anecdotes and examples. *The Pilgrim's Regress* promises a story (and there is a plot), but requires deep concentration on a range of matters that deeply concerned Lewis, and about which we may have limited knowledge. Here is arduous terrain to begin our travels—and, as they say, travel is broadening.

---

[2]For detailed help with *Pilgrim's Regress,* see the Wade Annotated edition by David C. Downing (Grand Rapids, MI: Eerdmans, 2014). See also Kathryn Lindskoog, *Finding the Landlord: A Guidebook to C. S. Lewis's Pilgrim's Regress* (Chicago, IL: Cornerstone Press, 1995).

The Abolition of Man

This book does not concern *Christian* belief, in the strict sense. We may call it a "pre-evangel," directed at those concerned with the education of our young, but who are not necessarily Christian. Of course, it also serves Christians who have not thought carefully about trends in philosophy and education. Phillip Goggins, in commending the piece to twenty-first-century thinking readers, makes an analogy between our time and King Lear:

> Shakespeare's *King Lear* tried to cast off the responsibilities of his office but retain its glory. He ended up homeless, isolated, despised, persecuted, exposed to the elements. Modern man, says C. S. Lewis in *The Abolition of Man*, is making the same mistake. . . . Kings have no choice but to fulfill the duties of the office they inherit. Likewise, argues Lewis, human beings have an "office" with moral responsibilities they cannot define or reject. Attempts to change these responsibilities result in . . . a giving up of one's humanity. . . . [Lewis's] goal is not to argue for the existence of God, but for the existence of an absolute moral order.[3]

This series of three interrelated essays, *The Abolition of Man*, was originally offered as a series of public addresses. The first talk, entitled "Men Without Chests," argues against the unexamined philosophy of "subjectivism" being foisted upon young students as a hidden yet corrosive part of their curriculum. Lewis disguises the textbook from which he takes his illustrations (which he calls "The Green Book"), so as not to embarrass the authors. He insists that to debunk all feeling as something detached from reality, as the authors do, is a teaching that will severely weaken those who follow this course, even possibly destroying them inwardly as human beings. The second lecture ("The Way") argues for

[3]Phillip Goggins, "*The Abolition of Man*— C. S. Lewis' Defense of Objective Morality," *Response* (web magazine), Seattle Pacific University, Fall 2000, accessed July 15, 2016, https://spu.edu/depts/uc/response/fall2k/abolition.html.

an underlying basic reality in the world to which morality corresponds, and thus against any futile innovation of an ethical system. Lewis names this underlying reality with its precepts "The Way," translating the Chinese word *Tao*. Every culture ever known, he says, has acknowledged a fundamental "givenness" of the world, which requires a human "way" of living: "natural law," "traditional morality," "first principles" or "first platitudes." On this common conviction, different human cultures have developed their (varying) moral instructions. In the third lecture, "The Abolition of Man," Lewis warns against those today who have adopted a thoroughgoing subjectivism that denies the existence of the Tao, while trying to bend human and material nature to suit their desires for a reconstructed reality. Any society persisting in such a course will eventually find not only the nonhuman world, but also its own rationality, "conquered." This is because it must deaden its own logic in order to match the newly constructed "morality." In following this course, it will become less human, even brutalized, rather than more sophisticated and in control. As we probe Lewis's argument, we cannot do justice to all its subtleties. Our purpose is to consider its points as they clarify our themes of rigorous thinking and godly ethics.

In the first essay, Lewis cautions against the damaging indoctrination of young people according to the positive and negative philosophy that was becoming common in the early and mid-twentieth century. The *approved* philosophy was subjectivism—the idea that all feelings about the external world are wholly governed by personal tastes, and are neither appropriate nor inappropriate responses to reality. The anonymous teachers who wrote "the Green Book" rejected Romanticism—an earlier generation's sense that a beautiful outer world compels strong (and apt) emotion and longing in the human breast.[4] Romanticism, which sometimes bordered on crass sentimentality, had been the prevailing

---

[4]Lewis himself, in his preface to *The Pilgrim's Regress* (1933; repr., Glasgow: Collins, 1977), speaks about the pliability of the term "romanticism" and his own particular use of it to describe an intense longing. See especially pages 10–12.

Western cultural outlook of the late nineteenth and early twentieth centuries, and was finally put to rest, it seems, by the sobering experiences of World War I.

The schoolmasters who wrote this text must have contracted this allergy to the Romantic. As teachers of literature, they use their influence to debunk an idea that had been held as foundational by many philosophers and thinkers right up to their own day—that human emotion can be a *merited and fitting* response to the beauties of nature, the loyalty of a tamed animal, or the mystery of a historical site. Our emotions about these outward things, say the debunkers, are wholly generated from within ourselves, and not actually elicited by the things themselves. The insistence of poets like Wordsworth that, in certain circumstances, such human emotions can be apt, is for them sheer human fancy and empty sentiment.

Even while many of the post-War generation debunked the dignity of that outside world, however, they unhappily retained from the Romantic school its frequent overemphasis upon human experience—what some have called "the turn to the *subject*," or the "I" who is doing the looking and describing. Sometimes the artist or poet of the Romantic era had spent as much (or more) effort in describing and relishing his or her own emotional and creative responses as in contemplating the object of desire or inspiration. Indeed, we see the vestiges of this in many of the popular Christian songs of our own day, which climax by wondering about the human response: "I could sing of your love forever," "Many times I've wondered at your gift of love, and *I'm in that place once again!*" (Surely it would be better to focus upon the wonders of the created world, on God's mighty acts than upon the worshipper's inner life. Instead, the songs fixate upon the inner life itself.) I hasten to add that Lewis, in his use of the word "romantic," agrees with the Romantic artists and poets concerning the worthiness of God's creation to be matched by human longing and awe: that human response, however, he never fastens upon as an end in itself. Rather, human longing and flashes of joy are meant to lead to the Source of all joy, the Creator of these marvels.

But the writers of the "Green Book" take an opposite path, scorning what Lewis approves, and holding up what he considers to be folly. They reject the romantic idea that facets of the outside world are innately worthy of human response, while also holding fast to the romantic emphasis upon subjectivity. In their new world, the educated and canny student is instructed to be well aware of his or her own desires and interests, without being swayed or confused by "sentimental" appeals to the outside world. Thus, in the name of passing on wisdom, they set the stage for a caustic and unfeeling society.

Lewis points out that by the time the 1940s textbook to which he refers was written, the Romantic movement had *already* long ebbed away as an influence. Contrary to the diagnosis of the anti-romantic schoolteachers, their actual pupils had seared and cynical hearts—more like a desert requiring cultivation than a jungle that required taming. Further, he complains that the wholesale "debunking" found in this and similar textbooks is at the very least seriously irresponsible, because young students are never told that sometimes art, literature, nature, or historical wonders deserve or rightly evoke human inspiration and awe. It is easy to dismiss bad art; it is not so easy to show the difference between crass sentimentality and well-expressed human sentiment.

Of course, in our day fanciful romanticism is back in vogue: Star Wars, Harry Potter, and even the (modified) film versions of Lewis's own work attest to this renewed appetite. The fantasy shelves in bookstores are replete with books, though often derivative and frequently not well executed. Romanticism has been revived, then, though arguably in art forms less admirable than those found in that past era: where are our Wordsworths, Shelleys, or even Tennysons? At the same time, unreflective subjectivism, as found among some Romantics, and perpetuated by Lewis's schoolmasters and their generation, has persisted, bringing with it untold danger not only for the individual, but for society. The main purpose of his first essay—to argue that the outside world may *merit* or *rightly* call for a human emotive response—thus retains enormous value for our day. Peter Kreeft, for example, speaks of *The Abolition of Man* as a pioneering ship that explored "this great, roaring river that is our common culture, now apparently headed for the falls."[5] Fr Thomas Hopko (of blessed memory) considered Lewis's book to be "the most important book in the past fifty [or] sixty years," and prophetic of our day: "Others [other books] can't come near the importance [of *Abolition*] as a critique of western culture, and [an explanation of] what happened to western people."[6]

Lewis warns: if we prejudice young people to reject, undiscerningly, any and all inward responses to what they see, read, or hear in the external world, we create "men without chests"—that is, human beings unable to respond in a human way to the world around them. Human beings, he reminds us, have minds that are designed to rule the flesh *through* the chest, or the seat of emotion, when this is rightly trained. Our reason we share with the angels; our body with the animals. But it is our chest, our heart, the seat of emotional knowing, that is characteristically human. Clearly some human emotions are inordinate, or out of place, or even perverted. But what happens to a generation that is brought up to dismiss everything known through emotion and feeling as merely subjective? Lewis answers: When this happens, our reason is deprived of the human element by which it can discipline the body. We are left "without chests."

Already in Lewis's day, then, teachers were fostering a generation that considered emotions to be wholly subjective, inward, and thus

[5]Peter Kreeft, *C. S. Lewis for the Third Millennium* (San Francisco, CA: Ignatius Press, 1994), 10.

[6]He recommends *Abolition* in the last of his list of recommended books, in this lecture: http://www.ancientfaith.com/podcasts/hopko/recommended_reading_from_fr._ tom_hopko. He further explores the significance of this difficult book, which he says needs to be read at least ten times, in http://www.ancientfaith.com/podcasts/hopko/ the_abolition_of_man. Last accessed September 2016.

arbitrary, and never corresponding to something outside of us, never merited by a natural wonder, or a loyal animal, or a traditional historical site. Such assumptions were enforced on the young, he argues, not by means of reason and argument, but by inoculation and propaganda. Budding scholars were miseducated to reject "old-fashioned values" such as awe in the presence of a mighty waterfall, or when visiting a key place of history. Such emotions were decried as simply "sentimental," with no basis in objective reality. A waterfall is only water pouring over a cliff and there is no factual reason to call it "sublime"; horses are simply working brute beasts, without any significant relationships with humans, who use them for work; nations are simply accidents of history, and so have no power to inspire national pride or courage in time of war. Any appeal to undergo hardship, or to persevere for the sake of courage, or to bravely travel in exotic lands, or to see animals as knowable and lovable fellow creatures is to be debunked by the clever and knowing modern person. If courage is a necessary trait to inculcate in young humans, it should be done on the basis of reason, and propaganda—for the propagation of the human species—and not by poetry or songs that speak of the sweetness of dying for one's nation.

Lewis notes that such a demolition job is easy when it is applied to crass sentimental literature or advertisements. Yet, such "seeing through" also robs students of the joy of *good* literature, which takes for granted common appropriate human responses. Pretending to teach about literature in an impartial way, the debunkers have actually "cut out ... the soul"[7] of the adolescent student, for they have taught him or her to believe that all emotions aroused by nature, music, or art are mere projections or taste.

Worse still, this is not simply a matter of calling human emotions subjective. Indeed, the debunking seems also to be fueled by a rejection

---

[7]C. S. Lewis, *The Abolition of Man: Or, Reflections on Education with Special Reference to the Teaching of English in the Upper Forms of Schools* (London: Oxford University Press, 1944; New York: HarperOne, 2001), 9.

of "the doctrine of objective value" as found in Plato, Aristotle, Stoicism, Oriental philosophy, and Christianity. Human beings teach authentically when they include the younger generation within their council, passing on traditions of living that work. That is, the teacher subjects himself or herself to the teaching, as well. True teaching, then, is more akin to "propagation" than "propaganda." This is entirely different than the kind of external training or conditioning that we would think appropriate to a nonhuman animal, one outside of the human species. It is a matter of initiating the new person, not conditioning him or her—as a bird teaches her young how to fly, rather than engineering the unwary fledgling's life as a poultry-keeper might do. Propagation is about "transmitting manhood to men," not training another for one's own use or for the good of an engineered society. Only careful thinking, including an education in which teacher and student share common values, can engender actual morality. Exploiters who implant an unreflective attitude that debunks authentic inner life and feeling soon become those who "condition" rather than actually teach the young— the instructors become human beings *using* other human beings for their purposes, rather than bringing the young into the mysterious fullness of human life.

Not for the modern debunker is the evangelical (and perhaps sentimental) hymnic sigh: "O Lord my God, when I in awesome wonder consider all the worlds thy hands have made."[8] Not for the conditioner is the Orthodox insight that the "Heavenly King, the Giver of Life . . . [is] present in all places and fills all things." This debunked and "useful" world is left wholly "unenchanted," unable to merit or elicit a response before such jaded eyes.

[8] This song, so well known in North America from evangelical rallies, details the beauties of creation, as well as the wonders of salvation. Further, it ends in speaking of the greatness of the creating and redeeming Lord. However, its emotional climax, at least as aided by the rising shape of the music, comes with a reference to the "subject" who is worshipping: "Then sings my *soul*, my Savior, God, to thee!" It is this lack of balance that gives it (in my estimation) a tinge of over-sentimentality: yet the singer does respond to earthly and heavenly wonders.

The "progressive" modern project, so hated by Lewis, thus goes far beyond unreflective debunking methods. It proceeds to suggest that morality *itself* is merely conventional, and entirely specific to cultures or individuals: there are no external standards that humans in general should acknowledge. Morality itself, then—the set of inner and societal values that prompt human action—must be cleverly reconstructed by the "Innovators": those who exercise coercive power over others "for their own good," either quietly or openly.

This dehumanizing result is what concerns Lewis throughout his second essay, where he mounts an argument for the objective "Way"— though variously understood or expressed in different cultures. In this essay he insists that true rigor of mind will look not only for what is convenient, but for what is real. Quoting Homer's Menelaeus (*Iliad* 17.628), he declares, *En de phaei kai olesson!* ("Zeus, if it be your pleasure to destroy us, do so in the light!") In other words, the most important thing is to see clearly, not to save one's own skin. Human beings are to follow through with their ideas in the clear light of day, even if these ideas are not, at first blush, practical—or safe.

But the "Innovator," like the "Debunker" of the first essay, is more concerned to compose an ethic that is pragmatic. The Innovator wrongly thinks that one can move from observation and habit to actual morality, from instincts (which are, in actuality, all over the map) to a sense of obligation towards others. Such a teacher does not take stock of the fact that our instincts are "at war" in this fallen world, and so cannot yield a secure system of values. Instead, such principles seem to have simply been *given* to human beings, across cultures. In every culture (as representative, Lewis considers Confucius, Locke, Terence, and the Torah) we find a kind of traditional morality or "natural law" that cannot be derived, but is simply a "given." Any "new" framework is simply a distortion of something more traditional, not a system unto itself: my older readers may remember, for example, the now-forgotten "Situation ethics" of the 1960s and 1970s. In the past, children were initiated into "the mystery of humanity," a framework of morality that was over teacher and student alike. But if this mystery is now debunked as subjective, then the innovators hasten to replace it with something that will serve, according to their own ideas of a good society. Indoctrination becomes the main mode of education, for the new system has nothing of real value to commend it. "The human mind has no more power of inventing a new value than of imagining a new primary colour."[9] Lewis is speaking about general human reflection, not the Christian faith, but we may remember the lament of God: "They have forsaken me, the fountain of living waters, and hewed out cisterns for themselves, broken cisterns, that can hold no water" (Jer 2.13). Without a foundation, nothing real can be built.

Finally comes the danger of the third stage—the power that human beings claim to have over ethics actually becomes a power *over* humanity, not a power *for* or *of* humanity. We may want to control "nature," but we are part of the natural order. "A . . . belief in objective value is necessary to the very idea of a rule which is not tyranny or an obedience which is not slavery."[10] This is seen, for example, in the science of eugenics, which permits total control of some human beings over others. We cannot arbitrarily or subjectively suggest that there is no objective set of values, or cook up a new standard of morality, and remain the same as we were before. Debunking leads to Innovation (for if we will not have the old set of values, we naturally will construct others to live by). Innovation, in its turn, leads to Conditioning, for one must train those who are younger to adopt this artificially constructed "morality." But Conditioning is for animals, not for humans. And the "Conditioner" himself or herself ultimately loses humanity, as well: "if man chooses to treat himself as raw material, raw material he will be."[11] In the end, the human who sees through all morals becomes inhumane.

[9] *The Abolition of Man*, 44.
[10] Ibid., 70.
[11] Ibid., 70.

To step outside the *Tao* is to step into the void: "Man's final conquest has proved to be the abolition of Man."[12] The person who tries to see through everything will end up not seeing at all.

So, then, these essays are a clearing ground in which Lewis tries to establish the imperative of objective reality and objective morality. In them he combats not only some of the sloppy thinking of his day (and ours), but the danger of current suppositions. For those less philosophically inclined, he makes the same points in his astonishing novel, *That Hideous Strength,* which we will consider in the next section of the book. Though we have only scratched the surface of Lewis's tightly constructed triad, we have been warned about the dangers of subjectivism, and have had put before our eyes the idea that it is human to hold a system of values as something given. Societies may differ as to which values are most important, and how to express these, but if they lose hold of the *Tao* altogether, they risk not simply chaos, but the loss of their humanity.

Sloppy thinking and skepticism concerning morals have conspired in the past three generations to produce students who are inoculated against an ethical imperative, and so have lost the very ground upon which they stand. Indeed, we have come to the point where many well-meaning people educated in this way insist upon society enforcing behaviors and ideas that they consider ethical, while at the same time denying the idea that there is any objective reality. Lewis's essays were prescient in seeing the oppressive potential of a majority view predicated upon a manufactured morality severed from what is real.

The three essays are not, however, an argument for Christianity in particular—since the Christian ethic fulfils, and is not itself, the Law. But they show where the difficulties of our generation lie in hearing the gospel. Relativism (on the one hand) and pragmatic, humanly-engineered standards (on the other) form obvious blinders, shading out the light. Besides these warnings, *Abolition* is important for highlighting our

[12]Ibid., 65.

common humanity, a matter that some pious Christians may discount. In these essays, Lewis puts into practice the well-known saying by Terence, *Homo sum. Humani nihil a me alienum puto* ("I am a human being. I consider nothing human to be alien to me"). This is salutary medicine for a narrow Christianity that will recognize truth only in explicitly Christian contexts. Of course, revelation (the Bible and Holy Tradition) and personal knowledge of the God-Man are the clearest means by which Truth personified may be found. But for the Christian who knows that the Holy Spirit "blows" where He wills and "is everywhere present," the recognition of sober thought and decency in other places than the Church is important. We can learn from the ancients—from their philosophy, as well as from their (distorted) mythology. God has not left the created order abandoned, nor has He simply "visited" it in a cursory way:

> The heavens declare the glory of God;
> And the firmament shows His handiwork.
> Day unto day utters speech,
> And night unto night reveals knowledge.
> There is no speech nor language
> Where their voice is not heard. (Ps 19.1–4, NKJV)

He has filled up the universe with his presence: with illumined eyes, we can see His traces everywhere!

Pilgrim's Regress

But we see Him most clearly with the help of Mother Church. *The Pilgrim's Regress* treads some of the same ground as *Abolition*, while going beyond it. John, the young Pilgrim, leaves his early home, the rigid training ground of "Puritania," in search of elusive joy, but also in search of an escape from the drudgery of responsibility. Early in the pilgrimage, he meets a travelling companion, Reason, but cannot accept

Reason's harsh insights: he tries to abandon reasonable thought. Eventually, coming to a dead end in his difficult travels, he has to "regress," to retrace his steps. Progression in the wrong direction is leading him nowhere but in a vicious circle. His regression leads, indeed, to his actual death, but then he gets Reason back—and much more! During his escapades, John follows through some of the thinking that may lead to "the abolition of man," but then returns to reason, and goes beyond reason to something greater: the gospel. The pattern of this book is not a "v," but a checkmark: John loses all, regains what he has lost in an unexpected manner, and then moves far beyond his first state.

Of course, Lewis's title recalls John Bunyan's seventeenth-century allegory, *The Pilgrim's Progress*. There is, then, a deliberately allegorical quality to the book, even while the piece reminds us of Dante's *Inferno*, since Lewis peoples his narrative with characters (not so thinly disguised) from the mid-twentieth century. Some have accused the book of trying to balance a Platonic idea of "forms" (which we discussed in our reading of *The Silver Chair*) with the kind of "fideism" (faith in faith itself) for which the theologian Kierkegaard was famous. I do not think that the book can be so easily slotted into either of these camps: Lewis is neither an uncritical admirer of Plato nor a theological Maria (in *The Sound of Music*) who "has confidence in confidence *alone*." Rather, he shows the attraction, strengths, *and* dangers of many schools of thought. Certainly he rehabilitates a form of Romanticism in the natural search for "joy" that John traces (and that Lewis also sought, as he admits, in his autobiography *Surprised by Joy*). Certainly he puts forth Reason as a necessary tool for humanity to use. But he also indicates where Romanticism and Reason reach their limits. They are put in their proper place, and not allowed to reign over John's entire life.

For example, Romanticism and Reason are John's needed defenses against the evils of Nazi ideology, subjectivism, nihilism (the idea that nothing makes sense), and ethical relativism. But romance and reason are not ends in themselves. They are meant to lead us, through death, to something (or Someone) else. Reason can slay the giants of nonsense for John. But Reason cannot tell him whether his longing for "the Island" is legitimate, or whether there is a transcendent "Mountain." And Romanticism, when it runs wild and is allowed to rule one's life, cannot satisfy, but can easily degenerate into sheer animal lust. Lewis situates Reason in the clear and cold north of the terrain John will tread; Romanticism lies to the swampy and warmer south.

Who are the "bad guys" in this strange story? Lewis has an insult for every major figure and for most "isms" popular in the first half of the twentieth century. All these come in for critique: Freud, Marx, Nazism, Hegelianism, pantheism, subjectivism (as highlighted in *The Abolition*), clever pragmatism, soft "artsy" living, pretentious and empty formal artistry, lust, pride, rigorous discipline *for its own sake*, "Broad" Church "generosity" that will retain no absolutes, and Epicureanism. (The last philosophy, in its classical form, assumed that humanity and divinity have no true meeting place, so that Humanity must create its own happiness: in its corrupt form it degenerated into a sheer love of pleasure.) These are the various ideologies that tempted or repelled Lewis as a young man, all jostling in competition for his attention, and so distracting him from Reality.

In contrast are the "good guys": Vertue (that is, Virtue, his alter ego and conscience), Reason, Mother Kirk ("Church"), History, Contemplation, and Wisdom. John traces his circuitous path from innocent but shallow "faith," through high and low terrain. Leaving his family's traditional faith, which was distorted by fear of God, he wanders by means of a path where he learns about desire and lust, and then through the philosophies and experiences of rationalism, thrill, romanticism, and artsy filth. Then he turns to the barren uplands of "Northern" philosophy (not the romantic north that Lewis loved, but a world barren of any joy). He has first sought joy, but then been disillusioned, and turned to facsimiles in his despair. Having rejected his family's faith, he assumes in his youth that everything is carnal, and that spiritual reality is nonexistent. Then he is rescued by Reason, while he also hears the story of Church but rejects it.

His traveling partner through much of this is Vertue, though the two do not travel together while he is engaging in lust. The rest of the novel is a dance between his loss of joy and Vertue's loss of power, though Vertue has more pluck than John. At one point, where Vertue can climb up while John falters, John is warned by a suddenly appearing and unknown "Man" that he must stay with his companion, or they will not "recover." The Man offers him a helping hand up the cliff where Vertue has gone, and John then finds, almost to his dismay, that he is *praying* for help. The duo follow a circuitous path and try to escape the inevitable, but through being taught by Wisdom and History, by engaging in Contemplation, and finally being trapped by Death, they arrive at the breaking point. Encouraged by Vertue's words and actions, John also jumps into the pool of conversion that he fears is an abyss. He then discovers that the Island, which he desired, and the distant Mountains, the home of the fearful divine Landlord, are one and the same. Indeed, he hears the voice of God, climbs the inside of the mountain, and is met by a whole host of other pilgrims who have followed the same path down, and then up. At last he sees his Island, in awe and in hope!

One would think that this is the end of John's journey. But it is really only the true beginning, for now, in Book X, a "regress," or retracing of steps, and a continual series of "deaths" must take place. He is instructed in this by a Guide called Slikisteinsauga ("Sleek-stone Eyes"), whose sharp vision can engender keen sight in others, as well. This Guide leads him, with Vertue, back through all the paths travelled before. John, however, on the other side of the pool, sees things differently, for he retraces his steps in obedience, as he dies to himself. He, the hopeful one, and Vertue, the strong one, travel together, both with more courage than they had during the first tour, and with more fear—for they see the dangers as they really are, huge dragons ready to devour them, rather than beckoning temptations! As they journey, they sing: this shortest part of Lewis's piece is replete with poetry, some of it quite didactic, but much of it also striking. There are some verses that are quite dour:

> Nearly they stood who fall;
> Themselves as they look back
> See always in the track
> The one false step. . . .[13]

There are others, such as John's reflection just before his final death, that give great hope:

> That we, though small, may quiver with fire's same
> Substantial form as Thou—not reflect merely. . . .
> God's we are, Thou hast said: and we pay dearly.[14]

The ultimate payment, of course, has been given by the Man who has appeared to John at crucial times. But Lewis here registers the arduous ascetical way laid down for the Christian who must follow the paths of the One crucified. Throughout this final journey, John and Vertue are led to humility, recognizing that God is in the little things and in their life's daily context, for God the Son took on human flesh. Both John and Vertue slay their final "Dragon," and they find themselves at the end of their journey, "full of light and noise."[15] The final sound we hear, at the end of chapter ten, is their voices, singing along with the guiding angel, who himself has never known sorrow, as they go beyond the Brook. By means of the nitty-gritty of time and place, "the tether and pang of the particular,"[16] they have been brought to the Eastern Mountain, by the Lord who knows his "own plan"[17] in bringing each of us there.

[13] *Regress*, 299.
[14] *Regress*, 249–50.
[15] *Regress*, 245.
[16] *Regress*, 249.
[17] *Regress*, 249.

Much of John's pilgrimage is understandable, though some of it will be obscure to those who are unaware of the dominant philosophical ideas in Lewis's own youth and early adulthood. Lewis himself comments upon its opaque narrative and the reasons for this. He was a new Christian in 1933, and unaware of the unusual progression that he had made from atheism to Christianity. No doubt he was unaware, too, of his extraordinary privilege, even in his own day, in having had a thorough classical education. On top of this, our current twenty-first-century tastes make it unlikely that many will immediately warm to the book's ironic allegories. Nonetheless, even in our era, the *Regress* offers some delight. Though the construction of the narrative is somewhat artificial, Lewis still has recourse to incipient myth (the Mountains, the Island), a lively use of metaphor, comic touches, poetry, and a search for reality and joy. Myth, metaphor, humor, and this longing search enliven what might otherwise be a wooden and difficult allegory, giving the piece some charm even while it instructs. Through the deluded and illumined eyes of John, we see these things for what they really are: subjectivism, idolatry, pretense, tradition, authority, and reason. Especially we learn that growth in holiness is not automatic, and that it may take us in unexpected paths. Here we encounter the potential drudgery of faithfulness, what one unlikely philosopher (Nietzsche) colorfully called the importance of "a long obedience in the same direction." Scripture is full of admonitions to keep struggling on: "Do not become weary in well doing" (Gal 6.9; 2 Thess 3.13, cf. Heb 12.3, Rev 2.3).

It is, however, in the pastoral letters (1 & 2 Timothy, Titus) that we get the best instruction on maintaining what we could call "spiritual pluck" (or courage). These letters, like Lewis's allegory, are not to the taste of many in our day, and so are often neglected. Typically, critical Biblical scholars of today have considered them less valuable than the undisputed letters of the Apostle Paul—pedestrian and lacking in the majesty of Romans or the psychological insight of the Corinthian correspondence. Their practical insights, however, are invaluable for the Christian who must train in holiness, in the same way that the instructions of the desert fathers have been helpful to so many. There is a certain tedium that accompanies our growth in holiness, calling for what the apostle called *makrothymia*—longsuffering, or persistence in hardship. 1 Timothy 1.3–6 warns the reader not to "swerve" from the way by giving attention to those things that "put forward speculations rather than the divine training that is part of faithfulness" (1 Tim 1.4, my translation), and then goes on to affirm the *proper* use of the Law. (No doubt it is this approval of the Law that influenced numerous critical scholars in their view that this could not have been penned by St Paul, the "apostle of grace"!) The Law, like admonitions to virtue and the right use of reason, is valuable for "the lawless and disobedient, for the ungodly and sinners, for the unholy and profane, for murderers of fathers and murderers of mothers, for manslayers, those engaging in sexual immorality, those engaging in same-sex eroticism, slave-traders, liars, perjurers, and those who do whatever else is contrary to sound doctrine" (1 Tim 1:9–10, my translation).

The letter goes on to speak of the mercy of God, and His desire to save sinners, of whom the apostle calls himself the chief. God alone is the immortal and solid One, yet in His servant Paul He has worked so that "Jesus Christ might display His complete *makrothymia* ('long-suffering') as an example to those who were to believe in Him for eternal life" (1 Tim 1.16). Our learning to persevere, then, enables us to echo the great endurance of Jesus, who persisted to the cross and the gates of hades.[18] Irksome duty takes its place within the grand drama of God's redemption of the world! It is by means of *personally* passed-on instruction, by

---

[18]I am aware that some of my non-Orthodox friends who read this may be uncertain about the doctrine of Jesus' descent into hades in order to free the dead. This is not the place to give a defense of the ancient doctrine, except to point out its honored place in an ancient creed (called the Apostles'), its acceptance by both East and West, and allusions to it also in Romans 10.7, Ephesians 4.9, 1 Peter 3.19, Matthew 27.52, and possibly Romans 1.4 (which speaks of the resurrection of the *nekrōn,* "the dead ones," as a past event).

oral and written word and deed, that we are meant to grow in the Body, just as John learned by means of others on his road: "Follow the pattern of the sound instructions which you heard while you were alongside me, in the faith and love that are in Christ Jesus; guard the truth entrusted to you by the Holy Spirit who dwells within us" (2 Tim 1.13–14, my translation); "But as for you, continue in what you have learned and have firmly believed, knowing from whom you learned it and how from childhood you have been acquainted with the sacred writings which are able to instruct you for salvation through faith in Christ Jesus. All scripture is inspired by God and profitable for teaching, for reproof, for correction, and for training in righteousness, that the man of God may be complete, equipped for every good work" (2 Tim 3.14–17). And the "equipping" goes right to the nitty-gritty in these letters—how to treat orphans and widows, how single women and men should behave, how Church members should take care of their leaders in practical ways, how families should care for their own if they can, how disputes should be handled in the Church, and even how a leader ought to care for his own body. (Consider the catalogue of detailed instructions in 1 Timothy 5). This detail reminds us of the dizzying and complex world that John encounters in his dubious Progress and Regress.

Just as we have seen in *The Pilgrim's Regress,* the solid and practical instruction of Scripture and the Christian Tradition does not come to us devoid of mystery. The pastoral letters break into enthusiastic adoration from time to time, changing the mode of their writing from sober instruction to praise. One example comes in 2 Timothy 1.10. The apostle begins by mentioning his vocation as an apostle, then spins into wonder as he considers God's plan for the universe: "God saved us and called us with a holy calling, not in virtue of our works but in virtue of his own purpose and the grace which he gave us in Christ Jesus ages ago, and now has manifested through the appearing of our Savior Christ Jesus, *who abolished death and brought life and immortality to light through the gospel*" (2 Tim 1.9–10). Faith and faithfulness are not simply human qualities to be inculcated, but are part of the great mystery of resurrection-life and immortality. In the final analysis, we see that the painstaking instruction that the older apostle offers the younger is undergirded by a great hope, a hope that corresponds to Lewis's longing for joy:

> But as for you, man of God, shun all this; aim at righteousness, godliness, faith, love, steadfastness, gentleness. Fight the good fight of the faith; take hold of the eternal life to which you were called when you made the good confession in the presence of many witnesses. In the presence of God who gives life to all things, and of Christ Jesus who in his testimony before Pontius Pilate made the good confession, I charge you to keep the commandment unstained and free from reproach until the appearing of our Lord Jesus Christ; *and this will be made manifest at the proper time by the blessed and only Sovereign, the King of kings and Lord of lords, who alone has immortality and dwells in unapproachable light, whom no man has ever seen or can see. To him be honor and eternal dominion. Amen."* (1 Tim 6.11–16)

St Paul, then, puts before his son Timothy's eyes the hope of glory. This becomes the incentive for perseverance during this present life, when we are apt to grow tired.

Wisdom: Let Us Attend!

It would seem, then, that both *The Abolition of Man* and *The Pilgrim's Regress* function in the same way as those biblical books that put forth wisdom—Proverbs, Wisdom of Solomon, and the pastoral letters. The books serve to remind us that acquiring "the mind of Christ," salvation, and growth in holiness, though spiritual gifts, do not come to us automatically. The effort that we must put forward in reading these books mirrors the effort to which all of us are called in living as Christians. Not everyone, of course, is required to understand the complexities of philosophy and logic that we find in these books by Lewis: some simpler minds have found more direct ways to the Mountain, the Island, and the Brook, as Lewis himself acknowledges. However, for those whose minds are drawn to philosophy, careful thinking must triumph over sloppy thinking. And for all Christians, dying to self and walking on the narrow way are imperative.

Some will find these books too prosaic and not to their taste. To these I would say that Lewis himself did not intend to address *The Pilgrim's Regress* to all readers (or even to all Christians), but to those who, like he, had been formally tempted and blindsided by the philosophies of the day. As for *The Abolition of Man,* its message remains an important one for anyone in the twenty-first century who has drunk deeply of the well of subjectivism. Those who find its tightly constructed arguments too difficult to follow will find picture-language that captures its main themes in some of the Narnian chronicles (*The Silver Chair; The Last Battle*) and in a book that we will consider in the next section of our study—*That Hideous Strength.* From the essays on the Tao, we learn the importance of careful thinking as a prerequisite (at least for some) to acting ethically. From John's pilgrimage, we see up close and in particular how longing and reason must work together, under God, to lead us to humility and to glory. It is interesting to see that, at the end of *The Pilgrim's Regress,* Lewis offers less discursive thought, and more images, mythology, and poetry. The allegory, with its one-to-one correspondence with ideas and other objects in reality, becomes less blatant. Here he poetically sketches places where he himself has not yet gone. Lewis himself is aware of how an allegory works, and how it differs from mythological writing, such as we have seen in his other books. He remarked in 1956 to a friend, "Into an allegory a man can put only what he already knows: in a myth he puts what he does not yet know and c[oul]d not come to know in any other way."[19] Allegory,

[19] *The Collected Letters of C. S. Lewis,* vol. 3: *Narnia, Cambridge and Joy, 1950–1963,* ed. Walter Hooper (San Francisco, CA: HarperSanFrancisco, 2007), 789–90.

by which Lewis communicates that which he understands, gives way in the end to myth. About thinking carefully he is clearly knowledgeable; acting ethically, however, leads to the path of following of Christ, which, even for the seasoned Christian, has its mysterious elements. So we turn again, as we travel in arduous places, to mythology, as used by Lewis in his extraordinary novel, *Till We Have Faces*.

CHAPTER 5

Theodicy, Spiritual Blindness, and Ascesis

(Till We Have Faces and St Athanasius' *Life of Anthony)*

I n Psalm 73 (LXX 72), the Psalmist Asaph cries out, trying to understand evil in the world; he shows how difficult it is to trust God's
goodness on the sole basis of common human experience. From the
onset he strongly asserts the covenant faithfulness of the Lord to those
who are "upright." (And his unspoken assumption is that the righteous
and holy Lord champions his holy people.) But then in the next fif-
teen verses he describes how he very nearly lost this conviction. These
tempting reasons to lose one's faith are compelling to any reader: the
arrogant are often spectacularly successful and popular, while the righteous frequently suffer. The Psalmist does not allow himself to dwell
in this dark place of thought, however. Instead, he cuts short his own
words as a plaintiff, recognizing that if he were to continue in this vein
of thought, he would be misleading those even weaker than he. To
fixate upon apparent injustice, where the evil flourish and the good
suffer, is a wearisome dead end. Then he enters God's house. There (as
we hear in verses 17–22) he sees the true instability of those who rebel
against God, and recognizes that he himself has been nearly seduced to
faithlessness. He does not tell us exactly how this epiphany comes to
him—only that it does. God takes him by the hand, guides him, and
brings him to a place where he can exult, "Whom have I in heaven but

Thee?" (verse 25). At the conclusion of the drama, the Psalmist declares his robust desire to stay near to God, to take refuge in Him, and to tell the truth about God's faithful acts to others.

Theodicy

The Psalter, especially this psalm, foreshadows the perfect empathy of the incarnate One for us. Indeed, the Psalter may be taken as God's verbal assurance to us that He understands our frailty and will enter into our situation to bring us aid. In our human condition, we do not always see things as they are: the fog of war and pain sets in. It is helpful to remember that though spiritual blindness may be due to moral failure, it is also a component of the human condition, due to our fallen state. (Though Eastern and Western Christians debate whether we inherit the first couple's "original guilt," there is no debate that we have inherited their feeble, mortal condition). To eyes compromised by the Fall, appearances are often deceiving. Even if we accurately see part of the present situation, we do not see the beginning and the end, nor the nexus of our life with that of others: we miss the whole picture. It is therefore natural, and not merely a sign of doubt, for us to bring our complaints before the omnipotent God. This is modeled for us by the prophets and some psalmists, who show, by their complaints, the paradox of *weak faithfulness* towards God, rather than outright rebellion. For the human being who believes that God is powerful and that He cares about His creation, it is quite in order to wonder what is going on, and even to lament, or cry out against suffering. The ancient Jewish people expostulated, in their exile, "Return! O Lord, how long?" And their longing is repeated by the saints in heaven, who have seen even more of the mighty acts of God (Rev 6.10).

The Jewish and Christian traditions, then, grapple with the reality of evil, while maintaining God's goodness and omnipotence. Out of the context of faith (albeit imperfect faith) emerges a particular brand of *theodicy,* that is, a literary or philosophical genre that affirms the "justice" (*dikē*) of God (*theos*) while recognizing the challenges to it. Indeed, the need for theodicy is registered most strongly where God is known to be all-powerful, all-knowing, and "personal"—that is, connected with humanity. In other cultures, the wearisome and tragic reality of evil is recognized, to be sure, but is explained by means of the capriciousness of certain divinities who do not love people (the common Greco-Roman myths), or by the nature of the physical world (the philosopher Plotinus), or by the general disinterest of the heavenly beings (Epicurus).

This difference between classical and Judeo-Christian theodicy is what makes the next piece on our menu, *Till We Have Faces,* so very intriguing. Its main character, Orual, lives in a fictitious pagan world that has been influenced partially by classical philosophy. Neither the old pagan ways nor her education offer her satisfying answers concerning the fluctuations, tragedy, and evil seen in the round of daily life. Thus, she finds herself caught between the high yet trite reasonableness of philosophy, taught to her by her Greek tutor ("the Fox"), and the deep but dark theology of her native land, where the fertility goddess and her son, the Shadowbrute, are immortal monsters who must be propitiated. The dissonance between these two views, the high and the low, leads to her quandary: neither the rational nor the pagan worldview fully explains the events in her life, or her deepest longings. She *knows* that she is blindfolded spiritually, that she cannot see beyond the darkness. Yet, against all hope, she thinks that there is a purpose to complaining against the divine powers that be, even if it is simply as a "catharsis"—a dramatic venting to clear the air and make herself less angry.

Spiritual Blindness

Among other themes, *Till We Have Faces* is concerned with the confusion of the world, the disease and cure of spiritual blindness, the temptations faced by one who has a mix of strengths and weaknesses, and the interplay of discipline with grace in that person's life. Though Orual is a pagan of an imaginary land called Glome, she treads the path laid down for all of us, from pride to humble repentance, from blindness to sight, from light to darkness. Quite literally, her road is arduous and takes us to high places (as she visits her idealistic sister on the mountain) and low places (as she plumbs the depth of the caves and sacred darkness of the goddess's grotto). Like the Psalmist, she feels justified in her complaint until she meets "the god." Then she takes back her harsh but limited words, recording a chastened understanding for any who will listen. Any of us who has cried out, or thought in the quiet of our hearts, "It isn't fair!" has much to learn from Orual.

Till We Have Faces was written in 1956, as Lewis's very last work of fiction, and has been well received by the literary community but not as enthusiastically by the general public. It was Lewis's own favorite from among his works—a writer's novel, so to speak. A difficult and mature work, it sums up the deepest of Lewis's thoughts. Moreover, Lewis had worked with the myth of Cupid and Psyche (upon which the novel is based) his whole life, rendering it in poetry, then in a play, and finally in this introspective novel, written in the voice of Orual. It is thus the fruit of a lengthy inner exploration and debate, long present in the mind of a subtle thinker. The novel's thick and absorbing plot line requires at least some understanding of Greek mythology, and he duly appends, at the end of the novel, an explanation of the underlying myth of Psyche and her sisters, and how he has used it. (The very subtitle of this novel, *A Myth Retold,* intimates that the reader should be aware of this element.) For this reason, I recommend that readers unfamiliar with the myth peruse the appendix before actually reading the book. It may feel a bit like cheating, like looking at *CliffsNotes*, but many in our generation do not know mythology—or, indeed, the Bible—well enough to have that "Aha!" experience that came so readily to our forebears. However, don't keep peeking at the myth while you are reading the book, or your reading will be reduced to the task of decoding. Rather, we are to let the character of Orual engage us, and let the story sweep us away, with the myth tucked into the back of our imagination.

The book is written so that we enter into Orual's mindset by retreading her steps, rather than being given directives by an omniscient narrator. Even Orual's blindness we do not at first see, but Lewis leaves it to us to recognize this by means of the story itself. (We will consider more about the effect of Orual as an "unreliable" narrator in the next chapter.) Further, the book has an open-ended quality that complicates matters. Despite Orual's visions, and her retractions or confessions, even at the end of the book we are left to wonder what is ultimately true and what has actually happened. Lewis also does not preach, or explicitly draw the parallels and differences between the deity in Orual's world and the true Christian God. Like an icon, designed to draw us in rather than to be assessed, the story calls us to inhabit Orual's story, rather than to hold the character and the novel at arm's length and to make judgments. It is, in the end, a story about *us*.

Lewis, of course, was a medieval scholar, and so it would have come naturally to him to write a novel that is, in some ways, similar to the fifteenth-century morality play called "Everyman," a play in which the major character stands in for any human being. We get an insight into Lewis's understanding of Orual as a kind of "Everyman" character through his conversation with an inquirer, Dorothea Conybeare:

How can they (i.e. the gods) meet us face to face till we have faces? The idea . . . was that a human being must become real before it can expect to receive any message from the superhuman; that is, it must be speaking with its own voice (not one of its borrowed voices), expressing its actual desires (not what it imagines that it desires), being for good or ill itself, not any mask, veil, or *persona*.[1]

Originally, we are told, he had planned to call the book "Bareface." It is a mercy that his editor did not allow it, since this would have given the initial appearance of a Western cowboy saga! Given what Lewis said to Conybeare, we may conclude that we are meant to read the novel as a description of any human being. Each of us has, in some sense, yet to become a real person, to be given a face, even though, in Christ, the veil of utter blindness has been removed (2 Cor 3.17–18). Still, the apostle Paul says that we see "through a glass darkly." It is helpful to remember the origin of the word *person*, which in the Latin (*persona*) and the Greek (*prosōpon*) refers also to a "character" or a "face." The word was first used to speak about the mask used in classical drama to signify a character (not to obscure a face), and then in Christian theological discourse it came to refer to the "persons" of Father, Son, and Holy Spirit. From there it came down into common discourse to refer to human persons, created after the image of God. Alongside this classical background, Lewis was surely also aware of the New Testament passage of 2 Corinthians 3, where the apostle Paul speaks about Moses' face being covered with a veil, and that there was a veil over the eyes of the Israelites, who could not see the true glory of God. In contrast, St Paul speaks of believers as having open faces that gaze at the likeness of Christ, the true Man, and so are transformed into his likeness. Much of Lewis's story turns upon Orual covering her ugly face during the main part of her reign as Queen, and then, even when she takes it off, using her unknown bare face as a disguise to hide her true nature.

Without a face, then, we are spiritually blind. But how do we get "real faces"? Orual learns two lessons that are seemingly in tension with each other: first, that authentic personhood is a divine gift; second, that

[1]From his letter to Dorothea Conybeare, in Rose Macauly, *Letters to a Sister*, ed. Constance Babington Smith (London: Collins, 1946), 261.

it does not come to us automatically. Paradoxically, it comes by way of sacrifice and arduous effort, though it is not primarily a human achievement. Just as John might have crossed the river without his circuitous path in *Pilgrim's Regress,* so Orual could have learned her lessons in her early life through her younger sister Psyche (whose name means "soul"). Indeed, she eventually does learn from her sister's example, but also follows her own tortuous path. Psyche, her sister, is the ideal human "soul" with an innate longing for the divine mountains and for joy, things both scorned and feared by the more pragmatic and less trusting Orual. The younger sister is prepared to give up her life, both for her people and for the sake of this longing; Orual, however, is driven by a self-protective and angry attitude to the vicissitudes of life.

We learn, then, by the contrast of Orual with her younger sister, just as there are contrasting psalms of doubt and trust. If Orual's biblical representation is Asaph's skepticism in Psalm 73 (LXX 72), Psyche personifies David's stance of hopeful attentiveness. Psalms 62 (LXX 61) and 63 (LXX 62) express this motif. Psalm 62 (LXX 61) begins: "For God alone my soul waits in silence; from him comes my salvation. He only is my rock and my salvation, my fortress; I shall not be greatly moved" (verses 1–2). Faced with adversity, and the arrogance of "men of high estate," David cries out:

> For God alone my soul waits in silence, for my hope is from him. He only is my rock and my salvation, my fortress; I shall not be shaken. On God rests my deliverance and my honor; my mighty rock, my refuge is God. (verses 5–7)
>
> ... Once God has spoken; twice have I heard this: that power belongs to God; and that to thee, O Lord, belongs steadfast love. For thou dost requite a man according to his work. (verses 11–12)

This psalm traces the path of searching, waiting, and looking for God's salvation, and declares that there is peace in depending on God alone, rather than on human power and riches. It ends by attributing to God two united characteristics—power and love—and sees these in God's acts of justice. Psalm 63 (LXX 62) follows a similar path, though it is even more dramatic. It is set in the wilderness, when David was completely dependent upon the goodness of the Lord: "O God, thou art my God, I seek thee, my soul thirsts for thee; my flesh faints for thee, as in a dry and weary land where no water is" (verses 1–2). David's thirst for God leads him to the sanctuary, where he exults in "beholding [God's] power and glory." The psalm moves into exuberant praises, speaking of God's goodness as though it were a rich meal, and wondering over how His presence is there, even in the darkness of the night:

> Because thy steadfast love is better than life, my lips will praise thee.
> So I will bless thee as long as I live; I will lift up my hands and call
> on thy name. My soul is feasted as with marrow and fat, and my
> mouth praises thee with joyful lips, when I think of thee upon my
> bed, and meditate on thee in the watches of the night; for thou hast
> been my help, and in the shadow of thy wings I sing for joy. My soul
> clings to thee; thy right hand upholds me. (Verses 3–8)

David cleaves to this confidence, even when threatened by those who seek "to destroy" (verse 9). Though still challenged by enemies, he looks to the time when lies will be stopped and enemies thwarted by the power and goodness of God.

Psyche is, in some ways, Lewis's King David, a woman "after God's heart," who meditates upon the divine in the watches of the night. Like all flesh, she cannot "see God," and so suffers from spiritual blindness. Yet from childhood she yearns for "the mountains" and immortality. Even when facing the prospect of a dangerous exposure on the mountain by her savage countrymen (who believe that her sacrifice will appease the gods), Psyche hopes that her desire will be requited: and it is. She comes to dwell in the high places, though at the beginning she is still forbidden to look upon the divine glory in the clear light. She too must grow and be transformed. However, Orual does not possess Psyche's yearning—or at least, it is a desire well suppressed by other concerns in her life. Scripture tells us that God has placed eternity in our hearts (Eccl 3.11), but it is there only in very small measure with the hardened and spiritually blind Orual. Possessed more by self-centeredness and rationalism, she must come to learn of eternal life and joy by a hard route. She lives a natural life of tragedy and disappointment, sees both the beauty and the inadequacy of her own loves, and "dies" slowly to herself.

As we begin the story, seen through Orual's eyes, the outside world is presented as the problem, and Orual is almost oblivious to her actual motives, her dark identity, and her need to change. Everything seems to conspire against her happiness: the intrusion of Redival, a third spiteful and shallow sister, who disturbs the harmony in the household; the removal of her beloved Psyche from the household to be offered to the Shadowbrute upon the mountain; Psyche's own "deluded" choice of the god over loyalty to her sister; the devotion of Orual's right-hand man to his wife, which Orual perceives as a threat to herself; the gradual distancing of her beloved Tutor, the Fox, due to age and finally death; her own inner conflict as she experiences nightmarish "visions" in her later years. She sees herself as attacked by the gods, stripped bare of any comfort, and bereft. And so, she believes, her complaint is valid.

The entire drama of the piece moves towards her formal complaint to heaven, which she offers before the heavenly beings in a vision, and the surprise finale that ensues. However, it is clear fairly early on that Orual is comfortable simply avoiding the gods, and that, left to her own devices, she would not embark upon the same journey as Psyche. Her default mode of thinking aligns with the Epicurean philosophy: she hopes that the divine realm will simply keep its distance, and allow humans their liberty to live life unhampered by any divine claim to them. Thus, though she registers horror and outrage at the pagan sacrifice of her beloved sister to the Shadowbrute, she is even more appalled by Psyche's choice of her divine husband over her natural family. Reacting to Psyche's delight that she is going to her husband (a fulfillment of Psyche's longing for "home"), Orual turns inward. She accuses her sister of never truly loving her, and of becoming cruel, like the gods whom Orual hates. Orual's full and convoluted disclosure of human-divine relations comes at the very end of Part I, before she has the visions that help her to begin to see:

> I say the gods deal very unrightly with us. For they will neither (which would be best of all) go away and leave us to live our short days to ourselves, nor will they show themselves openly and tell us what they would have us do. . . . But they hint and hover . . . to be dead silent when we question them and then glide back and whisper . . . in our ears when we most wish to be free of them. . . . Why must holy places be dark places?"[2]

Out of her own mouth, then, she condemns herself, for she does not truly wish to hear or understand, but to be left alone. Her spiritual blindness is not merely an unwitting condition, but a *chosen* state of self-will.

Personhood and Ascesis

Because the novel is focused upon the emerging personhood of Orual, it has a strong interest in the questions of identity. We hear about the goddess of Glome, Ungit, who is identical with Aphrodite/Venus, the goddess who has a thousand faces, manifest in different cultures. We hear about how, at the time of her sacrifice, Psyche is dressed with a painted mask so that she is not recognizable. The question of her identity is bound up with her relationship to her people, to her sisters, to her father, and (ultimately) to the god of the mountain. But it is the identity of Orual that proves most interesting, and that indeed occupies most of

[2]C. S. Lewis, *Till We Have Faces: A Myth Retold* (1956; repr., Grand Rapids, MI: Eerdmans, 1966), 249.

the narrative. Identity is highlighted in the novel both by terse questions ("Who are you?" "Who is Ungit?") and by declarations. Tormented in the delusions of dying, Orual's father is fearful of Orual's masked face, and calls on those around him to remove her from his presence, saying, "I know who she is." Later in life, Orual has illumining visions. One of them concerns her father (long dead) forcing her to recognize her own identity: "I am Ungit." Finally, towards the end of the novel, she is told by the god, "You must be[come] Psyche."

Bound up with the question of Orual's identity is her deep jealousy, which she must recognize and renounce. She has formed her own identity around the owning or enslavement of another person—that is, she is possessed by an inordinate or confused love. Her first inkling of this comes when she hears (but initially rejects) the priestly version of her own story, where Psyche's sisters are characterized as simply jealous of Psyche's desire and love for the divine. On hearing this version of the story, Orual jumps to the defense of the sisters, saying that they might indeed be able to say more about their motives than the myth disclosed. She is, however, reprimanded by the priest's comment that "The jealous always have . . . plenty to say about themselves."[3] What is not confirmed for her through lifelong experience and this religious tale eventually comes clear by means of inspired dreams. Finally, she admits that she herself is "that all-devouring womblike, yet barren thing . . . the swollen spider . . . gorged with men's stolen lives."[4]

Even before coming consciously to this self-revelation, however, we see our heroine working to pull herself out of the mire of self-absorption. Here, Lewis seems to have his cake and eat it, too, in theological terms: Orual is the proud pagan, trying impossibly to establish her own virtue by means of a disciplined life; she also becomes, by the end of the novel, the repentant one who models how a life of self-abnegation can be used by God in order to transform that person. It

[3] *Faces*, 247.
[4] *Faces*, 276.

is clear that we are meant to applaud the selfless exercise of Orual as she pours herself out for her kingdom; yet we are also meant to learn, through her escapades, that it is impossible to become virtuous simply through self-will and effort. As a pagan, Orual exemplifies the Stoic virtues that she has learned from the Fox, which cannot in themselves bring her to joy, but eventually do bring her to realize her inner bankruptcy. (Later, however, we learn that even these efforts are transformed by the energy of the gods, and have not been enacted wholly in vain.) We may be reminded of the wisdom of the pastorals: "Have nothing to do with godless and silly myths. Train yourself in godliness; for while bodily training is of some value, godliness is of value in every way, as it holds promise for the present life and also for the life to come" (1 Tim 4.7–8). Orual comes to reject the childish features of her homeland's mythology, especially the idea that she can manipulate the gods to give her instant success. Instead she pours herself into a doubly arduous life, influenced both by the Fox's leadership in classical philosophy, and by her disciplined military confidant, Bardia. Though a Queen, she is attracted to a frugal and disciplined lifestyle, as modelled to her in two different modes by her two closest friends, Bardia and the Fox. As a single and independent woman, she is in a position to practice *askēsis*—the self-discipline and rigorous training meant to bring forth a more fully rounded person. Both her status and background are conducive to this life. She is unmarried, answerable mostly to herself, and endowed with the classical teaching of the Fox and the martial training of Bardia, her right-hand man. In her efforts for her country we can perceive her desire to pour herself out for others—an impulse that first shines forth as she offers her own life instead of Psyche's, though that sacrifice was rejected. (This is paradoxical, considering Orual's self-absorption and self-justification throughout the novel, but it is as strong a theme as her weaknesses. Sorting out the motives and actions of Orual is complex: as complex as it is to take our own personal inward inventory.)

So, despite the loneliness, Orual's singleness becomes a means to her virtue. The Christian Tradition suggests that the complete ascetic state may be the particular path given to some of us who have been called "kings and priests" to God. Ascetic practice, in our sexually charged society, is a particularly difficult teaching, for our contemporaries are prone to measure personal health in terms of physically intimate relationships. Further, 1 Corinthians 7 reminds us of the inherent problem of pursuing asceticism in the entangled or enmeshed sphere of the family:

> From now on, let those who have wives live as though they had none, and those who mourn as though they were not mourning, and those who rejoice as though they were not rejoicing, and those who buy as though they had no goods, and those who deal with the world as though they had no dealings with it. For the form of this world is passing away.
>
> I want you to be free from anxieties. The unmarried man is anxious about the affairs of the Lord, how to please the Lord; but the married man is anxious about worldly affairs, how to please his wife, and his interests are divided. And the unmarried woman or girl is anxious about the affairs of the Lord, how to be holy in body and spirit; but the married woman is anxious about worldly affairs, how to please her husband.
>
> I say this for your own benefit, not to lay any restraint upon you, but to promote good order and to secure your undivided devotion to the Lord.
>
> (1 Cor 7.29–35)

Some scholars have seen this biblical passage as presenting a wholly historical concern, and assumed that it was only valuable at a time when it was believed that the Lord was coming imminently—or perhaps in times of great trial. Indeed, St Paul may have been giving advice in light of the obvious growing tensions between early Christians and their culture: "the time is short." Such tensions may well have been understood in the first century as a signal of the "wrath to come," and Jesus' warning concerning the difficulties that would come to those "with child" at that time (Mk 13.17). Perhaps the apostle had in mind the turmoil preceding the final return of Jesus; perhaps he was aware that there would be other historical moments of disruption that would point forward to that time. His advice is not limited to such moments of crisis, however. It speaks to all of us who are in Christ, whether we dwell in a relatively calm or a turbulent epoch. In a larger sense, "the time is short." We all have a general calling, which is to draw closer and closer to the Lord, recognizing that the current order is passing away. We may not assume either that the mere state of singleness will render a person less "worldly," or consumed with ordinary cares, than the married state. However, those who chose, for the sake of Christ, to live the life of celibacy make a valuable witness in an era which is mostly convinced that sexual expression is necessary for a truly fulfilled life. And, of course, not everyone has this calling: the married life also works for our completion, if we embrace it in such a way that we learn deep love and sacrifice. For each one of us (no matter what our position in life) is forcibly reminded, by the apostle's words concerning discipline, of the secondary nature of our human aspirations and loves. The Master, too, spoke mysteriously about "hating" family members for his sake: "If any one comes to me and does not hate his own father and mother and wife and children and brothers and sisters, yes, and even his own life, he cannot be my disciple" (Lk 14.26).

Were we not fallen creatures, blinded to the true light, such strong language would perhaps be unnecessary—our human loves would fall into place as expressions of our primary love for God. However, because our loves are disordered, we must heed the words of Jesus and Paul. At least a partial practice of the ascetic life becomes a necessary medicine in order to bring us back into reality: "If your eye offends you, pluck it out" (Mt 5.29; 18.9). In the end, Jesus' hard words and St Paul's call to be disciplined are not meant to "lay any restraint" upon the faithful, but to enable them to freely seek the Lord with a single and undivided mind.

So then, self-abnegation can and must be practiced in the midst of others, as we pour out ourselves for them, rather than closing in on our own desires. Each of us, not simply those who are celibate, is called to "take up our cross" and follow the Jesus "who did not please himself" (Rom 15.3). However, such actions are difficult given our natural inclination to confuse selfless love with need-love (as Orual does in her dealings with Psyche, Bardia, and the Fox). Why would I want to please my wife or husband? Perhaps because it makes things go more smoothly for me. And indeed, even if I please them without a thought for myself, sometimes my love may tempt me to do something contrary to God's will. Or perhaps my busyness for them may come to crowd out my larger and primary love for God.

Lewis is well aware of such temptations and weaknesses. And so the Fox reappears in a vision to Orual towards the end of the novel. There the far-seeing Fox prophesies, echoing Luke 14.26, and gesturing towards the Christian future (from the perspective of the novel), when the incarnate God will come to claim His own: "Mother and wife and child and friend will all be in league to keep a soul from being united with the Divine Nature."[5] His words are illustrated at the point in the novel where Orual violently dissuades Psyche from joining her true love, and also in the vision of Psyche's descent to Hades, where she is tempted to turn from her path when she hears the voices of those whom she loves. Orual, then, shows forth the opportunities of the single life, but she also becomes the means of tempting Psyche away from her devoted path: she is both a positive and a negative example for us.

---

[5] *Faces*, 304.

Christian Ascesis

In clarifying the ascetic life, we can amplify the pictures of Psyche's devotion and Orual's zealous self-denial with the life of an actual Christian saint. The most well-known example of the Christian ascetic life is found in St Anthony the Great. St Athanasius, in his *Life of Anthony* (fourth century), tells the strange but engaging story of an ascetic who learns piety in two steps—first, by seeking the company of good people who exemplify various virtues, and then, by leaving society to come close to God, first amongst the tombs, and then in the wilderness. At every point he meets the devil in many forms, and encounters many temptations, beginning with lust, and ending with spiritual pride. Throughout this ordeal, he learns from others, particularly with regards to humility, and eventually becomes an articulate defender of the faith against those who shallowly offer "Greek wisdom" as the answer to life's problems and temptations. But he also learns in solitude, by depending wholly upon the Lord, who strengthens him even while St Anthony is not able to see the divine presence.

St Athanasius tells the saint's story not simply to praise the saint, but also to offer an example to those who are young in the faith and seeking to follow the ascetic life. The watchword for St Anthony is that we should "Live as though dying daily." Throughout, too, the Scriptures are copiously cited, showing the connection between God's promises and the life of this extraordinary man. St Athanasius, in commenting upon the prowess of Anthony, is careful to give glory to God. In section seven, concerning an early extraordinary episode in Anthony's life, he explains, "This was Antony's first struggle against the devil, or rather this victory was the Saviour's work in Antony."[6] In Anthony we see a balance between the quest for personal piety and faithful adherence to Orthodox doctrine, as when he rejects the heresies of Arius and others. In the penultimate section, St Athanasius says that "the Lord shows [saints like Anthony] as lamps to lighten all, that those who hear may

[6]St Athanasius, *Life of Antony* 7 (*NPNF*[2] 4:197).

thus know that the precepts of God are able to make men prosper and thus be zealous in the path of virtue."[7] Though the biography is written to encourage monks, St Athanasius also says, in his final section, that the story will prove useful even among educated unbelievers, to show them what true piety and the complete human life look like. So, then, St Anthony's experiences are as important for the Oruals as they are for the Psyches in our world: his progress is put forward not only as an exemplary saint, but also as one who shows the fruit of dying to self, in whatever circumstance the Christian may find himself or herself. Both encouragement and evangelism are the fruit of asceticism, borne by any believer who denies himself as this saint did.

Orual's Progress: The Benefits and Dangers of Ascesis

Orual is a much more rough-and-ready "Everyman," though her world is as distant and exotic as that of the saint. She grows in personhood both as she lives and as she writes her memoirs. Like Anthony, the first stage of her progress occurs when she loses her innocence, experiencing the end of her childhood, the disappearance of Psyche, and the death of her father. She begins to live "as a Queen should."[8] She takes care to better know those under her, she revises and encodes the laws, and she makes geographic and architectural improvements. It is for accomplishing these things that she will be remembered, among her country-folk, as a good monarch, like Hezekiah or Solomon in the Bible. Yet, like Solomon in Ecclesiastes, she reflects that these things were distractions from a foundational "nothingness"—her loneliness dominates, as she wears the veil that separates her from others. The irony of her situation is filled to fullness when, having accomplished all her queenly tasks, she sets out on a journey through distant lands, only to make a disconcerting discovery: the story being told about Psyche and her sisters condemns *her* as one who was controlled by jealousy

---

[7]St Athanasius, *Life of Antony* 93 (NPNF² 4:221).
[8]*Faces*, 232.

rather than love. In anger at this "false" revelation, she concludes her
life of searching and her first book, asking the reader to judge in her
favor, for the gods have "no answer" to give to the futility of our lives.

Perceptive readers will notice Orual's maturation, coupled with her
emptiness, as they follow her initial first story. However, beneath the
surface, even more is happening to her, and this is finally disclosed in
her subsequent visions or dreams, found in Part II of the novel. (Part
II is appended by Orual to her complaint of Part I, in order to amend
what she has written in ignorance.) She tells us that after her long arduous first experience, she had a dream. The dream echoes the mythical
task set to Psyche in the classical tale: this dream demonstrates how
progress is not a gradual or strictly linear thing, but complex. In the
myth, Psyche is set to sort out myriad seeds into separate piles by the
goddess Aphrodite (Venus), an arduous—indeed, impossible—task for
a human being. Orual tells us that the dream comes as the "overflow"[9]
of her labor of writing. Indeed, she comes to see that her compulsion
to write again is actually part of the "gods' surgery"[10] on her person:
her writing pen becomes their instrument to "probe her wound." Just
as Psyche had to sort the seed, so Orual, in trying to write the truth of
her life's experience, must sort out her motives, her pretexts, and her
inner mental confusion. Part of the mythical task she accomplishes as
a human being, scrutinizing each "seed" between finger and thumb.
But then, in her vision, she is transformed into a little ant, carrying
upon her back the load of each enormous seed to its proper place. In
real life, she is so preoccupied with her project of writing a complaint
against the gods that she hardly notices that her trusty servant, Bardia,
is dying. Even while taking inner inventory, then, she remains fixated
upon herself. While writing she forgets her unhealthy obsession with
Bardia, only to replace it with neglect. In part, the writing takes her out
of herself; yet she herself remains the focus of her writing. Even still,

[9] *Faces,* 256.
[10] *Faces,* 24.

the dream of the seeds indicates that there is hope. She, the Queen, is prepared to become little, as little as an ant, in trying to accomplish the enormous task set for her.

For one like Orual who does not have a foundational belief in God's benevolence and protection, the disciplined life might seem, in a first resort, to be the only human hope. Though there is virtue in Orual's attempts, she eventually must come to realize that the task is impossible. She reaches that turning point of realization just after Bardia dies. Orual goes to visit Bardia's widow, where she takes off her veil to share a human moment of true mourning. In removing the veil, she reveals her ugliness, and acknowledges the vulnerability of their shared sorrow. Ansit, the widow, has a momentary empathetic moment, but immediately goes on the attack, detailing the Queen's utter self-absorption, and how she has "gorged"[11] herself on the lives of others. For Orual, the realization that even her intense love for Bardia had grown to be "nine-tenths"[12] hatred (for her exacting demands brought him illness and death) is devastating. She is left with utter emptiness, a state that renders her more open to further lessons about her depravity that will soon come by way of god-given dreams. However, she replaces the veil even after this encounter with Ansit, and thus shows that she still possesses a touch of self-protectiveness. Temptation and self-will are subtle, and can operate even in the life of one who, for a brief moment, has seen clearly. She has not yet learned deep humility, nor, like the Psalmist, cried "out of the depths" (Psalm 130). Once she fully admits and shows her true self, ugliness and all, things can be fully turned around.

She is accosted yet again by a divinely sent nightmare, a dream in which she meets her long-dead and terrifying father. Digging her own burial place, deeper and deeper, at the behest of her ghostly father, she is commanded repeatedly to throw herself down into the next (deeper) pit. In the very depth, he compels her to gaze in the mirror, where

[11] *Faces,* 264.
[12] *Faces,* 266.

she sees the face of Ungit, of death itself. Her father asks, "Who is Ungit?" and she responds, wailing, "I am Ungit!"[13] Soon after, assaulted by divine dreams, she comes to a point of despair, and plans to take her own life. As she goes out in the dark, she takes off her veil, and hopes that this, too, will be a disguise, since the townsfolk have not seen her face, and therefore cannot recognize her. As she is about to commit the act, she is told by a divine voice, "Die before you die! There is no chance after."[14] The digging down, the shutting up, and the fixation upon death must precede her coming into the light. It is not possible for her to "kill" Ungit herself, stringent though her ascetic activities have been. She must be undragoned by the gods, just as Eustace is in the children's novel, *The Voyage of the Dawn Treader.*

Yet her efforts have not been entirely useless. They have shown, at the very least, a disposition to distance herself from her own ugliness. In this sense, her own spiritual demon (the "Ungit" part of her) cannot be driven out without ascesis—"except by prayer and fasting" (Mk 9.29).[15] If she had not realized her spiritual bankruptcy in this manner, she would never have come to make confession before the god—"Lord, I am Ungit."[16] The path to that realization and to healing began when she desired "the death of our passions and desires and vain opinions."[17] The "death which is wisdom," taught by her philosopher-teacher, the Fox, was the first step in her remaking.

[13] *Faces*, 276.

[14] *Faces*, 279.

[15] Though the KJV includes them, most contemporary English translations leave out the words "and fasting," arguing that fasting was a later imperative in the Church, and that many manuscripts do not have these Greek words. However, at least one early manuscript does, and the reading is attested by numerous manuscripts. See Carsten Peter Thiede, "'By Prayer and Fasting'," *Tyndale Society Journal* 13 (August 1999): 17-23, http://www.tyndale.org/tsj13/thiede.html for Thiede's cogent argument that these words were not an afterthought, but part of the original story. At any rate, it is an integral part of the Church's tradition.

[16] *Faces*, 279.

[17] *Faces*, 281.

Yet she has more to learn. She must also realize that even her strong efforts are not strong enough. This itself is a step towards receiving the help that heaven can give. Once she has realized that her miserable identity is that of Ungit, Orual decides to turn her back on this life. But, like St Paul, who faces his own inability to follow the Torah (Rom 7.19), she learns, "I could not hold myself an hour."[18] Making her soul beautiful is even more difficult than changing her ugly face: "We bring our ugliness, in both kinds, with us into the world."[19] And so, she learns, we are ugly from the beginning. Yet, we also dream for a beautiful world from the beginning too—this was clearer in the case of Psyche, but also true of Orual, despite her tendency to cynicism.

And then comes another dream, one that corresponds to the second task of the mythical Psyche. Here, Orual finds herself by a bright river, gazing upon a flock of golden rams, in a scene bluer than blue, and greener than green, and with music as sweet as the air. She is filled with longing, but thinks that she can steal some of the beauty *for herself*. Crossing the cold stream and meeting the herd, she is very nearly trampled by their glad stampeding, and yet is not destroyed. Looking up, she sees another human figure at the borders of the field, gathering the wool that the rams had left behind, winning effortlessly what Orual had sought to take by force! So she learns that she indeed *did* have longings for the eternal world, and sees, in vision, the paradox: beauty and glory are gifts, not prizes to be snatched by those who would own them. This dream leaves her with despair, she says, and yet she becomes at this point a wise and careful judge over the disputes in her kingdom. Clearly, she has gained this ability because she is learning to lay her inordinate passions aside. We are able to discern the changes occurring in Orual, while she sees herself merely to have become aware of the vanity of life.

There remains one self-delusion of which she must be cured. This is the deception that has energized her entire story—her seemingly pure

[18] *Faces*, 282.
[19] *Faces*, 282.

love of Psyche. She may have oppressively confined her tutor the Fox and misused Bardia, but at least (she thinks!) in the matter of Psyche, the gods were wrong—she had loved her sister, and they had taken her away. She is soon to be disabused of this, by a sequence that she recognizes to be "certainly vision and no dream."[20] This vision begins with a hard trek through the sands, where she can just glimpse joy, but cannot arrive there on her own efforts. (We may be reminded of John in *Pilgrim's Regress,* who travels with the companion Vertue until he gets to mountains: the ascetic journey is finally too arduous for him.) Orual indeed now travels in arduous places, trudging in her visions up even to her waist in the sand of the desert. The trek lasts for hundreds of years, as she seeks for a well, and carries a bowl to capture the water of death that will make Ungit beautiful. Eventually she finds herself at the foot of an immense mountain, and is brought within it to stand before the heavenly court, before all the souls of the dead. There, her bowl has been transformed into a book, the book she has been writing. She brings her complaint against the gods, indeed, before the whole cosmos, and finds herself not to be a grand prosecutor of the gods, but simply naked Ungit, reading aloud, over and over, a shabby and spiteful book.

As she comes to the end of the recitation, her authentic self emerges—one consumed with jealousy of both Psyche and her true love. She cries out to the divine beings, "there's no room for you and us in the same world . . . we want to be our own. Psyche was mine and no one else had any right to her."[21] Even worse, Orual likens Psyche to a dog who was to be fed by *her,* receiving no tidbits from the table of the gods. She pictures the divine beings as seducers, though not the blood-drinkers and man-eaters whom her country-folk thought the Shadowbrute to be. And that they had stolen *her property* was worse than if they had killed Psyche outright! Orual is mercifully silenced in her reading. Her own spite, anger, pride, thanklessness, jealousy, and

[20] *Faces,* 285.
[21] *Faces,* 291–92.

moral bankruptcy disclose a preliminary answer to one of her early questions. Why could she not see the joyful beings, or experience joy? The answer is in her own small, straitened, heart. Unawares, she has found the water of death for which she was searching: the death of her own passions and self-deceit.

She sees, then, her own face. Asceticism—travelling for years over sand—finally comes to its end. It has played its part in exposing her frailty and in clarifying the temptations that have dogged her progress. By trying her hardest to follow its path, she has come to see her need. And we are reminded in the Scriptures, too, that asceticism is not merely for those who are searching, but also for those who have been on the road for some time (consider Matthew 4.2; 6.16, Mark 2.18–20, Luke 2.37, Acts 13.2–3, Acts 14.23, 2 Corinthians 6.5 and 11.27, and 2 Timothy 2.3–4). Orual might have been tempted to smugness in her queenly and ascetic activities; we, too, need constant reminders of our dependence upon God. Like Orual, we must face our own poverty, and allow our human rigorous actions to be made part of our transformation. The one who had fancied herself to be a brave opponent of the gods finally learns: "All . . . are born into the house of Ungit . . . must get free from her . . . or bear Ungit's son and die . . . or change."[22] (Here, of course, Lewis evokes the concept of atonement, as it is variously described: we will tackle this in our next chapter.)

The main question of this story, then, is "How can they [the gods] meet us face to face till we have faces?" This question does not allow us to keep Orual at arm's length, as a case study. Her blindness, her self-deception, her struggles, her efforts, and her resistance to the truth ring all too true for the reader. This is true even if we live in the twenty-first century rather than Glome, even if we have access to the Christian story, and even if we have not been privy to a single vision or unusual revelation. *Till We Have Faces* is difficult not simply because of its esoteric nature and its hard subject matter. Rather, the open reader sees

[22] *Faces,* 301.

himself or herself in Orual, and receives a bracing challenge: face up to your own emptiness and to the hardness of life. Through Orual we come to recognize that the real cave, the real death, the real darkness, can be internal.

Moving Towards the Unexpected

Yet we are not left in the depths. Rather, the divine work actually transforms the human soul once she has realized her poverty. She is brought out of her inner darkness. Just as Christ descends into the dark to grasp the bound and empty hands that are there, finally divine and burning hands greet Orual. The veil is removed for her, and she is unmade, overwhelmed by the advent of the god. In our next chapter, we will see that not only the immediately responsive Psyche, but also the resistant Orual can be made a "goddess," a "real woman," "a thousand times more her very self."[23] We will investigate the final visions of Orual, which disclose how the sisters' lives have been intertwined, even after they parted physically from each other. In the end, coming face to face with God also means that they are reunited with each other.

As we think about Orual's transformation, another (obscure) Greek myth makes its impact. When she was a young child, Psyche called her beloved Orual by the name of "Maia." Maia, in Greek mythology, was the eldest of seven daughters, known as the Pleiades, and she was both reserved and astonishingly beautiful. She attracted the attention of Zeus, and, like Psyche, the jealousy of a jilted wife. But Zeus retained his clandestine love for Maia, and also entrusted to her care the demigod Arcas, who in his turn eventually became a constellation in the sky. Our novel's Psyche evidently calls her older sister Maia because Orual displayed that nurturing capacity and had a hand in bringing her own "Arcas" to maturity, so that she could shine in the firmament. Orual, despite her flaws, had a mediating role in Psyche's glorification, as we

---

[23] *Faces*, 305–306.

shall see in the next chapter. Lewis's allusion to this outside story is subtle. He does not mean for us to decode the characters, or to offer a one-to-one correspondence between every character and every figure in the myth. Instead, he uses an impressionist's brush, allowing us to see Orual first in one way, and then in another. In this chapter we have seen how he pictures the sisters as different expressions of the human soul in search of, or fleeing from, divine joy. In the end, though both follow their separate paths, they merge in glory, before the face of "the god." By means of a heady cocktail of arduous adventure, introspection, mythology, and philosophical discussion, Lewis leads us to see the grave business before us all as we deal not only with ourselves, but with others:

> It is a serious thing to live in a society of possible gods and goddesses, to remember that the dullest, most uninteresting person you can talk to may one day be a creature which, if you saw it now, you would be strongly tempted to worship, or else a horror and a corruption such as you now meet, if at all, only in nightmare.[24]

The glory to which we and others may be led, in God's time, is wholly unexpected—as unexpected as Orual's transformation into Psyche.

---

[24] "The Weight of Glory," in *The Weight of Glory and other Addresses* (1949; repr., New York, NY; Macmillan, 1980), 21.

CHAPTER 6

Blessings and Curses: Justice, Atonement, and the Great Exchange

(*Till We Have Faces*, *Miracles*, and St Athanasius' *On the Incarnation*)

W e have seen that *Till We have Faces* is a rich work, though fraught with difficulty for some readers because of its idiom, form, and content. Besides the myths concerning Psyche (and Maia), and the introspective pain caused as we are drawn into Orual's character, we must also contend with the novel's complex subject matter. Here we find not only asceticism, but what Rudolf Otto called the *mysterium tremendum* (the divine mystery that makes us afraid). In particular, this mystery leads us to consider the significance of suffering and death, and various representations of atonement. Paradox is everywhere: freedom through self-sacrifice, blessing through curse, life through death. Lewis does not dispel these wonders, but leads us to appreciate them more fully, where they have been misrepresented or misused in some expressions of Christianity. With so much going on, the novel is not for the faint of heart, nor the feeble of mind!

A Scandal Not So Foreign

Some have dismissed the major scandal of Lewis's narrative, assuming that it is simply collateral damage that comes because he has used the ancient myth of Cupid and Psyche. Its premise (that the flawless girl

Psyche must be offered to the god of the mountain) is arresting, in the same way chapters seven and eight of Joshua are scandalous to the twenty-first-century reader. What are Christians to do with the idea of someone being placed, as the book of Joshua puts it, "under the ban"—that is, he or she becomes a curse, or paradoxically (in the logic of sacrifice) "a blessing"? Before turning to Psyche, let us consider these awkward chapters of the book of Joshua, concerning the execution of Achan. This event follows the unprecedented failure of the newly minted Israelite warriors at Ai, during their divinely sanctioned campaign to capture the Holy Land. In our era, when *jihad* is no longer merely a theoretical problem, contemporary readers immediately enter discomfiting territory. After the troops fail in their holy war, and their leader Joshua is devastated, the Lord "explains" the defeat and prescribes the dark solution:

> The LORD said to Joshua, "Arise, why have you thus fallen upon your face? Israel has sinned; they have transgressed my covenant which I commanded them; they have taken some of the devoted things; they have stolen, and lied, and put them among their own stuff.
>
> Therefore the people of Israel cannot stand before their enemies; they turn their backs before their enemies, because they have become a thing for destruction. I will be with you no more, unless you destroy the devoted things from among you.
>
> Up, sanctify the people, and say, "Sanctify yourselves for tomorrow; for thus says the LORD, God of Israel, 'There are devoted things in the midst of you, O Israel; you cannot stand before your enemies, until you take away the devoted things from among you.' In the morning therefore you shall be brought near by your tribes; and the tribe which the LORD takes shall come near by families; and the family which the LORD takes shall come near by households; and the household which the LORD takes shall come near

man by man. And he who is taken with the devoted things shall be burned with fire, he and all that he has, because he has transgressed the covenant of the LORD, and because he has done a shameful thing in Israel.'"

(Josh 7.10–15)

The booty supposedly "devoted" to the Lord was, of course, stolen by Achan, when it was either to be destroyed by fire as a holocaust, or, if made of precious metals, put into God's treasury. Instead, Achan was tempted by the spoils, despite a divine warning in the previous chapter (6.18–19). All the Israelite families therefore are brought "before the LORD" to be judged by the ritual casting of lots: the lot indicates Achan, who confesses all and is stoned with his entire family and their belongings, including the booty. This accomplished, the campaign against Ai is resumed successfully, with the whole city put "under the ban" since it is "devoted" to the Lord, as was Jericho. Following this victorious high point in Israel's campaign, a sacrifice is made (8.30) on the mountain, and during this ceremony, the Mosaic book of blessings and curses solemnly read:

Then Joshua built an altar in Mount Ebal to the LORD, the God of Israel, as Moses the servant of the LORD had commanded the people of Israel, as it is written in the book of the law of Moses, "an altar of unhewn stones, upon which no man has lifted an iron tool"; and they offered on it burnt offerings to the LORD, and sacrificed peace offerings. And there, in the presence of the people of Israel, he wrote upon the stones a copy of the law of Moses, which he had written. And all Israel, sojourner as well as homeborn, with their elders and officers and their judges, stood on opposite sides of the ark before the Levitical priests who carried the ark of the covenant of the LORD, half of them in front of Mount Gerizim and half of them in front of Mount Ebal, as Moses the servant of the LORD had commanded at the first, that they should bless the people of Israel. And afterward he read all the words of the law, the blessing and the curse, according to all that is written in the book of the law. There was not a word of all that Moses commanded which Joshua did not read before all the assembly of Israel, and the women, and the little ones, and the sojourners who lived among them. (Josh 8.30–35)

The embarrassing episode of Achan and Ai is not marginal to the book of Joshua. Instead, it leads up to this ceremonial climax, a ritual that involves the dedication of the Holy Land to the Lord and the solemn ratification of God's covenant, with its blessings and curses. In attendance is the entire community, including foreign adherents to Israel, with Joshua passing on to all the words of the Mosaic Torah. The solemn gathering to hear the proclaimed word of the Lord we understand. But the rest is in shadows, rife with dark mysteries. Why the bloody conquest in the first place? Why are the Israelites told to put conquered peoples and goods "under the ban"—that is, holy (in *destruction*) to the Lord? Why does Israel use lots to discover the transgressor? Why must a thief be executed, and why is his entire family punished?

Putting the episode in the context of the entire biblical story, from Eden onward, goes some way in making sense of our questions. It is helpful to keep in mind the fallen nature of humanity, the barbarous behaviors of those pagans among whom the Israelites had to establish themselves, God's historical actions to establish His particular people in that savage setting, and the ancient understanding of corporate identity in a time before the Enlightenment notion of individualism was adopted. Placing the story within these parameters is helpful (if not entirely satisfying).[1] Besides interrogating the story in terms of our con-

---

[1]My concern here is not to examine the Old Testament concept of *cherem*, and the embarrassment of "holy war" in the OT, but to consider more specifically the execution of Achan and his family. However, in dealing with the more general problem, it is helpful to remember that the trajectory of the Bible is away from violence towards the New Testament ideals of "turning the other cheek," predicated upon God's very own

temporary reaction, we may also fruitfully allow it to speak where we find it more congenial. For example, the story highlights the principle of mysterious holiness in a way that retains its power in our modern ears. Achan has sinned, after all, by trying to personally benefit from slaughter: his goal was to further his own interests rather than to participate in what God was doing and bring glory to God. Indeed, divine glory is highlighted in Joshua's lament before the Lord when Ai is not conquered. Fearful of pagans mocking the Lord, Joshua has asked, "What wilt thou do for thy great name?" (Joshua 7.9). Moreover, Achan confesses his transgression and does not resist his punishment, nor does he argue that his family should be exempt from the judgment.

In Jesus, we know a God who is not harsh and who has given a New Covenant that approaches matters of corporate identity differently. Both John 8.1–11 and Ezekiel 18.2–4 say that God does not visit the sins of the fathers on the children, as may once have been the case. Even so, we can, in reading the story of Achan, glean one insight: God may not be "used" for profit. To serve Him means to revere Him. Old Testament "holiness" is not a mere synonym for everything that we consider good. Rather, God's glory and holiness are in some ways unfathomable, veiled to the understanding of fallen humanity. Those

assumption of our death to Himself, the trampling down of death by death. We may also remember, when seeking to understand the place of the conquest in God's economy, that the Old Testament does not enjoin holy war as a normative action, and that we are dealing with narrative, rather than universal prescriptions. Origen, of course, famously dissolved the problem by reading the passages allegorically: helpful as this may be for Christian devotional reading, that is manifestly not their natural or original genre. Several more recent essays and scholarly books have been written on this topic, including those by T. R. Hobbs, Gerhard von Rad, Douglas Knight, Susan Niditch, and my colleague Jerome Creach, approaching the question from different perspectives. I have found particularly helpful the less complex treatment of Peter Craigie, *The Problem of War in the Old Testament*. He suggests that God, in working within our world, works within the conventions of a particular time and place, "getting His hands dirty," so to speak, but turning all to a just end. Thus such wars were waged by divine concession, and turned to God's will in recouping the fallen world, as God directed fledgling Israel, putting her in a more secure position to become a light for the world. Craigie avoids the temptation to dismiss the horror, even while insisting upon the integrity and compassion of God.

who are Christians may be tempted to exclaim, yes, but all is now revealed, and the fear of God is removed. I hasten to remind us that this is not the logic followed by the writer to the Hebrews, who speaks of the awe and fear surrounding the mountain of revelation:

> For you have not come to what may be touched, a blazing fire, and darkness, and gloom, and a tempest, and the sound of a trumpet, and a voice whose words made the hearers entreat that no further messages be spoken to them. For they could not endure the order that was given, "If even a beast touches the mountain, it shall be stoned." Indeed, so terrifying was the sight that Moses said, "I tremble with fear." But you have come to Mount Zion and to the city of the living God, the heavenly Jerusalem, and to innumerable angels in festal gathering, and to the assembly of the first-born who are enrolled in heaven, and to a judge who is God of all, and to the spirits of just men made perfect, and to Jesus, the mediator of a new covenant, and to the sprinkled blood that speaks more graciously than the blood of Abel. (Heb 12.19–24)

Did we think, after picturing the fear at Sinai, that the book of Hebrews would go on to assure the reader, "And so, we need no longer have any fear"? It does *not*, but instead follows a line of argument from the lesser to the greater: "See that you do not refuse him who is speaking. *For if they did not escape* when they refused him who warned them on earth, *much less* shall we escape if we reject him who warns from heaven" (Heb 12.25). The New Testament, though abounding in mercy, reminds us that God is holy, but not tame. Under the new covenant, then, there remains mystery that cannot be resolved by reason alone. And that mystery includes the idea of sacrifice. The "sprinkled blood" hints at a necessary but scandalous element that we cannot dismiss as foreign to the Christian faith.

Lewis was well aware of the scandal of holy sacrifice. Indeed, he accentuates the tension that we are certain to feel when reading *Till We*

Have Faces, as Orual, the homely older sister of sacrificial Psyche, tells her story. From the get-go, the "water" of Greek rationalism, taught to Orual by her tutor, the Fox, is presented with respect. But in the end its simple transparency does not satisfy. The Fox's maxim "The divine nature . . . has no envy"[2] rings true. Indeed, it is consonant with the Judeo-Christian view that God needs nothing, and so covets nothing. Yet that maxim stands in stark contrast with both the scriptural declaration, "I am a jealous God," as well as with Orual's intuitive knowledge of her nation's dark yet powerful tribal deity, Ungit. Perhaps it is true that the divine nature has no envy, or need of anything; but there remains the demand for worship, including sacrifice. The actions and words of the novel juxtapose the Fox's rational explanations with an awareness of enshrouded mystery, and so set up an argument in the reader's mind. Lewis does not reject philosophy, yet leaves us with the insight that reason cannot explain everything. Throughout the novel, reason and (sometimes dark) mystery jostle together and remain unresolved, even as they do in the Christian canon, and, if we are honest, in our own experience.

Nowhere is this competition more evident than in the novel's presentation of atonement and sacrifice. Here we must tread carefully, for the novel has its own logic, and lives within its own world. As with the Narnia stories, it is not a wooden allegory to be decoded in terms of Christian theology. Lewis's explicit foundation, after all, is the pagan story of *Cupid and Psyche,* that story of a divinely beautiful but mortal girl loved by a god, envied by a goddess and her sisters, warned not to gaze upon the divinity of her lover, punished by exile and various tasks for so doing, and finally restored to her bridegroom as a new goddess. Woven into the story is the conviction shared by many ancient cultures that divine beings may demand the ultimate sacrifice from their devotees. This perspective is also glimpsed in the story of Isaac's sacrifice: the Lord does not, in the end, require Isaac's death, but he *does* make the

[2] *Till We Have Faces,* 24.

demand. Service to the Hebrew and Christian God is not less arduous than service to idols. The path that Lewis takes here is risky, for there are elements of the pagan stories that are unworthy of the biblical, if sometimes inscrutable, portrait of God. Evidently, Lewis thought that the risk was worth taking.

In *Till We Have Faces,* the mature Lewis does for adults what he does for children in *The Chronicles of Narnia.* He spins an extended tale out of mythological material. His purpose in writing is not to delve *explicitly* into the problems of Good Friday. Nor is he writing an essay that holds on to vicarious suffering against contemporary theologians (some from the East) who insist that this is not how God works. As an avid reader of the Scriptures, certainly Lewis would have been aware of Jeremiah 32.35, where the Lord rejects the evils of pagan sacrifice: "They built the high places of Baal in the valley of the son of Hinnom, to offer up their sons and daughters to Molech, though I did not command them, nor did it enter into my mind, that they should do this abomination, to cause Judah to sin." Lewis, however, does not descend into the mystery of atonement by weighing Scripture with Scripture, or by delineating a careful doctrine. Instead, he fires our imagination with the story, while warning us through dialogue, and through Orual's mishaps, where we may lawfully go in thinking about God, and where we should not venture. By means of this ancient story, and the way in which it is told, Lewis "say[s] best what's to be said,"[3] without pontificating and without giving in to "the demon of compulsive explanation."[4] With the main characters, we enter high and low places, and are sometimes allowed to find our own way back to level ground. In fact, there are at least two atonement stories suggested in the book. Let's consider the surprising form that these stories take, and how the two juxtaposed pictures help

[3]"Sometimes Fairy Stories May Say Best What's to be Said," in *On Stories: And Other Essays On Literature* (Orlando, FL: Harcourt, 1982), 45. This article first appeared on November 18, 1956 in the New York Times.

[4]"On Three Ways of Writing For Children," in *On Stories: And Other Essays On Literature*, 37.

us to grapple with blessings and curses, divine judgment, and what St Athanasius called "the great exchange."

Competing Stories and Unreliable Storytellers

We begin with the unusual structure of the novel. Within it, we encounter astonishingly well-rounded characters with whom we empathize. In fact, our identification with them uncovers bits of *us* that we would prefer not to acknowledge. The story is an intricate reversal tale that surprises us like the cinematic psychological thriller *A Dangerous Mind*. We discover, through various twists and turns, and through subplots that amplify the story, that our narrator Orual is somewhat unreliable. Initially, we are taken in by her impassioned plea against "the gods," by her professed love for her sister Psyche, and by her version of reality. Then we change our minds as we see things through her changing eyes.

The story is told in four movements: Psyche's offering (which stresses sacrificial atonement), Orual's offering (which depicts atonement by victory), Orual's journeys to the heights and depths (which, we have seen in the previous chapter, emphasize discipline and self-understanding), and Orual's final visions (which stress judgment and encounter with the divine). As we read the story, we begin with an *anti*-theodicy, that is, an attack against, rather than a defense of the gods. Then we move into an exploration of human self-centeredness and frailty (as we explored in our previous chapter). Finally, there is a transformative and hopeful ending.

Sacrificial Atonement

Atonement is the most imposing theme. Most of the story revolves around it, as do the fates of the two major characters, the royal daughters Orual (or Maia) and Psyche (or Istra). Intriguingly, Lewis casts the two female characters as Christ-figures, though, as we have seen in our discussion of *ascesis,* they play other roles as well. Their gender is made necessary by the myth that he is retelling, and it also suits the biblical image of the bride of God. It is Psyche's messianic function that is most obvious to the Western reader. She is the sacrifice on the Tree, the Blessed and the Cursed, the beautiful one given up for many, the one who voluntarily goes to death, giving up her life that she may save her people. From the story's onset, we are enticed to love Psyche, as we see her through the eyes of her sister and their tutor, the Fox:

> [I]n one hour, I passed out of the worst anguish I had yet suffered into the beginning of all my joys. The child was very big, not a wearish little thing as you might have expected from her mother's stature, and very fair of skin. You would have thought she made bright all the corner of the room in which she lay. She slept (tiny was the sound of her breathing). . . . As I gazed at her the Fox came in on tiptoes and looked over my shoulder. "Now by all the gods," he whispered, "old fool that I am, I could almost believe that there really is divine blood in your family. Helen herself, new-hatched, must have looked so." . . . As the Fox delighted to say, she was "according to nature"; what every woman, or even every thing, ought to have been and meant to be, but missed by some trip of chance.[5]

Psyche, then, is the beloved and the blessed, loving "all manner of brutes," winning the heart of (nearly) everyone who meets her. She is believed to have healing powers of touch by the people of the land. As befits a Christ figure, she is betrayed by one of her own (the third sister, Redival) and rejected as the "Accursed" by those who had only just called her "Blessed." Christians recall the betrayal of Judas and the fickleness of the people in Jerusalem. She is also selected by the priest as the necessary offering to an exacting deity, "fit . . . [to] die for the people."[6] Her story of sacrifice is told with perfect timing, moving inexorably to

[5] *Faces,* 20–22.
[6] *Faces,* 61.

its poignant end. By subtle Christian echoes, it increases the foreboding of those who are biblically literate: "For hours she touched [in healing] . . . I saw her growing paler and paler. Her walk became a stagger";[7] then we hear, "The Accursed, the Accursed! She made herself a goddess";[8] and finally we listen to the awed comment, "That's the Holy Road . . . the way they took the Blessed."[9] Psyche herself describes her ordeal on the Tree:

> [T]he only thing that did me good . . . was hardly a thought, and very hard to put into words. There was a lot of the Fox's philosophy in it—things he says about gods or "the divine nature"—but mixed up with things the Priest said, too, about the blood and the earth and how sacrifice makes the crops grow. I'm not explaining it well. It seemed to come from somewhere deep inside me, deeper than the part that sees pictures . . . deeper than fears and tears. It was shapeless, but you could just hold on to it; or just let it hold onto you. Then the change came. . . . I was so thirsty. . . . At last . . . I saw him.[10]

Psyche's story leads us to ask the question, how can one be both the blessed and the cursed? We are told that she is the best that Nature had to offer, but her acclaim as "the blessed" changes very quickly into a charge that she is "the accursed." Similarly, the people initially believe that she has a healing power, until she becomes a scapegoat, and they are convinced that her touch instead has brought illness. Perhaps as readers we may discount the fickle crowd, and prefer instead to follow the cues of the story that she is blessed. However, the story does not allow us this escape, since she is described *both* as the beloved of the god of the mountain and the hapless one whom he will devour. Indeed, as Orual tells the story, we assume that Psyche has been made a victim *unjustly*. We react with Orual to the perfidy of self-centered Redival, the

---

[7] *Faces*, 32.
[8] *Faces*, 39.
[9] *Faces*, 95.
[10] *Faces*, 109–110.

cowardice of her kingly father, and the superstition of the people. Yet Psyche's sacrifice is also, mysteriously, the answer to her own professed longing for another life by means of death. She goes willingly, to Orual's horror. To be the blessed, she must accept the role of the accursed.

To the keen ear, these paradoxes parallel both the well-known words of the Eucharist ("On the night that he was betrayed, or rather gave himself over to death"), as well as complex passages in the New Testament letters:

> For all who rely on works of the law are under a curse; for it is written, "Cursed be every one who does not abide by all things written in the book of the law, and do them." Now it is evident that no man is justified before God by the law. . . . Christ redeemed us from the curse of the law, having become a curse for us—for it is written, "Cursed be every one who hangs on a tree"—that in Christ Jesus the blessing of Abraham might come upon the Gentiles, that we might receive the promise of the Spirit through faith. (Gal 3.10–14)

The letter to the Galatians also directly relates blessing to curse, suggesting that Jesus brings the blessing of Abraham by means of becoming subject to the curse of the law, indeed, by *becoming* a curse *for us*. Then there is the astonishing statement in 2 Corinthians 5.21 that the sinless Christ was *made sin* in order to bring about human transformation. In the letter to the Romans, St Paul explains more explicitly how this works. The curse of death, initiated in Adam, and continued by all humankind, has issued in sin, but is removed by means of blood sacrifice—an indication of God's great love. Christ's act brings about not simply reconciliation, but even the hope of "sharing the glory" of the immortal God:

> Therefore, since we are justified by faith, we have peace with God through our Lord Jesus Christ. Through him we have obtained

access to this grace in which we stand, and we rejoice in our hope of sharing the glory of God. . . .While we were still weak, at the right time Christ died for the ungodly. Why, one will hardly die for a righteous man—though perhaps for a good man one will dare even to die. But God shows his love for us in that while we were yet sinners Christ died for us. Since, therefore, we are now *justified by his blood,* much more shall we be saved by him from the wrath [of God].[11] For if while we were enemies we were reconciled to God by the death of his Son, much more, now that we are reconciled, shall we be saved by his life. Not only so, but we also rejoice in God through our Lord Jesus Christ, through whom we have now received our reconciliation. . . . If, because of one man's trespass, death reigned through that one man, much more will those who receive the abundance of grace and the free gift of righteousness reign in life through the one man Jesus Christ. (Rom 5.1–2, 6–11, 17)

These passages speak about hope and love initiated by God, but in the same breath talk about God's wrath and the curse, which Jesus assumes to himself. Such theological grammar understandably has scandalized some in our day. The mystery of atonement is amplified in Hebrews 2.9–18:

But we see Jesus, who for a little while was made lower than the angels, *crowned with glory and honor because of the suffering of death,* so that by the grace of God he might taste death for every one. For it was fitting that he, for whom and by whom all things exist, in bringing many sons to glory, should make the pioneer of their salvation *perfect through suffering.* For he who sanctifies and those who are sanctified have all one origin. That is why he is not ashamed to call them brethren. . . . Since therefore the children share in flesh

[11]"Of God" is not found in the original text, but the simple term "the wrath" is intended as a shorthand for the well-known phrase, which is found in its entirety in Romans 1.18.

and blood, he himself likewise partook of the same nature, *that through death he might destroy him who has the power of death,* that is, the devil and deliver all those who through fear of death were subject to lifelong bondage. . . . Therefore he had to be made like his brethren in every respect, so that he might become a merciful and faithful high priest in the service of God, *to make atonement for the sins of the people.* For because he himself has suffered and been tempted, he is able to help those who are tempted.

The language of solidarity seen in Romans is brought to the fore in Hebrews, where humans are aligned either with mortal Adam or the crucified and risen Christ. We must remember that both in St Paul's letters and in Hebrews, there is no playing off of Father and Son. Some have wrongly drawn a cartoon of a vengeful Father unjustly demanding the blood of His Son. No, God initiates, offering His best gift, and Christ takes on death, willingly atoning for sin by his suffering. Some English versions shy away from the language of atonement, fearful that we might see God as one like the "Shadowbrute" of Lewis's novel, who needs to be "propitiated" or made generous towards us by human sacrifice. Instead, they use the word "expiation" (a "sprinkling," or "covering," or "cleansing") to speak of what Jesus did to the sins of the people. But the Greek word used in Hebrews 2.17 is related to the word *hilastērion,* which is used in a sacrificial context of atonement.[12] Certainly, God does not require to be soothed, as pagans thought about

[12]My claim here about the sacrificial context of the Greek word is controversial among contemporary academics who (in my view) do not take seriously enough the sacrificial use of the term in 4 Maccabees 17.11–16, and stress that the "mercy seat" that covered the ark (for which the term is also used) was not an actual place of sacrifice. This is, of course, true, but I would argue that the blood was spilled upon the Lord's throne-cover not just to cleanse a place of meeting, but also to ratify that a sacrifice had taken place. Many, including some translators, continue to see sacrificial connotations of the word both here and in Romans 3.25. In the Septuagint, the term is used for several of the holy items in the temple, including portions of the altar (in Ezekiel and Amos), and is thus associated with the practice of sacrifice, whether or not it refers to sacrifice explicitly in every case that it is used in the Scriptures.

their deities: He is love and truth, and does not need to be "propitiated" in this sense. Still, actual blood or death is the means by which the reconciliation is accomplished. To this end, the Son "takes on flesh and blood," and suffers. God does not demand blood for His own arbitrary purposes; yet He does not simply declare us forgiven without the crucifixion and descent into hades. We remain in the realm of real mystery, where death is conquered by death, and sin removed by sacrifice.

The desire of English twentieth-century translators to avoid the idea of sacrificial atonement in the Bible may be seen as parallel to the cultic "improvements" instigated by the younger priest in *Till We Have Faces*. In the course of the story, the more enlightened priest places a palatable, nice version of the dark goddess Ungit in the temple, cleaning the statue and giving it a human beauty, so that it is less fearful. Similarly, he puts more windows into the temple, and allows the sweet reason of the sunlight to shine upon the events there. Something, however, is lost in the cleanup. When Orual speaks to one of her peasant countrywomen who comes to worship, the woman responds that there is power in the old, dark goddess, not in the refined one. It is almost certain that Lewis is gesturing towards what well-meaning revisionists have done in our day to the mystery of the faith, scrubbing its face, and putting it under human control.

All this is certainly not to suggest that the pagan notion of a bloodthirsty god is to be embraced. We have already seen the blindness of Orual, who cannot believe that the gods mean any good towards her sister. When faced with her sister's hope for transcendence, she is overcome with anger, and accuses her sister of liking "holy darkness" and being one of Ungit's temple prostitutes. Psyche knows that somehow sacrifice and true living are interconnected: and we are meant to believe her. After all, Psyche is not only a blessed and cursed Christ figure, connected with vicarious sacrifice; she is also Isaac, released from pagan notions of atonement. This challenges our easy identification of the gospel as something that may be rationally shown to be "good" in ordinary human terms. Throughout, Lewis contrasts Greek philosophy, like water, over against divine mysteries, like blood. These two perspectives are embodied in the learned Fox and the more provincial Bardia, Psyche's devout right-hand man and counselor. Fox introduces Orual to the bright light of reason, and later (wrongly) discounts any possibility of Psyche's sacrifice as propitiatory or effective. From his perspective, the saving rain after her sacrifice has come only by chance. Similarly, her rescue cannot have been miraculous, but must have been at the hands of a vagabond male, an unsuitable suitor for the royal princess. The philosopher insists that the gods are not jealous, that they do not intrude into the ways of humankind, and they remain unmoved by sacrifice. The Fox thus offers Orual a way of seeing the world that dismisses any notion of atonement, and all that it might entail. But it also dismisses the idea that the divine world is in any way connected with us. Bardia's world, on the other hand, is enchanted. For him, the dark fertility goddess Ungit and her son, the sacrifice-demanding Shadowbrute, are fearful, since "the loving and the devouring are one."[13] No water for him, but blood and wine! In their competing interpretations of Psyche's fate, Orual's two confidants embody the apostle's words that the gospel is "folly to the Greek and scandal to the Jew" (1 Cor 1.23). Whichever contrary version of Psyche's adventure Orual adopts, she has a ready-made excuse for disbelieving her sister's story of redemption and transformation.

Our author is playing a dangerous game. The Fox's explanation casts doubt not only on the interior myth of the story, but upon the Christian reader's desire for a faith that too glibly celebrates a personal connection with God. Any experience of mystery that we may have is notoriously fleeting, which lends power to the Fox's rationalistic argument. Orual is given only a split-second revelation of Psyche's god: we can well understand, then, her doubt and the attraction of the Fox's reasonable explanations. On the other hand, Bardia's adherence to the

---

[13] *Faces*, 49.

"dark side" reminds us of aspects of the Christian faith that we may prefer to underplay—for example, the sacrifice of the perfect Human Being. With Orual, we may be repelled by this aspect of "the holy." As we explore this difficult terrain, we must actually listen to *three* unreliable narrators, and not simply one: Orual, the Fox, and Bardia. Together, they conjure up a variation on the *tri*-lemma for which Lewis is famous: either Jesus is a liar, a lunatic, or the Lord.[14] In our story, Psyche is either in league with demons, delusional, or telling the truth.

The sacrifice of Psyche, then, is presented as either folly or scandal—unless there is a third alternative. Orual, in trying to come to terms with this, briefly argues with herself, like Tolkien's Gollum: "Do not meddle. Anything might be true. You are among marvels you do not understand. Carefully, carefully."[15] Her spiritual blindness, self-centeredness, and arrogance win, however, and she gives in to disbelief. Her communion with Psyche, and Psyche's own personal bliss are both destroyed.

Atonement by Victory

But Orual enacts her own story of atonement. This does not follow the dramatic and mythological atoning path of Psyche. Yet, after Psyche's disappearance, in her own subsequent living (related in chapters 16–19), Orual grows into a double of Psyche, and their stories interweave. Our last chapter stressed her self-abnegation, years of wearing the veil, and painstaking study, in terms of the theme of *ascesis*. These hardships come to a dramatic climax when, newly ascending to the throne, she is galvanized by the sound of moving chains on her castle well that come to her ear as Psyche weeping for release. As she leaves the castle, seeking to rescue the mourner, she plunges her hand into the darkness, and meets that of an endangered young prince whom she is destined to rescue by championing his cause in combat. In the Gethsemane-moments leading up to

---

[14] *Mere Christianity*, 52.
[15] *Faces*, 152.

Christ grasps Adam and Eve by the hand (icon of the resurrection; Chora Church, c. 1315)

the fight, she alternates between fear and determination. The young prince's question, "Where is your champion?" echoes the plaintive cry of the biblical Isaac to his father— "where is the lamb?" Both by the storyline and by this echo, we recognize Orual's life as a parallel to her sister's sacrifice. Orual comes to understand that she, too, may become an offering:

> So Psyche had gone out that day to heal the people; and so she had gone out that other day to be offered to the Brute. Perhaps, thought I, this is what the god meant when he said *You also shall be Psyche.* I also might be an offering. That was a good, firm thought to lay hold of.[16]

After she wins the contest, her friends also show awareness of the parallel: "Bardia (the Fox close behind him) came running up to me.... 'Blessed! Blessed! . . . Queen! Warrior!' "[17]

The Queen's triumph not only frees the young prince, but delivers her nation from ongoing turmoil and serfdom. At first, this story of victory seems more palatable than its twin, the sacrifice of Psyche. But it too has a shadow side. Orual, rather than basking in victory, enters into the dark night of the soul, losing hope of ever finding the weeping Psyche. She embarks on a long-term quest of dying to self: "I am the Queen; I'll kill Orual too!"[18] And so, in the third revelatory section of the book (chapters 20–21), the desolate Queen sets up a kingdom in which many benefit by her self-denial, with the exception of the Fox and Bardia, whom (as we have seen) she drains dry of energy. Hers is a double life. She is both the liberty-forging monarch, like Solomon of Ecclesiastes, and the embodiment of Ungit, the country's spider-like,

[16] *Faces,* 216.
[17] *Faces,* 220.
[18] *Faces,* 225.

rapacious goddess. In her later years, this revelation of her inner ugliness comes to her, for she has her kingdom in order and can travel, where she gains surprising insights into her own role in the unhappiness of her family and friends. Her journeys, then, are not merely geographical, but spiritual as well.

Orual's story shows us that atonement through victory harbors its own dark side, its own deep mysteries. Those who prefer the "Christus Victor" explanation of atonement, made popular in the twentieth-century West by Gustav Aulén,[19] sometimes argue that this view, *rather than* sacrifice, was the "classical position" of the Church. In this picture, Jesus descends into darkness and death to release those imprisoned there, rather than effecting atonement by means of his death on the cross. Certainly, the motif of Christ the Victor is dominant in the East (Christ "trampled down death by death"), and is found in older Western Easter hymns, too. However, to play off Christ's sacrifice over against victory does not do justice to Scripture or to the richness of the fathers. There, several ways of understanding atonement are often juxtaposed. Consider, for example, the numerous pictures or stories found in Romans 5 and Colossians 1.12–14. Atonement may be pictured as a judicial transaction, as sacrifice, as victory over the enemies Sin and Death, as liberation from slavery, as the deepest example of God's love for us, and as the payment of a debt.[20] Moreover, though the hymns

---

[19] *Christus Victor: An Historical Study of the Three Main Types of the Atonement* (New York: Macmillan, 1969).

[20] Later, in Western theology, the "debt" metaphor is modified by Anselm, who suggested, in medieval terms, that Jesus paid the debt humans owed to God, and thus settled the problem of God's insulted honor. In speaking of these myriad pictures by which we understand the mystery of atonement, and the current debate, Lewis gave wise advice: "You can say that Christ died for our sins. You may say that the Father has forgiven us because Christ has done for us what we ought to have done. You may say that we are washed in the blood of the Lamb. You may say that Christ has defeated death. They are all true. If any of them do not appeal to you, leave it alone and get on with the formula that does. And, whatever you do, do not start quarreling with other people because they use a different formula from yours" (*Mere Christianity*, 154). Some have suggested that this statement radically qualifies the necessity for atonement by sacrifice as something

of the East picture Jesus as Victor, the Divine Liturgy is saturated with
sacrificial imagery, centering around the Eucharist. These ways of gesturing at God's mysterious actions on our behalf are complementary,
not mutually exclusive alternatives: and all of them require us to look
into the darkness.

In *Till We Have Faces,* the "dying" implied in the Victor motif is itself
tortuous, demanding, and violent. Just as Lewis does not shy away from
portraying the "shadowbrute" side of sacrificial atonement, so he does
not mitigate the mystery here. Our narrator Orual cries out, "Why
must holy places be dark places?"[21] Because, it seems, *we* are in the dark,
that very place where atonement must be accomplished. And, so, as we
travel with Orual, we see not only the depravity of the human soul (as
we traced it in our last chapter), but also the uncomfortable aspects of
God seeking humanity.

Orual thinks that she is bringing the story of her sister and herself to an end when she insists, after her journey, that the gods have
"no answer" to give her. They cannot exonerate themselves from her
charges that they dwell in shadows and darkness. But the full answer
comes into focus in the story's "retraction" and the supplemental story,
which are designated Part II by Lewis. Here, Orual continues in her
quest to trample down death by death. Yet, she is also the one who
is being freed, and who undergoes the "surgery" of the gods. At this
point we are given more detail concerning the mythology believed in
Glome, Orual's domain. Orual has a conversation with the young priest,
and asks the meaning of the New Year celebration: she is not satisfied
with the answer that he gives her, that it pictures the natural cycle, and
the coming of the rains. Why would devotees talk about something so
perfectly natural as the crops in such a dark and mythological fashion?

that can be "let alone": notice, however, that Lewis says that *all* of these statements are
true. My suspicion is that his advice here is pastoral and ecumenical, and he hopes that
eventually someone who is put off by sacrificial imagery will be corrected as they enter
into worship and the Eucharist.

[21] *Faces,* 249.

Though it seems incomprehensibly unnecessary, there is something in the ritual itself that beckons to her. At the New Year, the Priest is "shut up" in the temple at sunset, and "fights his way" out at noon of the next day. In the midst of Orual's description of this ritual we pause for a moment. Orual, within the cave, observes one of Ungit's devotees at the Dark Stone, who offers a pigeon, and is comforted by the spilled blood and the darkness. Soon after this offering, Orual turns her face to the western door, and noon arrives, when the crowd acclaims him with cries, "He is born!"—a celebration that brings even the bitter enemies together as brothers, for the moment. (I am reminded of the traditional Orthodox Paschal jubilation: "It is the Day of Resurrection, let us be glorious, let us embrace one another and speak to those that hate us; let us forgive all things and so let us cry, 'Christ has arisen from the dead' "—Did Lewis know it?[22]) In the cave, we see both the sacrifice of the peasant who comes to worship, and the victory enacted by the priest. Sacrifice and Victory meet. By means of this conjunction, we, along with Orual, come to suspect that the rites have more to do with encountering divine mystery than with encouraging unseen forces to bring appropriate weather. That may be the lore of the people, but there is more going on. The darkness and the drama bespeak divine power, not human management of that power.

Immediately following this scene, Orual has her vision of digging down into the pit with her ghostly father, which we discussed in the previous chapter. Like the priest in the ritual, she sees herself shut up in the darkness, where she finally recognizes herself to be Ungit. The digging down, the shutting up, and the facing of death, are the dark complement

---

[22]This hymn is the doxastikon (the final stanza) of the Paschal Stichera. It is also quite possible that Lewis knew the opening words of St Gregory the Theologian's first oration, which this hymn paraphrases: "It is the day of resurrection and an auspicious beginning. Let us be made brilliant by the feast and embrace each other. Let us call brothers even those who hate us. . . . Let us concede all things to the resurrection." Oration 1.1, found in Gregory of Nazianzus, *Festal Orations*, trans. Nonna Verna Harrison, Popular Patristics Series 36 (Crestwood, NY: St Vladimir's Seminary Press, 2008), 57.

of the royal victory enacted by the priest. Orual will emerge from the
dark pit, in parallel to the New Year born out of darkness in the cave.
Ungit's cave is an integral part of the New Year celebration: life comes
by way of death in the battle, just as surely as comfort comes by way
of blood. At the very end of the book, when the Fox returns as a kind
of Beatrice or Virgil to guide the repentant Orual, we hear that these
dark myths are not the whole story, and that there is "a far distant day
when the gods become wholly beautiful, or we at least are shown how
beautiful they always were."[23] The day indicated, of course, is the Advent
of the God-Man.

Despite this hope for beauty, it does not seem that Lewis intends
to draw back from the inscrutability of the Victor story. Indeed, Orual
considers even a beautified divinity to be cold comfort: "Do you think
we mortals will find you gods easier to bear if you're beautiful? I tell
you that if that's true we'll find you a thousand times worse. . . . You're
a tree in whose shadow we can't thrive. We want to be our own."[24]
Moderns may have a similar reaction when they look deeply into a picture of Christ's divine Victory that relies on death and the recognition
of human bankruptcy. For the person who wants to be self-sufficient,
the scandal of Christ the Victor is as great as that of Atoning Sacrifice.
Self-denial and death still play a key part. We are drawn into a mystery
as thick as blood, a story as bracing as living water. The common reaction of Orthodox theologians to Western pictures of penal substitution
is right in rejecting the idea of a "contract" with God, or the notion
that our theory of atonement is meant to give a rational explanation of
mystery. But the theme of sacrifice cannot be excluded, for it is found
in Scriptures and in Holy Tradition. When the mystery of sacrifice and
the mystery of descending into hades are retained, the focus is rightly
trained upon the glory of the Sacrifice and the Victor, not upon the
logic of satisfaction or the mechanics of exchange.

[23] *Faces,* 304.
[24] *Faces,* 290–91.

After all, Christ enters the realm of death that we might live. This notion of ineffable exchange, and of the vicarious nature of life—depicted by the double story of these sisters—challenges our claim to autonomy. Like Orual, Christians do move beyond the pagan notion of divine blood-drinkers and man-eaters. Still our discomfort remains, for God "will have man; dark and strong and costly as blood."[25]

The Justice of God and Synergy

The problem for us, then, lies not merely in trying to understand atonement, but in contemplating the nature of God. Questions of divine justice and divine character are intertwined with the atonement stories of Psyche and Orual. The novel may remind us of the book of Job, with its unanticipated reversal, and a revelation of God at the end. Orual finally declares, "Lord . . . You yourself are the answer,"[26] as Job admits that he was ignorant and was relying on secondhand reports, but now has seen and heard for himself (Job 42.1–60). We learn, with Orual, that theodicy cannot be established by what we learn in daily experience alone. Instead, as with Psalm 73.17 (LXX 72), entrance into the holy place is a *sine qua non* (an absolute necessity) for perceiving reality. Like the Psalmist (73/LXX 72.25), the plaintiff is driven to confess, "Whom have I in heaven, whom do I desire on earth, but you?"

Yet the daily run of life does help us, in a modest way, to answer questions of justice. The entire sweep of *Till We Have Faces* (from its accusation of the gods, through self-awareness gained in ordinary life and divine vision, and then to Orual's self-judgment) ends astonishingly with a divine judgment in favor of Orual. Her transformation is the gift of the god who comes to judge Orual, but it is bound up with Orual's own efforts, and the efforts of Psyche, too. Lewis uses the four tasks set to Psyche in the classical myth to help us think about justice and judgment, divine help and mercy. There are actually two

[25] *Faces,* 295.
[26] *Faces,* 308.

tellings of this mythological sequence, the first of which we considered in the last section, where Orual is at center stage. Recall how in the penultimate part of the book, she sees herself as Psyche, sorting the seeds of her own confusion, trying to glean glory but being stampeded by beasts, carrying water of life in her unsubstantial hands. Finally, she undergoes a kind of death when challenged by the divine court. The sequence ends in human silence, which is an "answer." But, then, in the final sequence, the Fox appears to guide Orual's visions, and the whole sequence is revisited. This time, *Psyche* sorts the seeds, a task as impossible as the opening of the sealed scroll in Revelation 5, except for the strange help of the ants (and one of those ants must be Orual). Next, Psyche is bowled over by the irrepressible joy of the golden rams, but then, like a glory-tinged Ruth, plucks the wool that they have left on the edges of the field. Then, she toils across the desert (though somehow Orual is there, too) to fetch the water of death from the divine mountain. Finally, she remains determinedly silent, unyielding to temptation as she plumbs the depth of the underworld, "journeying always further into death"[27] to capture the beauty that will transform her sister. Like Jesus in the Eastern Christian hymn, Psyche "descends unto death, not being tempted thereby."[28] Orual's answer is twofold. First, she recognizes her own bankruptcy, seen in the first sequence of labors; second, she is shown the significance of mediating help in the second sequence.

In the story of the tasks, there is a blending of actors: the resolute bearing of one's own burden, with the ineffable help of others, either human or divine. As the Fox remarks, "She was all but unscathed. . . . Another bore nearly all the anguish."[29] Justice demands responsibility, and that the tasks be achieved; mercy acknowledges human frailty and so offers another to assume the burden. The four tasks help us to think

[27] *Faces,* 304.
[28] Troparion of the Resurrection in Tone 6.
[29] *Faces,* 300.

again about the two stories, how Psyche was willing to undergo her astonishing sacrifice upon the Tree, and how the second Psyche, Orual, offered herself in a less dramatic but lifelong quest. Both need the other; working in both lives, "the Divine Nature can change the past."[30] Love becomes true, and allows a genuine reunion to take place. Orual comes to see her love for even her greatest friends, Psyche, Bardia, and the Fox, as poisoned by self-love and jealousy: she must give up their affections to find them once again. Human life, like human speech and human love, takes its place in the story, but is overtaken at the end by a great Visitation from beyond. Before that divine face "questions die away."[31]

The judgment faced by Orual begins with the recognition that "All . . . are born into the house of Ungit . . . must get free from her . . . or bear Ungit's son and die . . . or change."[32] It moves on to the wisdom of the rejuvenated Fox: "Are the gods not just? Oh no, child. What would become of us if they were?"[33] All the same, human affection, toil, and burdens are not pictured as irrelevant. Instead, they take their place, and are given meaning when the one who has lived through them finally receives her face.

Lewis subtly uses his interwoven stories, images, and characters in order to make us think again. It is too easy to see these things opposed: sacrifice versus victory, works versus grace, human self-condemnation versus divine justice, daily experience versus divine revelation. Had Psyche not gone to the mountain, had Orual not fought as Queen, there would have been no story. Yet, in the end, they are both transfigured as a gift, and do not achieve their own "godding." The god is shown to be just, in answer to Orual's earliest questions: but beyond justice, there is mercy. The story and the characters give life to the dictum that Lewis uttered over BBC radio years before he wrote this

[30] *Faces,* 305.
[31] *Faces,* 308.
[32] *Faces,* 301.
[33] *Faces,* 297.

book: "Your real, new self . . . will not come when you are looking for it. It will come when you are looking for him."[34]

The Great Exchange

Till We Have Faces is about human personhood or identity. It is therefore about looking for and finding "Him," and thereby acknowledging the real world. The novel suggests on every level that the character of God, including His justice, is inevitably interconnected with how God acts in the human arena. We are helped in discerning how this works by remembering Lewis's study on *Miracles*. Recall how, in the chapter entitled "The Grand Miracle," Lewis discerns several interrelated principles in reality:

- the composite nature of humanity that distinguishes it from the animal world,

- the hierarchy of the created order,

- the pattern of death and rebirth,

- selectiveness,

- and vicariousness.

By giving weight to all these principles, Lewis shows the uniqueness and iconoclastic nature of Christianity. Christianity is neither a "nature religion" that declares the whole of biological life to be holy, nor a faith that suggests that nature, in its own right, is transcendent. Orual, then, is right in not trusting the explanations of the priest of Ungit regarding the meaning of rituals that speak so deeply to her. Mystery is not about biological life *in and of itself.* Instead, the natural world must be approached with rigor and with humility, as human beings acknowledge their place in it, and the temptations that it may pose for them.

[34] *Mere Christianity,* 188.

On the other hand, Christianity is not wholly pessimistic about the biological world. Even physical death may be turned to good.

Against easy answers, the Christian faith asserts that there is an order, a hierarchy in which we find ourselves, and that sacrifice is necessary at every point in that order—the lower gives up its life for the higher, but also the higher for the lower. This principle of vicarious suffering, suffering for the sake of another, is a major element in our story and a central part of the faith:

> We know that the whole creation has been groaning in travail together until now; and not only the creation, but we ourselves, who have the first fruits of the Spirit, groan inwardly as we wait for adoption as sons, the redemption of our bodies. . . . Likewise the Spirit helps us in our weakness; for we do not know how to pray as we ought, but the Spirit himself intercedes for us with sighs too deep for words. (Rom 8.22–26)

The apostle's picture is that of creation's groaning, enabled by the suffering prayers of Christians, enabled by the intercessory prayers of the Spirit, who sighs along with us. This *immanent* ("indwelling") power of the Holy Spirit is a correlative of the great visitation of God, the incarnation. Lewis suggests, along with the Apostle Paul and the Fathers, that the Spirit works among us not only for redemption, or forgiveness of sins, but also for glorification.[35] Similarly, the incarnation and the death of Jesus are bound up together, comprising the central chapter of the holy story. As St Paul puts it in 2 Corinthians 5.21: "For our sake, He made the One who knew no sin to become sin that we might become the righteousness of God in Him." A great exchange takes place—sin for God's own righteousness, curse for blessing, death for newness!

---

[35] *Miracles: A Preliminary Study* (New York, NY: HarperOne, 1974). First published 1947 by Macmillan, rev. 1960. For example, he says, "Redeemed humanity is to be something more glorious than unfallen humanity" (*Miracles*, 198).

Does all this seem strange? At one point in Christian history it would not have. The principles articulated by Lewis were taken for granted among ancient theologians. And so, we should heed what Lewis says, reading old books to help us "keep the clean sea breeze of the centuries blowing through our minds."[36] As he points out, though the ancients made their own mistakes, their errors were different from ours, and reading from the past will challenge us to reexamine our prejudices. One of the ancients whom he particularly recommends, and who speaks to the themes we have discerned in *Till We Have Faces,* is St Athanasius, who "stood for the Trinitarian doctrine, 'whole and undefiled,' when it looked as if all the civilised world was slipping back from Christianity into the religion of Arius—into one of those 'sensible' synthetic religions which are so strongly recommended today."[37]

Let us, then, consider what St Athanasius had to say about atonement, the incarnation, and the great exchange. The first thing to notice is that he sees the necessity of Jesus' death as sacrificial and substitutionary, while not limiting it to that purpose:

> Whence, by offering to death the body he had taken to himself, *as an offering holy and free of all spot*, he immediately abolished death from all like him, by the offering of a like. For being above all, the Word of God consequently, by offering his own temple and his bodily instrument *as a substitute for all, fulfilled in death that which was required*; and, being with all through the like [body], the incorruptible Son of God consequently *clothed all with incorruptibility* in the promise concerning the resurrection. And now the very corruption of death no longer holds ground against human beings because of the indwelling Word, in them through the one body.[38]

[36]Lewis's Introduction to Athanasius, republished in *On the Incarnation*, by Athanasius of Alexandria, trans. John Behr, Popular Patristics Series 44a (Yonkers, NY: St Vladimir's Seminary Press, 2011), 13. All further references are to this version.

[37]Ibid, 13.

[38]*On the Incarnation* 9 (PPS 44a:69) (in all quotations, the emphasis is added).

In this excerpt we see both substitution and representation. The saint is concerned both for sin and for death in the human condition. We also see a glimmering of the benefits that go beyond forgiveness: God will confer glory upon those who are redeemed. St Athanasius knits together themes, teaching that the incarnation of Christ was not simply a rescue attempt, a "plan B," so to speak, but radically consonant with God's creating activity:

> [B]y the love for humankind and goodness of his own Father he appeared to us in a human body for our salvation. . . . [The universe's] recreation was accomplished by the Word who created it in the beginning. For it will appear not at all contradictory if the Father works its salvation in the same one by whom he created it.[39]

Along with sacrificial language, St Athanasius dwells upon the victorious act of our Lord. Thus he celebrates Christus Victor, rejoicing that we are rescued from prison and brought into the light. Like the Apostle Paul, St Athanasius does not set Father against Son, but declares, "God was in Christ, reconciling the world to *Himself*" (2 Cor 5.18). Further, he does not stop at a reclamation from death, but offers hints of a higher level of life, casting Jesus as the great Mystagogue, the One who leads to mysteries on high:

> For it was not the Word himself who needed the gates to be opened, since he is the Lord of all, nor was any made thing closed to its Maker; but we were those who needed it, who he himself carried up through his own body. For as he offered to death on behalf of all, so [through] it he opened up again the way to heaven.[40]

It is interesting to note that the saint was well aware that human beings are unable by reason alone to pierce the purposes of God. The incarnation and crucifixion in this way become a means of pedagogy.

---

[39] *On the Incarnation* 1 (PPS 44a:53).
[40] *On the Incarnation* 25 (PPS 44a:105).

We see in them the very character of God, as Christ becomes our
exemplar:

> [T]hrough the incarnation of the Word the universal providence,
> and its giver and creator, the very Word of God, have been made
> known. For *he was incarnate that we might be made god*; and he mani-
> fested himself through a body that we might receive an idea of the
> invisible Father; and he endured the insults of human beings, that
> we might inherit incorruptibility.[41]

Here, too, the saint joins the themes of incarnation and crucifixion
("insults of human beings") with a shocking statement of *theōsis* ("being
made god").Though framed in terms of human perception, the logic is
that of an exchange of natures:"he endured . . . that we might inherit,"
"he was incarnate that we might be made god." The mystery of vicarious suffering is here upheld as part of the reason for the incarnation,
but not the whole of the mystery. We will not linger long on theosis
at this point, but will consider it more thoroughly in our discussion of
The Great Divorce. It is enough to register at this point that among saints
like Athanasius we find an awareness of that same interconnection of
the highest with the lower, as Lewis puts it. St Athanasius seems to have
informed Lewis's thinking in this matter. The saint, followed by Lewis,
speaks of creational hierarchy and the ability of the higher to "trans-
pose" itself into the lower:

> For this reason, the Savior rightly put on a body, in order that the
> body, being interwoven with life, might no longer remain as mortal
> in death, but, as having put on immortality, henceforth it might,
> when arising, remain immortal.[42]

St Athanasius' language is extravagant, and redolent of mystery in
the same way that Lewis's novel captures our attention. And he insists

[41] *On the Incarnation* 54 (PPS 44a:167).
[42] *On the Incarnation* 44 (PPS 44a:147).

upon the necessity for human rigor as we think about these things. An understanding of the Lord's ways and actions does not come automatically, even among those who search the Scriptures. With this careful balance, Athanasius marries together the three themes of careful thinking, acting ethically, and ascesis, with the mysteries probed in this present chapter. Redemption and theosis come as a gift from that country of light, and its King: yet those who want it may not rest idle, expecting it to be automatically given. Like Psyche, the faithful must long for that country; like Orual, they must chase from their lives all that hinder their perception of it:

> But in addition to the study and true knowledge of the scriptures, there is needed a good life and a pure soul and the virtue which is according to Christ, so that the mind, guided by it, may be able to attain and comprehend what it desires, as far as it is possible for human nature to learn about the God Word. . . . For just as, if someone would wish to see the light of the sun, he would certainly wipe and clear his eyes, purifying himself to be almost like that which he desires, so that as the eye thus becomes light it may see the light of the sun; or just as if someone would wish to see a city or a country, he would certainly go to that place for the sight; in the same way, one wishing to comprehend the mind of the theologians must first wash and cleanse his soul by his manner of life, and approach the saints themselves by the imitation of their works, so that being with them in the conduct of a common life, he may understand also the things revealed to them, and thenceforth, as joined to them, may escape the peril of the sinners and their fire on the day of judgment, but may receive what has been laid up for the saints in the kingdom of heaven, "which eye has not seen, nor ear heard, nor have they entered into the heart of man" (1 Cor 2.9), whatsoever things have been prepared for those who live a virtuous life and love the God and Father, in Christ Jesus our Lord, through whom and with

whom, to the Father with the Son himself in the Holy Spirit, be honor and power and glory to the ages of ages. Amen.[43]

Some may fear that the saint's emphasis upon such human effort borders on "works righteousness" or what is frequently (though anachronistically) called "semi-Pelagianism." Our reading of *On the Incarnation*, however, shows that human effort and divine initiative were not seen to be at odds with each other in past times.[44] Similarly, our reading of Lewis quickens our imaginations to a complex world in which God's unimaginable grace and our call to cooperation with it join together. At her trial, Orual finds herself speechless. Yet she finds that her human activities were not useless: she was, unawares, a participant in the divine mercy.

Conclusion

Throughout our reading, it becomes apparent how Lewis intended to tell his story as a tale for our day. In his epilogue, he speaks of Apuleius as a "source" for the Psyche myth, and not as an influence or a model. The story is directed instead to our era. Specifically, Lewis's decision to

---

[43] *On the Incarnation* 57 (PPS 44a:173).

[44] Contemporary Christians continue to be unreflectively shaped by the way Martin Luther read St Paul's words on faith and justification. In reaction to the merit-driven atmosphere of the medieval Roman Catholic Church, Luther directly appropriated the apostle's words concerning "works" for his own day, seemingly unaware of the first century context. The apostle was not speaking about human effort in general, of course, but in particular about "the works of Torah" (especially Sabbath-keeping, circumcision, and food regulations); these, he said, had been mistaken as the means of salvation when they were instead pointers to Christ, and evidence of the community's faith. As a result, Luther had difficulty with "the epistle of straw," James, which appeared to have a higher view of "works": but James was, in using that word, speaking not of "works of Law" but about positive human activity, which Paul celebrates as "fruit." This dichotomy between works and faith has colored a good deal of Christian discussion up to our day, and makes it more difficult for many Christians to see value in the ascetic life, or to recognize God's approval of human effort. Unfortunately, it has led many to ignore whole sections of the Gospels—particularly that of Matthew—and aspects of the letters that speak about "synergy" with God (e.g. 2 Cor 6.1).

make the divine castle of Psyche largely invisible to Orual is a master stroke. It beautifully depicts our plight in a nearly disenchanted world, which can enjoy satyrs and orcs in films, but no longer sees creation as mysterious. Even more intriguing is the way that he uses mythology and symbolism to portray characters that are fully rounded.

The younger sister evokes the sacrificial story of atonement, and the second sister, the theme of Christus Victor. Yet my selection of passages threatens to reduce a powerful tale of love, heartbreak, and mysterious transformation to a mere vehicle for theological ideas. My exposition of the story cannot convey Lewis's uncanny ability to evoke the internal life of his female characters, without psychologizing. He has learned well from masters of story-craft. One of his models comes from the Torah, especially Genesis, which Auerbach (with Lewis's approval)[45] describes as dependent upon what is "done and said" to convey pathos. The biblical author tells a spartan story and does not psychologize. Instead, he expresses a whole world of meaning in such phrases as, for example, Isaac's plaintive question, "Father, where is the ram for sacrifice?" Besides the Genesis model of storytelling, Lewis, as we have seen, uses the myth or fairy tale. These forms he celebrates because they provide helpful restrictions that prevent verbose explanation on the part of the author.[46] Psyche, Redival, Orual, Batta, and Ansit are not merely ciphers for ideas, but emerge both as persons and as icons. They are like the woman at the well in the Fourth Gospel, who is both believable and symbolic. Ranged against them, the male characters pale. Though their portraits are an artistic triumph, they also speak theologically, for, as we have seen, his book stresses the gaining of "faces," or robust personhood.

---

[45]Auerbach is cited by Lewis in "Modern Theology and Biblical Criticism" (sometimes printed with the title "Fern-seed and Elephants"), where he evidently refers to page 44 of *Mimesis*. It is likely that Lewis also noted Auerbach's description of sparse OT narrative in the first essay of Auerbach's book, "Odysseus' Scar," since the reserve of the Genesis author in psychologizing exactly matches Lewis's own delighted description of the constraints of the fairy tale.

[46]"On Three Ways," in *On Stories,* 37.

It is unusual for such a traditionalist as Lewis to use feminine characters to portray the love of God in Christ Jesus. But we have seen, too, that the mythology is meant only to hint at the Christian story, and that the heroines are also there to remind us that we are made, body and soul, for more than ourselves. And so, having travelled in arduous places, looking at the interwoven themes of atonement, blessing and cursing, justice and exchange, we are ready to consider the extreme heights and depths of Lewis's thought and the biblical story. Before us are the challenges of human depravity, the final condition, and the iconic or sacramental nature of gendered humanity and of reality.

Part III

PLUMBING THE DEPTHS AND CLIMBING THE HEIGHTS

"If I go up to the heavens, you are there;
if I make my bed in the depths, you are there."
(Psalm 139.8)

CHAPTER 7

Depravity and Possession

(*That Hideous Strength* and Jonathan Edwards's
Sinners in the Hands of an Angry God)

O sinner! Consider the fearful danger you are in: 'tis a great furnace
of wrath, a wide and bottomless pit, full of the fire of wrath, that
you are held over in the hand of that God, whose wrath is provoked
and incensed as much against you as against many of the damned in
hell: you hang by a slender thread, with the flames of divine wrath
flashing about it, and ready every moment to singe it, and burn it
asunder; and you have no interest in any mediator, and nothing to
lay hold of to save yourself, nothing to keep off the flames of wrath,
nothing of your own, nothing that you ever have done, nothing that
you can do, to induce God to spare you one moment. . . .

All the kings of the earth before God are as grasshoppers, they
are nothing and less than nothing: both their love and their hatred
is to be despised. The wrath of the great King of Kings is as much
more terrible than theirs, as his majesty is greater. "And I say unto
you my friends, be not afraid of them that kill the body, and after
that have no more that they can do: but I will forewarn you whom
ye shall fear; fear him, which after he hath killed, hath power to cast
into hell; yea I say unto you, fear him" (Lk 12.4–5).[1]

---

[1]Jonathan Edwards, *Sinners in the Hands of an Angry God: A Sermon Preached at
Enfield, July 8th 1741, at a Time of Great Awakenings; and Attended with Remarkable Impressions on many of the Hearers* (Boston: S. Kneeland and T. Green, 1741), 16–17 (edited for
modern style in capitalization and punctuation).

There is probably no Christian sermon more distant from contemporary sensibilities than that for which Jonathan Edwards is most famous, his *Sinners in the Hands of an Angry God*, preached to the congregation of Enfield, Massachusetts in July 1741. It is found in many anthologies of western Christian writings, but usually taught as a cautionary tale today for would-be homilists. Its fiercest critics label it as a prime example of "the bleak, cruel, and hell-bent outlook of Edwards and his Puritan predecessors."[2] A more charitable view would respond that the preacher's purpose was to awaken his careless congregation, who were indifferent to judgment, rather than simply to frighten them. In the sermon, Edwards painfully and imaginatively draws for us his picture of the "weight of sin, the wrath of a holy God, and the unexpectedness of the moment when God will execute justice."

Here I will neither hold a brief for Edwards's approach, nor will I analyze the usefulness of its rhetoric, either in his day or in ours. We might, however, acknowledge that our Lord Christ gives more than a few warnings concerning judgment, complete with some colorful imagery, in the gospel accounts. However, Orthodox teachers (including myself) typically balance Jesus' warnings that we must *watch* with the assurance of God's love, and His desire that none should perish. As a result, homilists in the Orthodox tradition rarely give themselves over to unqualified scenes of doom. We should also notice that the Puritan Edwards himself stressed darkness and judgment as only a *part* of his larger vision of reality. Perhaps we can approach his sermon as a kind of verbal equivalent to the eastern icon of the Ladder of Divine Ascent, and the fearful prospect that it conveys to those who glibly presume that they are immune from falling as they climb.

---

[2]This common assessment is noted in the introduction to his sermon, reproduced in the "Works of Jonathan Edwards Online" project blog by the Jonathan Edwards Center at Yale University. For this introduction to the full text of the sermon, see http://edwards.yale.edu/research/major-works/sinners-in-the-hands-of-an-angry-god.

As for C. S. Lewis, we have seen that much of his writing is marked by hope, joy, and glory, even though he is famous for that topsy-turvy examination of evil, *The Screwtape Letters*—a piece which Lewis confessed he did *not* enjoy writing. The dark themes are tackled head-on (without the irony of Screwtape) in some of his other books, particularly in the aptly named novel *That Hideous Strength.* While human beings are called to glory by our Creator, we may become our own worst enemies, and unleash, from within our midst, an inhuman "hideous strength" for which we are no match. This novel

Ladder of Divine Ascent (Russian illuminated manuscript, 1560)

explores that fearful depth, alongside the promised height of humanity through redemption. There are many themes, including positive ones, in this novel, but we will approach it in the first place as a way of thinking about evil and its influence, about human depravity, and even possession.

In *That Hideous Strength*, the evil elements and their doom unfold with a kind of inevitability, reminiscent of what Edwards has to say at the outset of his sermon concerning depravity that refuses the grace of God: "[Consider] Deut 32.35, 'Their foot shall slide in due time.' . . . Notwithstanding all God's wonderful works . . . and . . . under all the cultivations of heaven, [they] brought forth bitter and poisonous fruit." Edwards goes on to detail Psalm 73 (LXX 72), which we have read in connection with the problems of innocent human suffering and theodicy. There the Psalmist also learns that those who rebel against the Lord are, by their very position, exposed to destruction. Their judgment may indeed come suddenly, for they stand upon slippery places. In a single verse (73/72.18), their final end is pictured *both* as the action of God *and* as the natural consequence of a life that is lived apart from God, once the appointed time arrives. A similar double vision of judgment is to be seen in 2 Peter 2, paralleled more briefly in Jude 5–16, where the apostles give us ample evidence that it is in God's nature to judge: he casts the fallen angels into darkness, does not spare the world before Noah, and pronounces judgment on Sodom and Gomorrah. Yet, their condemnation is also inevitable, occurring as the natural consequence of their actions (2 Pet 2.3): they bring destruction upon themselves (2 Pet 2.1).

Contemporary pastoral sensibilities may prefer to speak about the inevitable results of a rebellious life, rather than to cast God in the role of Judge. Indeed, C. S. Lewis himself was prone to speak about judgment as self-inflicted, and of the door handle to exit hell as on the inside, available to us to turn and pull the door open, so to speak. However, Scripture and the full Tradition of the Church will not allow us wholly to escape the picture of God as the One who actively judges, nor does Lewis entirely neglect this fearful prospect. As we Orthodox pray on Meatfare Sunday, in preparation for Great Lent: "The trumpets shall blow, and the graves shall be empty, and all mankind shall rise trembling. They who have done good shall rejoice with joy, expecting their reward; and those who have done evil shall tremble greatly, moaning and shaking, as they are sent to suffering, separated from the elect. Wherefore, O Lord of glory, be compassionate toward us, and make us worthy to be of those who love thee; for thou art good."

That Hideous Strength is not only about the danger into which particular rebels place themselves, but also about the confusion, darkness, and peril that Lewis saw threatening the twentieth century. It is therefore about individual but also corporate sin and doom. We have seen already in our study of *The Abolition of Man,* and in the picturesque scenes of *Pilgrim's Regress,* how spiritual "dragons" may be conjured when intellectuals jettison the idea of objective truth in theology, in ethics, and in the material order. Such drastic moves in the twentieth century were, in his estimation, the beginning of a flirtation with the demonic, possibly leading to a point of no return: "there are progressions in which the last step is *sui generis*—incommensurable with the others."[3] His novel, *That Hideous Strength,* clothes the argument of *The Abolition of Man* with flesh and blood, though the people in the novel are fictional. Here we meet characters of various temperaments and observe their dealings with each other, so that we can see in a vibrant fashion how the creation of "men without chests" might proceed. (We should hasten to add that some of these characters have a larger-than-life or cartoonish quality, adding an element of lampoon to a serious plot. This dark humor somewhat relieves the glimpse of hell afforded us here.) And so in the novel we meet several generations of academics, scientists, and behaviorists swayed not by argument but by high-sounding propaganda. Some of these have come to believe that emotions are wholly subjective, and that old-fashioned values have no foundation in reality, but are simply sentimental. The end result is that when they gain (or *seize*) places of notoriety, they do so in an attempt to recreate truth and to master nature. The final result is that, after destroying the weak, those who initially survive then end up subjecting *themselves*, and thus they are made subordinate to the worst impulses of a fallen nature— even to the demonic world.

The novel may be read as a standalone volume, but is better understood by way of the first two books of the trilogy, *Out of the Silent Planet* and *Voyage to Venus* (also known as *Perelandra).* The hero of the stories, who increases in stature throughout them, is Elwin Ransom: both his first and last names tell us something of his character. He is "a friend [*win,* Old English] of God [*el,* Hebrew]" and therefore associated with the great "Ransom" provided for humankind. Our hero is a professor of philology—the science of language formation—who in the first book finds himself abducted by two ruthless associates, Weston and Devine, and taken on a dangerous trek to the planet Malacandra (Mars). They

[3]From the concluding paragraph of *The Abolition of Man.*

have plans to exploit the planet for their own purposes, using Ransom as a sacrificial bargaining chip with its inhabitants, whose nature they have actually misunderstood. Ransom immediately notes the similarities and differences between Earth and Malacandra. He discovers that there are three types of reasonable inhabitants there, none of them humanoid, but all of them foundationally innocent of evil—the *hrossa*, the *pfifltriggi,* and the *séroni*, each group with their own strengths and occupations. He also learns about the *eldila*, who are super-rational beings, some of whom, called *Oyérsu,* guide the life of the various planets. He learns the dark mystery that the *Oyarsa* of earth has turned against the great Being who heads all the *eldila* (indeed, all life everywhere), and so has been quarantined, along with his fallen planet, so as not to infect the rest of the universe. When Ransom finally returns home after many adventures and a critical rescue out of the hands of his evil friends, he speculates that the term *Oyarsa* is related to the Greek *Ousiarch* ("Head/Source of Being"), a term approximated in Paul's letters for the unseen "powers and principalities."

Ransom's adventures continue in the second volume, where he is whisked to *Perelandra* (Venus), and finds himself battling against the possessed Weston's evil plot to seduce the first woman of that planet into sin. In this novel, we are aghast at the depth of depravity, as well as disgusted by its mundane and snivelling quality. Unlike Milton, who pictures the grandeur of Satan's rebellion in his *Paradise Lost,* Lewis exposes the banality of evil, without dismissing its power for those who succumb to it. Indeed, in Lewis's tale, Weston, who has conflated good and evil in his own imagination, actually loses his name and becomes known to Ransom and the reader as "the Un-man." This sober assessment of evil serves Lewis well in describing the drama that unfolds in the pristine and foreign world of Perelandra (whose fate I will not reveal), and also in depicting the dismal complexities of our own world, crystallized around the urban university context of *That Hideous Strength.*

In the final novel, the villain Devine (known now as *Lord Feverstone*) is surpassed by more thoroughly evil characters. His own weakness is a shallow opportunism, but those who lead the cast of reprobates (all associated with a group ironically named N.I.C.E.) become increasingly unrecognizable as humans, like the Un-man in the preceding novel. Even as they sink down to the depths, the others who join the "good party" in the novel, associated with the community at St Anne-on-the-Hill, grow in their vitality and in their abilities to make informed and godly choices. Indeed, even the animals who form part of the St Anne's community come to take on human characteristics, while the humans give the reader a glimpse of immortality. This is not so with the N.I.C.E. crew, whose members are parasitic and prey upon each other as well as those outside the group. What appears at first simply to be a takeover bid by the college's "Progressive Element" (a group of ideologues and scientists associated with N.I.C.E.) is finally revealed to be an out-and-out battle of good against evil, angels against demons, Christians against those who are wholly self-absorbed.

Let's consider the characters and their interactions as indicators of depravity that leads to actual possession by the dark side. As we plumb these sordid depths, we ask the Almighty and the host of saints to protect us. (I recommend prayer before and during a reading of the novel, as well.) The dangers of training our focus upon evil include temptations to pride as we compare ourselves with others, to despair concerning God's strength and goodness, and to a sordid fascination with those things that dwell in the darkness. Against these and other wounds that we may receive in this quest for understanding, we ask God's help.

> I bind unto myself today
> The strong Name of the Trinity,
> By invocation of the same
> The Three in One and One in Three.

I bind this today to me forever
By power of faith, Christ's incarnation;
His baptism in Jordan river,
His death on Cross for my salvation;
His bursting from the spicèd tomb,
His riding up the heavenly way,
His coming at the day of doom
I bind unto myself today.

I bind unto myself the power
Of the great love of cherubim;
The sweet "Well done" in judgment hour,
The service of the seraphim,
Confessors' faith, Apostles' word,
The Patriarchs' prayers, the prophets' scrolls,
All good deeds done unto the Lord
And purity of virgin souls.

I bind unto myself today
The virtues of the star lit heaven,
The glorious sun's life giving ray,
The whiteness of the moon at even,
The flashing of the lightning free,
The whirling wind's tempestuous shocks,
The stable earth, the deep salt sea
Around the old eternal rocks.

I bind unto myself today
The power of God to hold and lead,
His eye to watch, His might to stay,
His ear to hearken to my need.
The wisdom of my God to teach,
His hand to guide, His shield to ward;

The word of God to give me speech,
His heavenly host to be my guard.

Against the demon snares of sin,
The vice that gives temptation force,
The natural lusts that war within,
The hostile men that mar my course;
Or few or many, far or nigh,
In every place and in all hours,
Against their fierce hostility
I bind to me these holy powers.

Against all Satan's spells and wiles,
Against false words of heresy,
Against the knowledge that defiles,
Against the heart's idolatry,
Against the wizard's evil craft,
Against the death wound and the burning,
The choking wave, the poisoned shaft,
Protect me, Christ, till Thy returning.

Christ be with me, Christ within me,
Christ behind me, Christ before me,
Christ beside me, Christ to win me,
Christ to comfort and restore me.
Christ beneath me, Christ above me,
Christ in quiet, Christ in danger,
Christ in hearts of all that love me,
Christ in mouth of friend and stranger.

I bind unto myself the Name,
The strong Name of the Trinity,
By invocation of the same,
The Three in One and One in Three.

> By Whom all nature hath creation,
> Eternal Father, Spirit, Word:
> Praise to the Lord of my salvation,
> Salvation is of Christ the Lord.[4]

Moreover, let us remember that, though Lewis intends to expose the powers of darkness, the first character whom we meet in the novel is not one of these. Rather, it is the relatively innocent Jane Studdock, who, despite her imperfections, becomes a rescued heroine in the story. Lewis's book, though concerned with evil, is not wholly fixated upon it, nor should we be.

Here, then, is the lineup of those who indulge in depraved attitudes and actions. Jane's husband, Mark, is a stand-in for the soul in danger. An ambitious young academic, he is flanked by Busby and Curry, older academics who are, so to speak, only *moderately* bad. (One of these meets his end as collateral damage in the battle, and the other, it seems, escapes with his silliness intact.) The naïve but self-centered Mark is brought beyond this outer circle further into the plot by Devine (Lord Feverstone) and Miss Hardcastle, power-hungry and despicable people who are associated with "N.I.C.E.," the progressive institute that is loosely connected with the college where Mark teaches. Finally, he is introduced to the fearful foursome of N.I.C.E.—Straik, Filostrato, Wither, and Frost. Besides these human protagonists, the novel traces the more mysterious influence of superhuman powers: one evil (the possessed "Head," served by the four leaders of N.I.C.E.) and several good beings associated with St Anne's. These remain mostly on the sidelines of the human action—until its climax—but are, all the while, involved in helping it. Even the godly powers, whose mere presence is overwhelming to mortals, have no power compared to that of Maleldil, who alone is to be worshipped, and who is the guide for Ransom, the leader of St Anne's.

[4]This prayer is the beloved English versification of the Lorica, or Breastplate of St Patrick, composed by nineteenth-century poet Cecil Frances Alexander.

We begin with the most innocuous pair, two professors at the college where Mark teaches, who are being manipulated by N.I.C.E. to help the Institute, which includes the acquisition of a historical piece of land that the college owns. (We don't find out until later that the land is coveted because it supposedly harbors the grave of the ancient magician Merlin, whom the leaders of the Institute hope to resuscitate and use to their own ends.) Busby is depicted as a one-time clergyman who still clings to his foggy values. Here is a man who cares nothing for the particular people that he meets, but who is wholly absorbed by an ideological desire to preserve the human race. His ideal is too glibly acknowledged by Mark, who calls the value "a pretty rock-bottom obligation." At the same time, it is scorned by the pragmatic Devine as a shallow "Busbyism" (a religious platitude) that can be "explained psychoanalytically."[5] (Of course, Devine thinks that self-interest is a far more powerful force for action.) Comically, Busby becomes expansively religious when drunk, while his friend Curry shows himself to be an unrealistic dilettante for the technological progress of society. This duo becomes handy pawns in the hands of the inner circle of the "Progressive Element," who care nothing for religion or technological progress except insofar as these things will give them power. As the novel progresses, we see how Busby's humanist principles can be twisted by one of the inner circle. Wither applauds the "progressive self-definition of an organic whole":[6] that so-called progression permits him to engage in murder and unthinkingly embrace his own unhappy death. "The whole" obliterates the claims and even the lives of its individual members, including himself.

Indeed, the entire N.I.C.E. contingency is marked by unreality and pretense, as is seen most clearly in Lord Feverstone (Dick Devine). Since he himself is consumed with arrogance and pride, he knows well how to implicate the ambitious Mark in N.I.C.E.: he ridicules those

[5] *That Hideous Strength* in *The Cosmic Trilogy* (1938–45; repr., London: Bodley Head, 1990), 386.

[6] *Hideous*, 401.

who do not know what the Institute is up to, while insinuating that Mark has what it takes to get into the inner circle. He treats Mark to a heady brew of scorn and "belonging," advising him to curry favor with the leaders of N.I.C.E. for his own gain. In practice, this means that Mark must, without question, perform the little tasks of publicity and disinformation asked of him, while hoping that eventually he will be ushered into the inner circle. Mark instinctively tries to walk back his missteps in conversation with Devine, where he misspoke concerning the importance of other players in N.I.C.E.; similarly, he accepts the vague comments of Devine concerning Mark's own proposed role, for he fears appearing crass or simplistic. It is from Devine that he learns "Man has got to take charge of Man. . . . [S]ome men have got to take charge of the rest."[7] But the "giddy sensation"[8] that he experiences in being admitted into a higher level of secrecy blinds him to the despotic and cruel nature of Devine's pragmatism. *He* will not be a pawn like Curry or Busby, but one of the initiating actors, like Devine.

Of course, the true nature of the devouring leaders of N.I.C.E. should have been apparent immediately to Mark, as they are to his wife Jane, who finds the self-importance and the sharkish appearance of Devine not only distasteful but also alarming. Their practice of arrogance and mockery aimed at those colleagues who are intellectually superior, but not with the times, studs the earliest part of the book. Tellingly, they mock Hingest—one of the professors who unfortunately has joined N.I.C.E.—as "Bill the Blizzard," for his reactionary cleaving to the objective element in scientific inquiry. This character, who warns Mark against joining the Institute, tries himself to leave it, and is murdered for his efforts. The cynical nature of his colleagues emerges when they engage in a moment of silence after engineering his death. They also treat others of the old guard in the college disrespectfully to their faces, or ridicule them behind their backs. Mark sees all this, but

[7] *Hideous,* 388.
[8] *Hideous,* 384.

convinces himself that the important business of the N.I.C.E. must call for ruthless measures. He himself hopes for advancement through association with them.

The uncivil conduct among the members of the group is only a symptom of something far more deadly—their policies of entrapment through making a new candidate like Mark indebted, and eventually enslaved. His new mentors acknowledge no Tao or code, and routinely flout expected behavior: for example, they tell Mark who was responsible for his hire at the College, refuse to give him actual parameters for his new job with N.I.C.E. (on a pretense of needed flexibility), and close doors behind his back to make a return to his old position impossible. Mark comments upon Devine's lack of loyalty to him when he learns that there is no way to turn back the clock: "I thought you were my friend." Devine responds that Mark is an "Incurable Romantic!"[9] In dealing with their deceit, Mark has one redeeming quality: he wants to "do something that is worth doing."[10] It will take some time before he realizes the real purpose of N.I.C.E. and discover that they have no real interest in him, but are using him in order to gain access to his clairvoyant wife. This epiphany will be almost too late.

As distasteful as Devine, but even more ruthless, is the "Fairy," Miss Hardcastle, whose appearance and demeanor are anything but ethereal. (Had he been writing today, Lewis would certainly have had the Institute members call her "Ms.") Lewis's repugnance at militant feminism is undisguised in his description of this stolid, cigar-smoking, short-skirted, lipstick-smudged virago, whose bite is every bit as bad as her bark. Later in the story, she will attempt to torture Jane with the cigar in order to extract information about Jane's mystical experiences. Mark's first impression of her is that she fixes him "with a gaze of cold intimacy."[11] As Mark becomes acquainted with this woman who has run

[9] *Hideous,* 463.
[10] *Hideous,* 407.
[11] *Hideous,* 407.

the gamut in personae, from suffragette to pacifist to British Fascist,[12] he is alternately fascinated and repelled. As the one who runs the special police of N.I.C.E., she is wholly devoted to power, but has enough personal magnetism to draw this new member into her web. As a sociologist (she explains), Mark will be invaluable in helping to advise how to bring others under control. She models her controlling tactics on Mark, calling him "Sonny" and insisting that he must resort to "elasticity," doing whatever he is told, and not bothering those higher up.[13]

It is the *quality* of the secrecy at N.I.C.E. that is so dangerous. When nothing is made clear, there is no responsibility of the inner circle to the newcomers, and thus no protection for the latter. There are mysteries at St Anne's as well, but these are not for the purpose of controlling others, but for the good of all, and dispelled at the right time for those who want to actually become members of the company. Jane, upon coming to know the St Anne's group, is neither seduced nor coaxed into joining, for this must be her own decision. When asked if she shares their faith, and she is uncertain about her answer, her reserve is taken seriously.

The members of N.I.C.E. also boast of a "family" relationship: this, however, is something like the story of the emperor's new clothes. Hingest, a chemistry professor, plays the part of the child who exposes the lie:

> If I found chemistry beginning to fit in with a secret police . . . and a scheme for taking away his farm and his shop and his children from every Englishman, I'd let chemistry go to the devil and take up gardening again. . . . I happen to believe that you can't study men; you can only get to know them, which is quite a different thing. Because you study them, you . . . want to take away from them everything which makes life worth living and not only from them but from everyone except a parcel of prigs and professors.[14]

[12] *Hideous,* 416.
[13] *Hideous,* 472.
[14] *Hideous,* 418.

Hingest deplores the demonic tendency to objectivize and *use* others, though he does not realize the wholly bloodthirsty nature of his opponents. Mark, however, is quickly infected by this cocktail of ill-conceived and fuzzy principles, arrogance, mockery, and unreality. We overhear his thoughts as he composes a deceptive speech to convince Jane about the integrity of his new position. He is clearly delighted with his own "amusing, confident phrases," which "drove out of his mind the real experience he had undergone."[15] This planned speech, with its misshaping of the facts, and its deletion of salient points, is created almost without Mark noticing that he is, in fact, lying to himself, as well as to his wife. His "breezy and buoyant" attitude is also wholly manufactured as he tries to look "big" in the eyes of his wife, and suppresses the cautionary instincts that he has also felt while being introduced to the Institute. The narrator pictures him as a male bird "display[ing] his plumage"[16] for the benefit of its mate. And so unreality and manipulation settle into their already fragile marriage.

Filostrato, Straik, Wither and Frost are the real movers and shakers. Filostrato is motivated completely by pragmatism, so that he has no qualms in engineering a riot among the public (aided by Mark's propaganda) for his cause. He harbors no sentimentality, and has a complete trust in humanity's ability to conquer nature. For him, the advantages of an artificial tree with no vegetation, of a non-material person who need not be born, breed, or die, and of the "conquest of death [which means] of organic life"[17] are obvious. The bleakness of the lunar landscape is idyllic to him. Yet, in some ways he is "a dupe,"[18] for he has not truly understood the purposes of Frost and Wither, nor does he fully grasp what is going on. He believes that he has actually resuscitated and is sustaining just the *head* and mind of a dead (and murderous!) scientist, François Alcasan. This monstrous experiment is, for him, the model for

[15]*Hideous*, 438.
[16]*Hideous*, 439.
[17]*Hideous*, 531.
[18]*Hideous*, 724.

a sterile prolongation of human life for some select human beings in the future. The intellectual prowess of this artificially sustained Head is a matter of pride to him, and in preparing Mark to meet the monstrosity, he declares that "The Head will assume your obedience."[19]

His colleague, Straik, emphasizes the religious aspects of this great secret, rather than the scientific potential. Where Filostrato sees the Head as the first human being to live beyond animal life, Straik celebrates it as "the beginning of Man immortal and Man ubiquitous."[20] Straik's religion is as horrifying as Filostrato's desire for sterile, unbiological existence. "Man on the throne of the universe" is his aspiration, so that Man (or perhaps, a single man) becomes God, living forever, and ruling forever.[21] For Straik, N.I.C.E. (and its leadership) is God himself. All the religious language of Christianity is bent by Straik to refer to this Frankenstein-like endeavor. Indeed, he realizes that what they are doing is "a message of absolute despair to organized Society,"[22] because the present-day English society must be overturned (even by violence) to make way for the new order. As Straik associates Jesus' name with this scientific-mystical monstrosity, Mark has the grace to blush—and is surprised at his own reaction.[23] To his ears, Straik appears (quite simply) mad, for he is unaware of the depth of this bent mystic's apostasy, aspiration to manipulate God, and blasphemy against the Spirit. But the sound of the name "the Lord Jesus" in Straik's filthy mouth makes him uncomfortable. Again, at a critical moment that comes later in the novel, Mark is compelled to actually perform blasphemous actions, and is strangely reluctant. Mark is not quite the atheist that he thinks he is. The only true thing that Straik tells him is that no one can leave N.I.C.E. without suffering loss.

[19] *Hideous,* 516.
[20] *Hideous,* 532.
[21] *Hideous,* 533.
[22] *Hideous,* 427.
[23] *Hideous,* 427.

As distorted as Straik is, Wither and Frost are the most depraved leaders of the Institute. Wither is characterized by a complete loss of personhood and personality, which we discover towards the climax of the novel has been caused by close association with demonic powers. The Institute calls these powers "Macrobes," and Frost and Wither understand that it is by means of the artificially sustained "head" that they communicate not with the dead scientist Alcasan, but with an unearthly "Head" that possesses what remains of the man—an evil eldil under the power of the "bent" (fallen and rebellious) *Oyarsa* of earth. At one point, Mark has the misfortune of trying to speak with the Deputy Director during one of Wither's disassociating moments, and thinks that he is actually dead. On realizing that Wither is alive, but dissociative, Mark comments, shuddering inwardly, "It was impossible to speak to a face like that."[24] He has, in fact, looked into the face of one possessed, *withered* from the inside by contact with evil.

Frost's character is similarly depleted, though he is not prone to mystical wanderings. Cold as his name, he has been wholly captivated by the doctrines leading to "the abolition of man," and has drained all emotion and human response from his consciousness, so that he can concentrate upon the workings of N.I.C.E. He does not even enjoy his part in the battle against humanity, as does, for example, the masochistic Hardcastle, who delights, as one of the "enemies of the human race," in distressing her "patients."[25] With Wither and Frost we see the end result of what happens with a deliberate perversion of justice, and a desire for infinite mastery over others. Their methods are depicted clearly in the incarceration of poor "Mr Maggs," who no longer has a debt to pay to society, but will nonetheless be imprisoned until he is "cured" to the satisfaction of his captors.[26] It is neither punishment nor rehabilitation that the directors seek, but total compliance with their actions from any who are allowed to live.

[24]*Hideous*, 544.
[25]*Hideous*, 508.
[26]*Hideous*, 718.

The final evil figure, the mysterious "Macrobe," remains, for the most part, in the shadows. But Mark himself meets it as it attacks both his consciousness and his conscience, taking him "by the throat."[27] In the attack, Mark has a sense of all things being sucked into a great black hole, so that all his previous feelings, experiences, delights, and fears are rendered completely irrelevant. "These creatures . . . breathed death on the human race and on all joy."[28] It is telling that this attack only occurs at the point where Mark has decided to stand against the crew at N.I.C.E. And he is alarmed that, when so accosted, he has been unable to put up any resistance. During the dark death-eating experience, he has been both repelled and fascinated, and has even seen a kindred bond between himself and Wither. The black hole of evil has forcefully beckoned to him—and yet, he cries out for help against it, wherever help may be.

In our characters, then, we have seen a swirling and dismaying combination of fuzzy thinking, arrogance, mockery, cruelty, self-absorption, masochism, power-seeking, and, in the end, possession that destroys humanity and personality. It is impossible to do justice to the strength of Lewis's characterization, and his manner of presenting the drab sameness of these many different characters who are curved in upon themselves, even when they appear to follow lofty principles. They are the living epitomes of overlapping vices listed in 2 Peter and Jude, in which the apostles aim to attack heresy and blasphemy, and warn against any conspiracy with evil: blindness, false and heretical prophecy, denial of Christ, flattery in order to gain advantage, the ability to induce others to follow them, covetousness, lust, presumption, vanity, self-will, deception, bestiality, and emptiness. Those who are entangled in these vices "promise liberty, but [are] servants of corruption, bringing others into bondage" (2 Pet 2.19), pervert the Scriptures (2 Pet 3.16), mock (Jude 18), and "speak evil of those things which they don't understand, [while] corrupting the

[27] *Hideous,* 629.
[28] *Hideous,* 629.

natural things they do understand" (Jude 10). Jude, indeed, calls them "*twice* dead ... wandering stars" (Jude 12–13), which may cause us to recall the black-hole appearance of both Wither and the Macrobe. It is their nature to have light, but they are dark, and make everything in their wake dark as well. A listing of these dark characteristics sounds almost melodramatic and tempts us to dismiss such desolation as overstatement. Our imaginations may, perhaps, be more convinced when we add to the warnings of Scripture the scenes of Lewis's novel, where we can eavesdrop on the psychology of the characters while watching their horrifying actions: the sheer multiplicity of fallen souls shows us the potency of evil. Their hollowness depicts how we are emptied of our humanity the further we get from reality, and ultimately, from God.

Perceiving Their End

Psalm 73 (LXX 72) explains how the Psalmist saw the apt "end" of those who rebel against God. Lewis's novel dramatically describes such endings, suiting each doom to the fatal flaw of the character. At the turning point of the story, each of the members of N.I.C.E. meets an appointed end, illuminating how evil can ravage a human being, and why a just God cannot allow such self-destruction to go on interminably. The judgment of the individual members is preceded by a general scene of judgment, which uncannily resembles the story of Babel in Genesis.[29] The leaders of the Institute think that they have discovered the resuscitated magician, Merlin, whose magical body, Frost and Withers believe, will be an apt vehicle for the Macrobe, a new and more powerful Head than the one they are keeping alive. (Merlin has been asleep for centuries, entombed in a part of the College property N.I.C.E. deceptively acquired, but he has awakened and exchanged places, and clothing,

---

[29]Indeed, it is clear from the title of the novel that Lewis has the story of Babel in mind; the title is drawn from *Ane Dialog*, by Sir David Lindsay (c. 1490–1555), who describes the tower of Babel thus: the "Shadow of that hyddeous strength / Sax myle and more it is of length."

with an ordinary tramp, whom the Institute leaders have mistaken for Merlin himself.) They have gathered together for a formal and celebratory dinner, with "Merlin" (the tramp) as the guest of honor. But as the speeches commence, pandemonium descends. The figurehead of the organization, who knows nothing of Macrobes, experiments, or Merlin, begins to spout some very strange ideas and "words" in his opening address. When Wither finally silences him, and himself begins to speak, it appears that the same malady has struck him, as well. "Tidies and Fuglemen . . . ," he begins. Soon, the entire company, discovering that aphasia has hit them all, descends into chaos.

In the midst of the riot that ensues, the *real* Merlin, who has been occupied in releasing the wild animals kept on the premises for experimentation, sounds the word of doom in Latin: "*Qui Verbum Dei contempserunt, eis auferetur etiam verbum hominis*" ("As for those who have despised the Word of God, from them shall the word of man also be taken away").[30] As with Babel, the directors of N.I.C.E. have sought to take the place of God and to make a name for themselves; as with Babel, their means of communication (and also their mastery over the created order) is stripped from them. In the midst of the melée, Merlin discovers Mark lying on the floor, douses him with cold water, and pronounces "*Surge, miselle*" ("Arise, miserable boy!").[31] He thrusts a letter into Mark's hands, telling him to join his wife at St Anne's quickly, and forcibly propels Mark to the exit, thumping him on the back to get him running. Mark's own legs, however, propel him out: he will be the only human rescued from this house of darkness. The rescue of Lot from Sodom and Gomorrah comes to mind.

In the scenes that follow, we see the fates of the entire evil crew, of the passionate misanthrope Hardcastle, the opportunist Devine, the dupe Filostrato, the devotee Straik, the initiate Wither, and the non-person Frost. Their ends are fitting. Devine, driven by his ambition, is killed

[30]*Hideous,* 718.
[31]*Hideous,* 719.

by his own driving as he seeks to escape, after remarking "Well, I'm damned." One hopes not. Hardcastle, as befits one who has destroyed others by her passionate pleasure, is crushed amidst the panic of the Babel scene. Straik and Filostrato, the religious and political ideologues, are both sacrificed to the cause by Wither, who slaughters them before the Head. Wither himself is devoured by a bear who has, in the confusion, breached the inner sanctuary, but hardly cares about his death: as he discovers, "[t]he last moments before damnation are not often so dramatic."[32] And Frost, controlled by the evil powers, kills himself. For one brief moment, light glances into his soul, offering him a chance to repudiate all that he has done and been, but he "wholly hates"[33] that light and clings to his illusions. The leader of this program, devoid of mercy or compassion for others, finally denies his own existence.

All of these scenes are horrific and pathetic, yet Lewis manages to relate the various judgments without devolving into what frequently accompanies the destruction of villains—*Schadenfreude,* that is, delight in the pain of others. His narration is neither detached nor sentimental, and is shockingly effective because he adopts the perspective of each of the characters. Our ability as readers to listen in on the mindset of each who meets his or her doom is in itself instructive. The horror does not dominate, except in the depraved inner sanctuary where twisted worship and sacrifice takes place. Instead, the ending evokes three reactions in readers: pity for the depraved human condition that has gone so far into the darkness, a sense of relief that evil has been stemmed and justice served, and an apt concern or suspicion that at least *one* of the characters shows forth a fatal flaw of our own, to which we should attend.

In this sober but resolutely non-sadistic description of final judgment, Lewis takes on the same tone as those epistles that we mentioned earlier—Jude and 2 Peter. There is the tragic possibility that a human being may go too far along the path of the reprobate: there is the

---

[32] *Hideous,* 721.
[33] *Hideous,* 726.

"unpardonable sin" that is mentioned not only in the Gospels (Mk 3.22–30; Mt 12.31–32), but in Hebrews 10.26, in 1 John 5.16–17 and, by implication, in 2 Peter 2.20–21 and Jude 13. The possibility exists, but all is not bleak. Mark's salvation, out of the pandemonium and hatred, illustrates what the apostle instructs concerning how to rescue those embroiled in evil: "save some with fear, pulling them out of the fire" and keeping a safe distance from the contamination that could occur (Jude 22–23). In both the anti-heretical epistles of Jude and 2 Peter, and the novel of Lewis, serious evil is treated with both severity and compassion. In the next section of this study, we will entertain the hope of some, like George MacDonald and Hans Urs von Balthasar, that the warnings will remain warnings, and never crystallize into *final* doom for any of those whom God has created. This we cannot declare—it goes beyond what we know—but in the particular case of any human being whom we love, for that mercy we can pray. In the end, we must reckon, however, with the impossible possibility that God's will for all to be saved can be thwarted by human willfulness, godless ambitions, and the refusal to embrace light. Whoever gives himself over to darkness is liable to become darkness himself.

We return to the initial fear of Jonathan Edwards that was the catalyst for his colorful sermon: "Men's hearts harden, and their guilt increases apace at such a day as this, if they neglect their souls: and never was there so great danger of such persons being given up to hardness of heart, and blindness of mind."[34] Lewis, also, was issuing a wake-up call to his blind and hard-hearted day, which he feared was running pell-mell in its philosophy and action into "the abolition of man." *That Hideous Strength* issues the warning by weaving a tale around the danger, and peopling it with characters who are certainly extreme, but not in every way totally distant from ourselves. In the end, what could be a worse fate than the judgment of Merlin: "*Qui Verbum Dei contempserunt, eis auferetur etiam verbum hominis*"—"As for those who have despised the Word of God,

[34]Edwards, *Sinners*, 24–25.

from them shall the word of man also be taken away."[35] If we will not worship the true God, we will cease, eventually, to be human.

The End of the Matter

But the Macrobes and their human co-conspirators are no match for righteousness. Lewis's picture of evil is by no means set in a dualistic framework. The great literary theorist Northrop Frye claimed to find a parallel structure in biblical imagery, which he set out in charts, in which Jesus is set opposite Satan, good against evil. Lewis would not agree. There are bent *Oyérsu* and then there are those who obey and worship Maleldil. But there is no figure opposite Maleldil in this novel: he is in a category all of his own. And his Word prevails. The story does not close, as do some parables, with weeping and gnashing of teeth, but comes to its conclusion in the unifying house of St Anne's. There, the "Director" Ransom emerges as the redemptive figure, the figure of hope, a visible human icon of Maleldil himself. Those who are savvy concerning medieval legend will see in him a representation of the "Fisher King" or the "Wounded King" from the Arthurian cycles. This character is called to guard the Holy Grail, and there are many versions of his story with different details. All of them, however, have him wounded, either in his legs or groin, and so impeded in his movement. His injuries affect his entire land, which becomes a wasteland. He fishes in the river near his castle, while many come to try to heal him. Only one knight succeeds, who is called Percival. Sometimes, though, the stories have two wounded Kings, one who lives in the castle, while his son is more active. This particular detail seems to be an echo of Father/Son theology.

Ransom, also, has sustained a serious wound from his contest with the Un-man in Malacandra. In Celtic mythology, one of the characters in the story of the Fisher King asks his followers to chop off his head and take it back to Britain. The head, miraculously, can speak, and magically

---

[35] *Hideous*, 718.

sustains the characters of the story for almost a century in a castle. In a Welsh version of the story, there is also a severed head, which the Fisher King presents on a platter to a main character of the story, telling him that he must avenge this person's death. The details of Ransom's wound, which makes it difficult for him to travel, and the centrality of a head, both recall this legend of the wounded king. It is helpful also to realize that "fish" is in itself an ancient sign for Jesus—since its Greek name, *ichthys,* was read as an acronym for the Greek "Jesus Christ, Son of God, Savior"—and to remember that the disciples were to "fish for men." Ransom's main position at St Anne's House has been not only to help stem the evil coming into the world, but also to attract those like Jane and Mark who may be rescued from it.

He himself is not Christ, but bears in his body the marks of Christ, as did St Paul. Moreover, in spinning this tale about Ransom and his friends and enemies, Lewis is not following the structure of the Fisher King story, as he did the Psyche plot in *Till We Have Faces.* He has been, however, marked by its imagery, and turns these details into potent pictures for his own story of doom and salvation. At the end of Lewis's story, Ransom is given the respite of leaving this planet, to be with the *eldila* and Maleldil. His work on earth is over. But the climax of the story also includes the rejuvenation of those who will continue as an influence for good in Britain, for they are members of the spiritual Britain, called Logres, which is known only to a few (Logres also is part of the Arthurian legend). Mark and Jane are reunited, after they have seen as much as they can bear of the divine Light. So too are Mr and Mrs Maggs, animals in the house, and others, in a thoroughly satisfying and traditional ending, complete with bridal imagery. Those who have seen the films (or better, read the works) *Much Ado About Nothing* and *Pride and Prejudice* can recall in their mind's eye the delightful closing of those works, with their joyful weddings. The light has shone in the darkness, and the darkness has not overcome it (Jn 1.5).

CHAPTER 8

Blessings and Curses Revisited: Heaven and Hell

(*The Great Divorce*)

How should we think about heaven and hell? Our discussion of depravity and rescue, as opened up by *That Hideous Strength,* leads us to Lewis's evocative *The Great Divorce*, a book that tackles these final questions more thoroughly. What about eternal bliss, eternal separation from God, and our present position on earth—how *are* these related? It is often said that heaven is a state of mind; some say this about hell, as well. Well, yes, Lewis might answer, since we begin our trajectory to eternity in the here and now. But to limit our understanding of final things to a present state of *mind* is not a sufficient answer, especially where heaven is concerned. First of all, we are told in the Scriptures that we can hardly imagine, from our position on earth, what will come later (1 Cor 2.9). Secondly, the incarnation and the resurrection of the God-Man make it clear that the material world is important. Thirdly, in the Christian tradition, the eternal state of bliss is pictured not as a solitary, internal thing, but as communion with God and others who love Him. To relegate heaven to a mere mental state is not helpful, since it dismisses the distinction between earth and God's realm, it ignores the significance of matter, and it forgets the importance of our relation to others.

In this chapter, we will follow Lewis through *The Great Divorce* as he gives us a tour of two strange places—or perhaps, as gives us spectacles with which to see places that are not *entirely* strange to us. For both locales, the grey city and the shining land, also offer reflections upon our present state. As we consider the "last things," it is helpful to also think about *why* we would engage in such speculative thought. Why is this so important? We might respond that this quest extends the concern for blessings and curses that we broached in our reading of *Till We Have Faces*. Blessings and curses, we have it on good authority, are not for this present life only.

Evil from Outside?

When we think of hell and heaven, do we picture goodness and evil as equal and opposed forces? And do we primarily think about spiritual danger as something that comes from the outside? Certainly this is one way of looking at those things that may destroy us. Probably the most picturesque scriptural depiction of this external attack is found in Revelation 12, where a noble woman and her newborn child are being pursued mercilessly by the dragon:

> And a great portent appeared in heaven, a woman clothed with the sun, with the moon under her feet, and on her head a crown of twelve stars; she was with child and she cried out in her pangs of birth, in anguish for delivery. And another portent appeared in heaven; behold, a great red dragon, with seven heads and ten horns, and seven diadems upon his heads. His tail swept down a third of the stars of heaven, and cast them to the earth. And the dragon stood before the woman who was about to bear a child, that he might devour her child when she brought it forth....
>
> And when the dragon saw that he had been thrown down to the earth, he pursued the woman who had borne the male child. But

the woman was given the two wings of the great eagle that she might fly from the serpent into the wilderness, to the place where she is to be nourished for a time, and times, and half a time. The serpent poured water like a river out of his mouth after the woman, to sweep her away with the flood. . . . Then the dragon was angry with the woman, and went off to make war on the rest of her offspring, on those who keep the commandments of God and bear testimony to Jesus. (Rev 12.1–4, 13–15, 17)

St John is given, and passes on to us, a series of images in which a woman and a dragon are in mortal combat. The dragon is pictured as a usurper, one whose natural habitat is not the earth, but who has been cast down as the result of an unholy war. His initial rebellion has been staged in order to devour the woman (who represents, in the first place, God's Old Testament people) and her child (the Messiah). Once he has been removed from heaven, he turns his attention to her *other* offspring—us. The danger comes from *outside* of the human community, and in fact is perpetrated by a being who is only rampaging through earth because of his rebellion. Of course, the seer is well aware that wickedness can also be internal to the human community, and even lodged in members of the Church. He deals with such infidelity elsewhere in his Apocalypse. However, we should notice that in *this* sequence the danger is extrinsic. It is so much on the outside of believers, in fact, that their very suffering is seen as participating in God's victory over this evil one. A heavenly oracle declares, in the midst of the battle, that "they conquered him [the Dragon] by the blood of the Lamb and by the word of their testimony [or martyrdom], for they loved not their lives even unto death" (Rev 12.11).

This view of evil as external is dominant in both *That Hideous Strength* and Lewis's better-known book, *The Screwtape Letters* (which we will not, alas, consider in any detail in this study). Peril, both physical and spiritual, comes in terms of temptation and attacks from outside the person, by unseen principalities and powers, with their human accomplices, who are determined to bring us to destruction. Of course, both Mark and Jane (and the devil's "patient" in *Screwtape,* as those who have read the book will remember) bear some responsibility: the temptation to join the dark side appeals to something *within* them. We are aptly given some insight into the choices made by the N.I.C.E. crowd as they embrace evil for various reasons. But this aspect of the drama remains an accent to the main action. Mostly we are concerned with what is *happening to* our two young protagonists, and how they are being swayed. The main emphasis is laid on the power of evil and the ability of evil beings (whether human or unseen) to seduce and beguile. *That Hideous Strength* is a cautionary tale suggesting to its readers that there is more to evil than meets the eye: we are contending with unseen enemies, and need the armor of God. The "abolition of man" is being hastened by actors, both unhuman and inhumane, who are bound to destroy everything around them, for their own pleasure or power. A contest is taking place for the souls of our main characters. The implication is that the same war is being waged in our world at large: we should not be naïve.

Evil Within

That is, of course, not the only way for a Christian to consider the power of darkness. James 1.14–15 gives us food for thought: "[E]ach person is tempted when he is lured and enticed by his own desire. Then desire, when it has conceived, gives birth to sin; and sin when it is full-grown brings forth death." In *The Great Divorce*, the focus shifts to such personal responsibility. Though there are external powers at work as well, the contest is largely portrayed here as going on within each person. Hell is presented as a dangerous choice, a place of residence that both closes in upon and is embraced by the person who inhabits it. In taking this angle, Lewis reminds us of the fearful freedom given to humanity, a freedom that enables us to turn good things—graces and blessings—into an enslaving curse. In this, Lewis follows the fathers of the Church in insisting that evil is not a thing in itself, but a "privation" of good—a thing that has declined from the good, and is parasitic upon the good for existence.[1]

We see, then, that Lewis considers the origin and force of evil from two different perspectives, and commends both of these to us. First, evil attacks us from without; but then, we also must take responsibility, and admit our wayward tendencies from within. In reading *The Great Divorce,* we are compelled to gaze into the human soul, fearing the abyss that it may become, and hoping for the glory to which we are called by God. In the last chapter, we prayed for protection as we considered the specters of those possessed, or strongly influenced by the demonic. As we consider last things, eternal things, we also need to recognize our vulnerability. To probe into such depths in the wrong way is perilous. Concerning careless speculation about such hidden matters, the ancient rabbis made this solemn declaration: "Whosoever gives his mind to four things—what is above? what is beneath? what is beforetime? and, what will be hereafter?—and whosoever gives no thought for the honor of his Maker, it were better for him if he had not come into the world" (*Mishnah Hagigah* 2.1). This is not simply an odd reserve registered by repressed Jewish religious leaders. St Basil the Great, among other Church fathers, East and West, also counselled, "Put then a limit to your thought . . . [avoiding] curiosity in investigating the incomprehensible."[2] Protestants, too, have their luminaries, like John Calvin, who railed about the danger of such curiosity.[3] Thus, Lewis is

[1] This longstanding patristic tradition regarding evil is frequently attributed to the Blessed Augustine—see especially *The Enchiridion* 11 (NPNF[1] 3:240)—though it was already articulated a century earlier by St Athanasius—see especially *Against the Heathen* 1.2 (NPNF[2] 4:4–5) and *On the Incarnation* 4 (PPS 44a:59).

[2] Basil, *Hexaemeron* 1.9 (NPNF[2] 8:7a).

[3] Calvin's warning may be seen throughout his commentaries whenever he is touching on mystery, and is even applied to excessive curiosity about his signature doctrine of predestination, cf. *Christian Institutes* 3.21.1.

in line with a long and varied tradition when he shares this caution. We have seen it already in those places where he darkly pokes fun at the meddling "scientists" in *That Hideous Strength,* and we will encounter it again as he showcases impious speculation among some of his academic characters in *The Great Divorce.* And he demurs, in the preface to *The Great Divorce*: "The last thing I wish is to arouse factual curiosity about the details of the after-world."[4]

But we go too far if we say that any contemplation of last things ("eschatology") is beyond the pay grade of the faithful. After all, in the Scriptures we receive glimpses into eternity, including much—perhaps too much for our comfort—regarding final damnation. Consider only one chapter, Matthew 25, where Jesus narrates three parables: the tale of the foolish and wise virgins, that of the talents, and that of the sheep and goats. To "be cast out"—a refrain that runs throughout these parables—is a major theme of Scripture, and commends itself to our attention. This is a topic, then, initiated by our Lord: we are to give our minds to this terrible possibility, while holding to the hope of everlasting communion with God. Why? Because even though "this is my Father's world," which He has reclaimed and is healing through Christ, our present weakened state and the earth itself remain (for now) an arena for the enemy. Our lot here is interconnected with worlds that we can hardly fathom. The stakes are very high.

The question of final judgment is, then, something to which we must give our sober attention. But do we want to think about it? In a central chapter of the late first-century Jewish book of wisdom and visions, alternately called *4 Ezra* or *2 Esdras*, there is a vision reported to the reader. In it, an unidentified woman is lamenting in the wilderness, but is told by the prophet "Ezra":[5]

[4] *The Great Divorce,* (1946; repr., Glasgow: Collins / Fontana, 1972), 9.

[5] The book is pseudonymous, written in the late first century, so we are not to think of "Ezra" as the actual Ezra who, with Nehemiah, is associated with the rebuilding of the first Temple and the establishment of early Judaism. The visionary who wrote this book no doubt considered "Ezra" a good pen name, since he had seen the destruction of the

Now ask the earth, and she will tell you that it is she who ought to mourn over so many who have come into being upon her. From the beginning all have been born of her, and others will come; and, lo, almost all go to perdition, and a multitude of them will come to doom. (4 Ezra/2 Esdras 10.9–11)

Clearly the prophet believes that most human beings will be destroyed, and passes on his gloomy perspective to the visionary woman figure with whom he is speaking. This is supposed to help her put her own grief at losing her husband and son in perspective, but it certainly strikes our contemporary sensibilities as cold comfort. However, several verses later, the visionary (with the reader) discovers that the woman is not an ordinary person in grief. Rather, she is transformed into a great City, Holy Zion, in the process of being built, and "Ezra" is amazed at its magnitude—its ability to include myriads of God's people. It would seem that this revelation is given to undo his pessimism, though the narrator leaves us to draw our own conclusions. Will many perish or will many be saved?

Lewis famously suggested that the devil likes to send errors into the world in pairs, so that folks, consumed with which error is the worst,[6] are distracted from the truth. With regard to the topic of damnation, even Christians have fallen prey to this tactic. Some adopt an ostrich-like attitude of denial, while others embrace the specter far too cheerfully on behalf of those whom they think deserve such a fate. Our tendency, of course, in the twenty-first century, is to follow the first course. But *Schadenfreude* (which, it will be remembered, is glee concerning the misfortunes of others) was a more common response in the ancient world, and its presence was so prevalent in theological

second Temple, and the decimation of the Jewish people by the Romans: he hoped for a renewal, a period like that of Ezra and Nehemiah, following this tragedy. Would that the Jewish author of this chapter (scholars agree that chapters 3–14 were written by a Jewish author) had seen this possibility of resurrection in the Messiah Jesus!

[6]*Mere Christianity*, 153.

texts that some of these nearly made it into the scriptural collection. *The Apocalypse of Peter*, frequently read in the second century, peoples hell with all kinds of sinners, describing their punishments in such detail that we suspect that the author intended to entertain his readers as they meditated upon these scenes. The scenes are too sordid, in my opinion, to be reproduced here: if you decide to investigate, be prepared. Though much less extreme, the closing Christian additions to the Jewish book of *2 Esdras/4 Ezra* also express an intense interest in God's vengeance against those who have harmed Christian people. (This book, complete with its Christian framework, was not added to the Deuterocanonical/ Readable Books in either the Roman or Orthodox context, but it was appended to the Latin version known as the Vulgate, and to the Slavonic Bible in the Russian Orthodox Church, and so it holds a certain measure of authority in some quarters.) Its Jewish core, from which I have quoted above in the sequence of the Weeping Woman and "Ezra," is, in my estimation, a remarkable book that bears resemblances both to Job for its wisdom, and to the Apocalypse of John for its striking visions. On the other hand, I am somewhat embarrassed that this Jewish classic was normalized for Christian use by the addition of a severe framework that concludes with these verses:

> For all unbelievers shall die in their unbelief. Beware, says the Lord, I am bringing evils upon the world, the sword and famine, death and destruction. . . . My right hand will not spare the sinners, and my sword will not cease from those who shed innocent blood on earth. And a fire will go forth from his wrath, and consume the foundations of the earth and the sinners, like burnt straw. Alas for those who sin and do not observe my commandments, says the Lord; I will not spare them. Depart, you faithless children! Do not pollute my sanctuary. For God knows all who sin against him; therefore he will hand them over to death and slaughter. (4 Esdras/2 Esdras 15.4–5, 22–25)

One might respond that even the canonical book of Revelation is rather uncompromising. Yet in the final book of the New Testament, we sense a difference in tone. To those who are in danger of infidelity, God pleads, "Come out of her, my people" (Rev 18.4); throughout the sequence of plagues, the narrator registers disappointment that those who have been so judged do not repent. Finally, at the end of the visions, the New Jerusalem appears, peopled with many from various nations, as God enlightens and dwells with them, and the rulers bring their riches into the holy city. Though final condemnation is seriously presented, the hope for salvation is robustly presented (indeed, accented) in the climax. In early Christian literature at large, however, we can trace a form of writing in which the eternal suffering of the reprobate is detailed. Perhaps this begins with the Christianized version of 4 Ezra and *The Apocalypse of Peter*, and finds its most mature (and least petty) expression in Dante's political and theological writing, *The Inferno* (the first section of his *Divine Comedy*). So many Jewish and Christian pieces in the first millennium AD elicited *Schadenfreude* in this manner that a biblical scholar named Martha Himmelfarb delineated them as a subgenre of the apocalypse genre, called "the tour of hell."[7]

Lewis's book is different. It is, instead, a tour *away* from Hell. As the narrator dreams, he boards a bus that is leaving "the grey town," which may be taken as either a holding place (like, but not identical to, purgatory) or a permanent abode like hell. The travelers enter a glorious land of light, where they are offered the opportunity to exchange their drab and self-centered existence for something real. It would seem that Lewis named his book as a rebuke to the eighteenth-/nineteenth-century romantic poet William Blake, who constructed a complex and heterodox poem entitled "The Marriage of Heaven and Hell." Again, if you decide to investigate Blake's striking poetry, be prepared for shock and awe, as well as for much confusion. Blake, despite his literary genius,

[7]Martha Himmelfarb, *Tours of Hell: An Apocalyptic Form in Jewish and Christian Literature* (Philadelphia: University of Pennsylvania Press, 1983).

was influenced by the philosopher Swedenborg, and maintained that there were two opposite and powerful energies, the angelic and the demonic. The artist, he implied, has special need of demonic potency in order to write with verve and commitment. John Milton is declared by him, for example, to have been "of the Devil's party" without knowing it, which is why he could create the masterpiece *Paradise Lost*. (Blake may, indeed, be correct that Milton's personification of Lucifer is far more compelling than his characterization of Christ. This may be due more to a deficit in Milton's ability to inhabit purity than to the innate power of the dark side, however.)[8] At the climax of Blake's extravaganza, heaven and hell are unified in the poetic imagination, creating a new "gospel" for the bold artist, who must not be afraid of blasphemy and darkness. *En route*, the angelic figures in the book are exposed as priggish and short-sighted by Blake, and the idea of God's judgment, at least in the traditional sense, is mocked.

The problem is that Blake considers darkness necessary for life, and cannot conceive of a world without shadows. The idea of evil as a "privation" of good would be nonsense to him, and submission itself is seen as the archenemy of freedom. Lewis would not agree. For he has fully embraced the scriptural and patristic vision of God's completed and renewed world, which embraces godly order, and which is so bright that it chases out the darkness:

> There shall no more be anything accursed, but the throne of God and of the Lamb shall be in it, and his servants shall worship him; they shall see his face, and his name shall be on their foreheads. And night shall be no more; they need no light of lamp or sun, for the Lord God will be their light, and they shall reign for ever and ever. . . . Blessed are those who wash their robes, that they may have the right to the tree of life and that they may enter the city by

---

[8]For Lewis's astute discussion of why it is easier for most writers to depict evil characters than good, see chapter thirteen of his *A Preface to Paradise Lost*.

the gates. Outside are the dogs and sorcerers and fornicators and murderers and idolaters, and every one who loves and practices falsehood. (Rev 22.3–6, 14–15)

In light of this sober but hopeful picture, *The Great Divorce* refuses to give in to easy answers. It neither denies the inevitability of divine judgment nor relishes the judgment of others; nor does it put forward moral confusion in the name of paradox, such as we see lurking in the art of William Blake. Instead, Lewis gives us a touchstone in the preface to his book:

> We are not living in a world where all roads are radii of a circle and where all, if followed long enough, will therefore draw gradually nearer and finally meet in the center.... If we insist on keeping Hell (or even earth) we shall not see Heaven: if we accept Heaven we shall not be able to retain even the smallest and most intimate souvenirs of Hell. [9]

With this great divide firmly in place, Lewis carefully but compellingly explores this difficult topic for a contemporary audience, offering us his own miniature version of Dante's classic, *The Divine Comedy*, complete with a glimpse of hell (or a place of purgation) and heaven. The reason why we cannot clearly identify the grey town with which the book begins—and to which, alas, some of its characters return—is that Lewis sees our present life in continuity with the life to come. If errors are not undone, then the sins of earth can slide into the settled enmity of hell—though Lewis presents the hope that evil can be undone even after a person's death, if there is even a kernel of reality left within that person's life. This suggested possibility has unsettled Protestant readers, who take as rigidly programmatic the brief Bible phrase: "It is appointed for men to die once, and after that comes judgment" (Heb 9.27). However, Lewis is not alone in the view that after death human

[9] *Divorce,* 7–8.

beings are either refined in their integrity, or tragically hardened in their godlessness. Hence, we find Church fathers referring to the climb of the Holy Mountain that lies before the pious dead[10] and the efficacy of our prayers for Christians who have fallen asleep.[11] In the Eastern Church, this idea of postmortem refinement is not expressed in terms of deficit and merit, nor as an actual place called purgatory. Lewis's refusal, then, to unequivocally decode his grey town for us is apt, and in harmony with Orthodox tendencies.[12] He is not positing purgatory as a place. Instead, he intimates that there is an uncanny relationship between space and time, between this world and the next. Indeed, in the preface he comments that our present state, if preferred to heaven, will "turn out to have been, all along," a part of hell, whereas if our desire for earth is subordinated to heaven, then it will become "from the beginning" an actual part of heaven.[13] Here, again, we see Lewis holding together two ideas: that heaven is far beyond our present state; but that the joys of earth are not unimportant or irredeemable. The same God who has created this world and called it "good" has promised to remake rather than ultimately destroy it.

Throughout *The Great Divorce* we encounter Lewis's vision both of the transcendent beauties (all gloriously different from one another) seen in human beings glorified by God, and of the potential ugliness of humanity gone wrong. The beauties refresh our spirit, while the prospect of ugliness issues a dire warning. In his inimitable style, Lewis does not shy away from the complex matters of the faith. Instead, we join him in a fantastic journey into depths and up to heights. As we journey, we are compelled to engage in sober, hopeful, and caution-

[10]St Ambrose, *Funeral Sermon of Theodosius* 36–37.

[11]St John Chrysostom, *Homilies on 1 Corinthians* 41.8; St Cyril of Jerusalem, *Mystagogical Catecheses* 5.9–10.

[12]Elsewhere he uses the term "purgatory," but also agrees that the Protestant objections to the teaching, as it has developed in the Roman Catholic context, are appropriate. See, for example, C. S. Lewis, *Letters To Malcolm: Chiefly on Prayer* (1964; repr., London: Collins / Fontana, 1966), 109–11.

[13] *Divorce*, 8.

ary reflections on reality. The book reminds us that we are not made simply for this world, while it also suggests that what we do, how we think, and who we are in this world matter. All the while, we are led to go further in and further up, reveling in the depths of God's love and humility in the incarnation. Those matters that are difficult to declare in plain words are brought to life by means of images and story. Lewis suggests that our present moments are interconnected with salvation history, and with the astounding glory for which God has designed us. This book is not for the faint of heart. However, its complexity is not due to a demanding reading level, but to the subject matter—the tenderness *and* holiness of the Lord who makes his claim on each one of us. If it is challenging on a doctrinal level for Protestants (because of its suggestion that one can be purified or grow in grace after death), it is challenging on a spiritual level for Catholics and Orthodox. Its vignettes strike close to home, quickening the imagination to teachings that we may be prone to accept only on an intellectual level. In this way, the book works in a similar manner to Jesus' parables. It instructs those whose dogma may be too circumscribed, but also questions those who have merely given assent to truths that should constantly astonish. Again, I strongly recommend this chapter as a tour guide of the book for those who have already read *The Great Divorce*. I will try, however, to avoid too many spoilers for those who have not yet jumped in, and hope that this study may whet your appetite.

What is real?

As we began our study of Lewis, we zeroed in on Lewis's view of reality, contrasting it with *The Matrix* and Morpheus' challenge to Neo: "What *is* real?" *The Great Divorce* also compels us to consider reality and our preconceptions concerning it, by putting before our eyes a series of images.

Lewis, in speaking about the genesis of his Narnia books, says that they began with an image, a picture of a fawn in the snow, holding an umbrella.[14] The impact of *The Great Divorce* for adults demonstrates, at least for me, how we share his childlike propensity for pictures: it is the images (even more than the arguments) that lurk in our memory, once we have read the story. We are left with a dread of the ghostlike grey town, smaller than the chink between two blades of grass, yet vaporously expansive because its denizens steadily move further and further apart from each other in hellish solitude. Alongside this we recall the brilliance and solidity of that other land, made all the more apparent because the denizens of the grey town are ghostly apparitions on its bright landscape. And then, we remember that in the distance beckon the "impossible steeps" of the Mountains, where the blessed may climb and dwell.

In order to understand even this terrain, our narrator, who writes of his journey in the first person, is provided with his own mentor, his own Reepicheep (or Virgil), whom he identifies as the nineteenth-century author of children's books such as *The Princess and the Goblin*, George MacDonald. The narrator himself has seen the bleak town, and has come by bus to the "foothills" of heaven, but has not seen the shining mountains except in a glimpse—though he does witness some of the blessed transformed so that they are able to move towards the highlands, and disappear, in the distance. "MacDonald"[15] explains to him, like the heavenly angel does to the prophet Daniel, what is happening, and where they are going. He also converses with the narrator (whom we will call "Lewis") about the meaning of the landscape, and about the persons involved the dramas that are envisaged. Each of the visitors has his or her own guide or mentor, someone who has reached the shin-

[14] "It All Began With A Picture," in *Of This and Other Worlds*, 78–79.
[15] I will put "MacDonald" and "Lewis" in quotation marks when referring to the characters depicted in *The Great Divorce*, since Lewis imagines how MacDonald might answer, and indeed modifies some of that writer's recorded views. He also states that he has *not* had visions, and so distances himself from the "I" who narrates the story.

ing land before them, who comes back to meet and help them. The insubstantial nature of each visitor proves problematic: even the grass is so solid, in contrast to their human feebleness, that it hurts the visitor's feet to walk. Indeed, one scene shows a spirit-guide offering his arm so that the beloved visitor can lean on him in this harsh but beautiful environment as they go towards the mountains. She is, paradoxically, both too ashamed and too proud to receive the help. "Lewis," however, does take the arm of "MacDonald."

Thus two of Lewis's convictions about human nature are linked: we are not "real" enough to manage in God's own realm, and we require help in order to survive in it. Indeed, there is a third conviction—that God frequently works through the help of other human beings. Our investigation into the character of several of the visitors helps us to accept the truth of his observations concerning the unimaginable solidness of eternity, our present need of help, and the aptness of being offered help by others like us. The significance of human mediation has already been seen as a major theme in *The Pilgrim's Regress*, *Till We Have Faces*, and *That Hideous Strength*. Lewis has no intent, of course, to dishonor the Great Mediator, the One between God and Man. Rather, he acknowledges, along with the Great Tradition (beginning with the Scriptures themselves), that this One characteristically *uses* those who love Him in order to bring others to a place of reconciliation. Consider, for example, how the Lord directed Philip to the Ethiopian official's chariot (Acts 8.26) to interpret Scripture for him and then whisked him away: why not simply speak to that seeker, through the Holy Spirit? And to Saul/St Paul, God spoke directly, but then required that great sinner to seek out the Christian community in Damascus for baptism and further instruction in the faith.

As we become acquainted with the travelers while they wait in line for the bus, travel together on it, and arrive in the shining land, we are forcibly reminded of their former state in the grey town. There, all was drab, grey, and the same. There, we witnessed the customary bickering

and posing of the realm, as each visitor tried to claim his or her place
in line or on the bus. There, almost all of the apartments and businesses
on the street were boarded up—because, we learn later, everyone in the
town feels driven to move further and further away from each other.
Along with self-centeredness and a lack of substantiality, then, goes isolation. "The trouble is," says one of the travelers to "Lewis," "that they're
so quarrelsome."[16] In fact, so is the bus-partner who makes this observation. On the bus, "Lewis" meets a young "poet," an "intelligent man,"
and a fat man, all of whom, in various degrees and combinations, show
forth the characteristics of selfishness, arrogance, lack of interest in the
outside world, inability to experience joy, and greed. Ancient theologians would describe such people as "turned in on themselves" (*curvatus
in se*). So, the young poet speaks incessantly of not being understood by
his parents, peers, teachers, and girlfriend, and opines that in the shining land he will finally be appreciated. Indeed, he is sure that "Lewis"
will appreciate his writing—could he just read something from his
manuscript to him? The "intelligent" business man in a bowler hat then
converses with "Lewis" about the grey town's tendency to expand but
thin out, and of his scheme to bring back "*real* commodities" to the
town, which everyone will want. His hope is to become wealthy, but
also to be acknowledged as a benefactor by the denizens of the town.
In the third place, "Lewis" speaks with a fat man of culture, who insists,
in contradiction to the intelligent schemer, that twilight is not turning
to darkness in the grey town, but that the light is coming—the twilight is not to be feared, but is rather the promise of dawn, "a sublime
thought!"[17] The way that the cultured man waxes rhapsodic here makes
us realize that he is engaging only in wishful thinking.

The visitors' reactions to the real world, when they arrive there, are
also instructive. Orthodox readers may think of the awed reactions seen
in iconic representations of the apostles Peter, James, and John, when

[16] *Divorce*, 19.
[17] *Divorce*, 24.

they behold the glory of Christ with Moses and Elijah on the Mount of Transfiguration—shielding their eyes, looking away from the glory, or concentrating on it with rapt joy. We would expect that kind of response from our busload of insubstantial visitors, but this is not the case with most of them. One of them, called the "Big Man," has gained his place in line by brute strength, and expects to be met when the bus lands. His arrival has in fact been anticipated, but he is not at all pleased with his appointed mentor, a repentant murderer, who tries to convince the bully that he needs help. Despite his obvious flaws as a bully and a violent man, the visitor is comically self-righteous and refuses to be helped by someone he considers more morally bankrupt than himself. In the end, he adopts the stance of the fox with the "sour" grapes, preferring to tell himself that the shining land is all a hoax. He wants no "Bleeding Charity"—and so rejects the very cross itself. When the drama then turns to the fat, cultured ghost, we listen in on a conversation in which he demonstrates his inability to rethink his theology, and his mistaken conviction that there are no sins of the intellect, since (in his view) the whole purpose of thinking is to be self-willed and ingenious. He is met by an old friend who, it seems, studied theology with him. When he learns that his entire avant-garde school of thought has had no lasting value, and is wholly forgotten on earth (let alone in the shining land), he resolves to go back to the grey town to read his planned paper for that Friday—a paper that suggests how Jesus might have matured in his theology had he lived to a riper age! Delusion and intellectual pride blind him to the glories all around him, not least to the transformation of an old friend. Then there is the intelligent entrepreneurial ghost, who simply wants to plunder the shining town for one of its glorious artifacts, and another hard-bitten skeptical ghost, who can see nothing valuable in the glory because he is wholly unsuited to that land. Alongside these, there is the ashamed ghost who hides, refusing to take her mentor's arm, because she cannot endure admitting her need and does not want to be seen by anyone in her ghostly condition.

All of these, in various ways, are tiresomely the same in their self-centeredness. They show forth, in different ways, the self-centeredness of a life not oriented towards God. In listening in on their self-disclosures, we may be reminded of St John's vision of Babylon: "She glorified herself. . . . [I]n her heart she says, 'A queen I sit, I am no widow, mourning I shall never see' " (Rev 18.7). Babylon's destruction comes from within—she simply implodes, and all those associated with her also turn against her. Her seeming wealth and knowledge all fail her in the end, and she remains desolate, without any festivity or joy in her streets. In following our visitors to the deep places of their barren souls, we come to see how individuals can, in varying ways, participate in Babylon's fruitlessness. "Lewis's" mentor, "George MacDonald," explains: "There are only two kinds of people in the end: those who say to God, 'Thy will be done,' and those to whom God says, in the end, 'Thy will be done.' All that are in Hell, choose it. Without that self-choice there could be no Hell. No soul that seriously and constantly desires joy will ever miss it. Those who seek find. To those who knock it is opened."[18] Yes, it is true. Each of the resistant ghosts wants to keep something of hell with them, even if it makes for misery—and that something cannot be kept in heaven. Each of them reminds us of Satan's words in *Paradise Lost,* "Better to reign in hell than serve in heaven." Each of these characters has shown a variation of stubborn pride: petulance, wrath, vengeance, "self-respect," or the need to prove themselves tragically great, even by way of suicide.

Alongside these ones obviously motivated by variants of pride, there are some characters who exemplify what appear to be "lesser" sins: the wife who is constantly "helpful"; the "smother mother" who refuses her child any autonomy and so makes the object of her love a slave; the grumbling ghost who can see nothing good; those who want to do nothing but instruct others; those who were "famous" on earth and cannot abide a place where they have little notoriety; and those who

---

[18] *Divorce,* 66–67.

despise or hate others. The latter, it turns out, can actually be converted because they still harbor some passion, and are, at least at the point of their hating, turned outward. (We are reminded of St Paul and his persecution of the early Church, and of Jesus' words concerning those who are hot or cold and not merely lukewarm). Some of these sinners seem hardly evil enough to "deserve" punishment—and some are, in fact, rescued. But Lewis pictures them so colorfully and with such insight that we are led to see how even the "lesser" sins of petty conceit or the constant overshadowing of others can lead to an utter lack of reality, and an inability to appreciate what is real, and free, and joyful. A person who will not repent of these may well lose whatever life remains in him or her. With regards to, for example, the grumbling woman, "Lewis's" Teacher explains, "The question is whether she is a grumbler, or only a grumble. If there is a real woman—even the least trace of one . . . it can be brought to life again. If there's one wee spark under all those ashes, we'll blow it till the whole pile is red and clear. But if there's nothing but ashes we'll not go on blowing them in our own eyes forever. They must be swept up."[19] We are reminded of Isaiah's words about the Servant, our Lord Jesus: "a bruised reed he will not break, and a dimly burning wick he will not quench" (Is 42.3; Mt 12.20). As we stoop with Lewis in these depths to see if there is something there, we find ourselves back at the question, "What is real?"

Enslavement and Freedom

Caught up in the matter of reality is the perennial human struggle against enslavement, and for freedom, however it is understood. We see this connection between freedom and reality even in the topsy-turvy world of Neo and Morpheus (to return to *The Matrix*), who can be "free" only when they accept the truth of their enslavement in a grim world. Lewis, because he is nurtured by the Christian story rather than

---

[19] *Divorce*, 68.

a gnostic myth, aspires to a more frank and full liberation. Indeed, he follows the hope of the apostle Paul in looking to the liberation of the entire cosmos and the human body—not simply the human mind or conscience. We are reminded by the apostle in Romans 8 that the entire universe, creatures and all, has been bound both because of the misstep of our first parents and because of their necessary confinement at the hands of God. However, Christ has taken on all that it is to be human in order to undo this imprisonment:

> [T]he sufferings of this present time are not worth comparing with the glory that is to be revealed [in] us. For the creation waits with eager longing for the revealing of the sons of God; for the creation was subjected to futility, not of its own will but by the will of him who subjected it in hope; because the creation itself will be set free from its bondage to decay and obtain the glorious liberty of the children of God. We know that the whole creation has been groaning in travail together until now; and not only the creation, but we ourselves, who have the first fruits of the Spirit, groan inwardly as we wait for adoption as sons, the redemption of our bodies. For in this hope we were saved. (Rom 8.18–24)

Lewis follows the wisdom of the Scriptures and Holy Tradition as he speaks about the acquisition of true freedom—something reserved, indeed, for the resurrection, when there will be, as the Apocalypse puts it, "no more curse." We are alternately disgusted and delighted by the plight and liberation of the "be-lizarded" Ghost, who, with the ministrations of a shining helper, becomes a "new-made man." The deforming lizard, a personification of lust sitting on his shoulder and whispering obscenities in his ear, must be killed, but with his consent—and the struggle of the poor man against losing what he assumes is his connection with the natural world is very fierce. At the end, though, he gives his permission, and the little red beast is destroyed. Our patient, in the vision, is subjected quite literally to Jesus' advice, "If your eye offends you, pluck it out" (Mt 5.29; Mt 18.9; Mk 9.47). The ghost, after the amputation, takes on a shining and gargantuan appearance, as the reptile itself is transformed into an imposing and glossy stallion. Together, in joy, they ride off towards the holy High Country, bringing tears to this reader's eyes.

As he gallops through the shining land, the once tortured and besieged man now hears the cosmic song concerning his newfound authority: "[A]ll natures that were your enemies [have] become ... backs for you to ride, and firmness for your feet to rest on.... [W]e desire the beginning of your reign as we desire dawn and dew, wetness at the birth of light.... Master, your Master has appointed you for ever: to be our King of Justice and our High Priest."[20] Here is true freedom: to allow whatever enslaves us to be killed, or to die to this thing, so that we (and whatever is good about us) can be raised to new life. The newly made man takes his passion, his "energy of desire,"[21] newly ordered, with him to the high country, because it, too, in its place, and not as a controlling master, is of God. Body and bodily matters are significant: but they find their place in the en-Spirited resurrection body not as our masters, but as our servants. True freedom comes by way of sacrifice and transformation—and it includes the proper ordering of our composite natures, in the way God intends the created order (and the new creation) to be. This vignette gives us an imaginative glimpse into what St Paul might have meant when he spoke of Creation, personified, keenly anticipating the "liberty of the sons of God" (Rom 8.21–23). Our liberation means joy for the entire cosmos, whose creatures will no longer be in rebellion against humanity. Even more, our own bodies will no longer rebel against our wills, and against right reason. Instead, made anew after the resurrected Christ, they will blessedly be in submissive harmony with our remade wills and our godly desires.[22]

---

[20]*Divorce,* 94–95.

[21]*Divorce,* 95.

[22]For a cogent discussion of the probable *necessity* that human freedom (including

Freedom does not simply involve the integration of each person, but also the wholesome relationship of that person with another (or others). At the close of the story concerning the stallion-riding new man, "Lewis" engages in conversation with his Teacher: if such a menial characteristic as lust can be so transformed, then what might happen in the resurrection to one characterized by a mother's love, or deep friendship? We are about to find out.

Approaching us as we read is what appears to be a dancing, light-reflecting, undulating river. It turns out to be a procession that heralds the coming of an unbearably beautiful woman, whose "clothing" does not hide her luminous and clearly perceptible body, but adorns it. Lewis's astonishment at her is similar to that of Dante, who speaks of his "sweet guide" Beatrice, who smiles and shoots forth beams from her celestial eyes.[23] This woman is not to be Lewis's mentor, however, but the guide of a wholly unworthy visitor. We discover that this shining woman was no one important on earth, but who in her motherly service became glorious, attended by sons and daughters, animals, and all the richness of life. She is, evidently, "mother" to all who cast the flowers before her arrival and dance for joy, as she is the caretaker to the myriads of animals who attend her way.

We are shocked to see this one, full of the "abundance of life," stoop to kiss and greet a shrunken, dwarfed ghost—a dwarf connected, by a chain, to a huge, thin, but even more insubstantial second ghost. The small ghost holds the chain to the larger, but paradoxically it is the larger repulsive figure from whom he takes his cue, who overshadows him and who speaks for him. This large figure is entirely unreal, seemingly a projection of his own psyche, and yet he converses with him: readers who know *The Hobbit* may think of the pathetic "conversation" between Gollum and himself about "his precious." The contrast is com-

the breakdown of reason-will-flesh) be limited after the Fall, see chapter five of Lewis's *The Problem of Pain* (1940; repr., New York: HarperCollins, 2001), 63–85.

[23]Dante, *Paradiso,* Canto III, 22–23.

plete—this free and lively woman with her many attendants, and this restricted vestige of a man, willingly chained to a specter (aptly called "The Tragedian") that does not really exist.

What About Names?

The introduction of the shining Lady, whose name is "Sarah Smith" of "Golders Green," compels us, as a kind of sidebar, to consider *names* in Lewis's book. Sarah Smith and "Ikey," the intelligent-looking business-man (in the round bowler hat) from the bus, make an interesting duo. "Ikey," of course, is not the man's self-designation, but a short-form of abuse for Isaac, given to the man by the bullying "Big Man" on the bus. Both Ikey and Sarah are clearly Jewish: Ikey corresponds to the stereotypical idea of the Jewish financeer, and Sarah, who is iconoclastic, comes from a Jewish area in London—Golders Green was sometimes nicknamed "Goldberg's Green."[24]

Elsewhere, Lewis avers that in the Middle Ages, Jewish people, stripped of their land, were driven "into occupations remote from the soil,"[25] unlike their biblical ancestors. Clearly, then, he is not caricatur-ing "Ikey" in a malicious manner, with an intent to vilify the Jewish people, though some today will be offended by his stereotype. We do not know Ikey's fate, only that he must heed the voice saying that his entrepreneurial scheme is useless in the shining land, if he is going to find joy there. But Sarah has, in every sense, arrived, though she had no notoriety while on earth. One analyst of this text shrewdly observes that "Just as Ikey is the only nickname used in *The Great Divorce*, Golders Green is the only location used in *The Great Divorce*. And just as Ikey indicates Jewishness, so Golders Green indicates

---

[24]For a more detailed explanation of these two characters and their unmistakably Jewish character, see the splendid analysis of Kathryn Ann Lindskoog, to whom I am indebted at this point: *Surprised by C. S. Lewis, George MacDonald and Dante* (Macon, GA: Mercer University Press, 2001), 34–36.

[25]*Reflections on the Psalms* (1958; repr., San Diego, CA: Harcourt, 1986), 76.

Jewishness."[26] As a result, the careful reader is compelled to pair the two figures and to contrast them. Sarah presents to us the blessedness of a motherly person, transformed by God—like her Biblical namesake, the matriarch, she is the mother of those who are free (Galatians 4.26). And even the unfortunate Isaac, abused by the bully, is addressed by the divine voice, and invited to see the shining land for what it truly is. Lewis clearly deplored the anti-Judaism that was rife in his day, and that was at least a partial catalyst for the Second World War that was raging at the time when he wrote this book. (As Christians we should be alarmed, I believe, at its resurgence in the third millennium, often cloaked under a critique of the modern state of Israel! The latter question is appropriate for debate, but hatred and dismissal of the Jews is another matter.)

We should not be surprised that when Lewis finally married, it was to a woman who had embraced Christ, but who had a Jewish American background, with all the cultural characteristics entailed: many of his friends did not appreciate the shining quality of Joy Davidman, but fixated upon her brash American ways. There is no indication, however, that "Sarah" had converted to Christianity in her earthly life—only that her motherly openness had proven fertile ground for God to work. Now, in paradise, she is "*in* love . . . [and] loves truly." We may take her, together with the exotic figure of Emeth in *The Last Battle,* as an example of those who will be found to be in Christ at the end, despite their being hampered from such a conscious faith while here. Paradoxically, those who today are physically related to the ancient people of God may now be pictured (since they have been for so many years separated from the physical presence of their Messiah) among the sheep "of the nations," in Jesus' parable of Matthew 25. We should remember that the sheep put to his right hand were astounded to hear that they had responded in kindness to Jesus, since they had never heard or seen him.

[26] *Surprised by C. S. Lewis,* 35.

Damnation and Non-Being

Let's return to the drama between Sarah and the Dwarf-with-Tragedian.
We hope to see a transformation of the pitiful ghost, kissed, like a frog,
by this great Lady. It is not to be. Instead we see that sin (in his case, self-
pity and the use of this as blackmail against others) is a mortal cancer,
consuming him from the inside out. The Lady pays no attention to the
antics of the tall figure, who expresses the little figure's self-pity in the
most bathetic and childish manner. He acts the part of the "Tragedian"
when he discovers that she has not "missed" him in heaven because of
the joy there. She steadfastly addresses her love to the real person—or
what is left of him, trying to draw him into reality and into the joy that
surrounds them both. In the end, he will not budge, so accustomed he
has become to playing the martyr, and trying to hold her hostage to her
own winsome disposition of pity. She speaks with earnestness, sternness,
humor, reason, and entreaties—but in the end, "Frank" disappears, and
the Tragedian alone remains, for a moment. In encountering the tall
specter alone, she asks, "Where is Frank?" We are dismayed to see how
one who has made himself miserable, and has tried to make everyone
around himself miserable, can in the end lose all touch with reality. The
Lady remarks, "If it would help you and if it were possible I would go
down with you into Hell: but you cannot bring Hell into me."[27] But,
in the vision, there is no one left for her to visit in those depths, even
if she could. Self-imposed unreality has swallowed the one clutching it.
The "freedom" to embrace misery and spread it has become a deadly
tyrant. Instead of transformation, then, we have seen the demise of the
Dwarf-turned-Tragedian. But Lewis is not concerned to give us a scene
of damnation. Rather, he is intent to show the incompatibility of utter
Love with a lie.

The Scriptures also talk about the potential for self-destruction,
the sheer emptiness of those who embrace, and will not renounce,

---

[27] *Divorce,* 109.

falsehood. At one point in their conversation, Frank (who is anything but "frank") catches a glimpse of the truth that his beloved is speaking to him. But Sarah's reason cannot prevail against his desire to make her pity him and so enter into his misery. He thrusts away the snatch of light that comes to him, and returns to wallow in his whining ways. We have already considered a passage in the words of 2 Timothy against the heretics as we analyzed the deceptive crew of *That Hideous Strength*. Some of N.I.C.E. even dared to co-opt Christian language to spread their deceit. Such actions bespeak a hardness of heart that is difficult for even the divine light to pierce. Speaking of those who have once known Christ, but who have embraced error, the apostle says:

> These are waterless springs and mists driven by a storm; for them the deepest darkness has been reserved. For they speak bombastic nonsense, and with licentious desires of the flesh they entice people who have just escaped from those who live in error. They promise them freedom, but they themselves are slaves of corruption; for people are slaves to whatever masters them. For if, after they have escaped the defilements of the world through the knowledge of our Lord and Savior Jesus Christ, they are again entangled in them and overpowered, the last state has become worse for them than the first. For it would have been better for them never to have known the way of righteousness than, after knowing it, to turn back from the holy commandment that was passed on to them. It has happened to them according to the true proverb, "The dog turns back to its own vomit," and, "The sow is washed only to wallow in the mud." (2 Peter 2.17–3.1)

These Scriptures warn against deceit without pity. And yet . . . and yet . . . even if they *deserve* it, even if this is in the nature of their lies, how can the blessed be happy knowing that some are not in this joy? How can there be heaven where there is also hell? The Teacher in Lewis's story takes various approaches in responding to our disquiet. We have already heard of his explanation that it is foolish to continue to blow "ashes in the eyes" when there is no spark left to flame. In his ongoing conversation with "Lewis," the mentor also distinguishes between the *action* of pity, which is eternal, and the *passion* of pity, the suffering that accompanies it, which will not live for ever. For it cannot be used as a "weapon" against those who are good by those who are loveless: that would give evil the prerogative of "blackmail."[28] Another answer given is that "all hell is smaller than one atom . . . of the Real world"[29] and that there would be no space in hell, were the Lady to have tried to follow Frank into unreality to save him. All that grey town that Lewis saw, with its vast empty expanses, is smaller than the space between two blades of the eternal, shining grass!

The Great Transposition, Universalism, and our Transformation

But what about mercy triumphing over judgement (Jas 2.13)? Are God's hands tied as much by our potential unreality as by our sin? Here, too, we receive a paradoxical answer through Lewis's mentor. Sarah could not go between the blades, but One can, and did. "Only the Greatest of all can make Himself small enough to enter Hell. For the higher a thing is, the lower it can descend—a man can sympathise with a horse but a horse cannot sympathise with a rat. Only One has descended into Hell. . . . There is no spirit in prison to Whom He did not preach."[30] The answer to our question is not a doctrine, but a Person. Jesus descended, and has made provision for all. That is what we need to know. More can we learn only by living in time, through to the end.

We are driven, by the words of the Teacher "MacDonald," back to Scripture: "The one who descended is Himself also the one who ascended . . . that he might fill all things" (Eph 4.10). Our imaginative and reasonable ascent and descent with Lewis is only possible because

[28] *Divorce*, 111.
[29] *Divorce*, 113.
[30] *Divorce*, 114.

there is one who has actually made the tour before us. And his purpose
was to fill all things. And so, we pause. What is the force of this "all"
language? Is the filling of all things automatic, since Christ has won
the victory? Other passages of Scripture might lead us to think so. We
are told to pray for everyone, especially those in authority, because
"God our Savior ... desires all men to be saved and to come to the
knowledge of the truth" (1 Tim 2.3–4). Romans 5.12–18 contrasts the
effect of ancestral sin with the victory of Christ in a way that suggests
universal salvation:

> Therefore as sin came into the world through one man and
> death through sin, and so death spread to all men because all men
> sinned—sin indeed was in the world before the law was given, but
> sin is not counted where there is no law.
>
> Yet death reigned from Adam to Moses, even over those whose
> sins were not like the transgression of Adam, who was a type of the
> one who was to come. But the free gift is not like the trespass. For
> if many died through one man's trespass, much more have the grace
> of God and the free gift in the grace of that one man Jesus Christ
> abounded for many.
>
> And the free gift is not like the effect of that one man's sin.
> For the judgment following one trespass brought condemnation,
> but the free gift following many trespasses brings justification. If,
> because of one man's trespass, death reigned through that one man,
> much more will those who receive the abundance of grace and the
> free gift of righteousness reign in life through the one man Jesus
> Christ.
>
> Then, as one man's trespass led to condemnation for all men,
> so one man's act of righteousness leads to acquittal and life for *all*
> men. (Rom 5.12–18)

However, lest we be too expansive in our reading of the "all" in the
final sentence, we must supplement it with verse nineteen: "For as by

one man's disobedience many were made sinners, so by one man's obedience *many* will be made righteous" (Rom 5.19). And earlier in the passage, the word "many" was used, rather than "all." Yet we have still to contend with the apostle's words that the Father's intention was "through [Christ] to reconcile to himself *all things*, whether on earth or in heaven, making peace by the blood of his cross" (Col 1.20). This is consonant with Ephesians 1.10, that God's "plan for the fulness of time [was] to unite *all things* in him, things in heaven and things on earth." Hebrews is more circumspect in speaking of "Christ, having been offered once to bear the sins of *many*" (Heb 9.28). But 2 Peter returns again to God's universal desire: "The Lord is not slow about his promise as some count slowness, but is forbearing toward you, not wishing that any should perish, but that all should reach repentance" (2 Pet 3.9). Finally, we have to account for Jesus' own programmatic promise: "I, when I am lifted up from the earth, will draw all men to myself" (Jn 12.32).

These verses that speak of "all" provide a strong case—though not an iron-clad argument—for those who, like Rob Bell (author of *Love Wins*),[31] would like to declare that, in the end, Christ will rescue us all. Yet we have the warnings of judgment vividly before us in Scripture too. Are we permitted to say, as Bell does, that these are *simply* creative metaphors by the biblical writers, or warnings with no substance? To do so would be to picture God as the harried mother who typically issues a vacuous warning to her children, "If you do that *one more time*. . . ." This being said, we remember that the Lord did issue an unqualified warning to Ninevah, which He did not in fact enact. In the case of Jonah's warning, God's judging words were not strictly predictive, but "propadeutic"—for the purpose of *instruction*. And the warning *worked*. They repented, and God did not destroy the city.

---

[31]Rob Bell, *Love Wins: A Book about Heaven, Hell, and The Fate of Every Person Who Ever Existed* (New York: HarperOne, 2011).

Lewis acknowledges that the flesh-and-blood George MacDonald wrote as though he were a thoroughgoing universalist.[32] But in his dream, *The Great Divorce*, "MacDonald," the Mentor, draws back from such certainty. He says that "it may be" true that all will repent, but that it is not our business to declare it. Here, he utters sage words consonant with those of Hans Urs von Balthasar, who himself quotes from Lewis's *Great Divorce*,[33] concerning the varied nature of human self-centeredness. With Lewis, von Balthasar dared to *hope* that all be saved from the solipsism of hell, but refused to declare it: "To push on any farther into these deep waters is not permitted us. We have to stop at this observation: it would be in God's power to allow the grace that flows into the world from the self-sacrifice of his Son to grow powerful enough to become his 'efficacious' grace for all sinners. But precisely this is something that we can only hope for."[34]

It is the element of time that is crucial, as Lewis also remarks: "Every attempt to see the shape of eternity except through the lens of Time destroys your knowledge of Freedom."[35] It is not for humans, then, to declare what they have not yet seen—even though they may hope for it. This caution rules out both unconditional universalism (of the declaratory, not hopeful variety) and rigorous predestinarian thought. We simply cannot solve the puzzle of God's sovereignty and human freedom. The piece that is missing is our experience, our living through time to eternity, so as to see the entire picture. Both human freedom and God's omnipotence are assumed in the gospel, but to us they look mutually contradictory. Moreover, we are taking about *persons*—all mysteriously made in the image of God—not theorems.

[32] *Divorce*, 114.

[33] Hans Urs von Balthasar, *Dare We Hope "That All Men Be Saved"? With a Short Discourse on Hell,* trans. David Kipp and Lothar Krauth (San Francisco, CA: Ignatius Press, 1988), 91–94.

[34] *Dare We Hope*, 210.

[35] *Divorce*, 115.

When we encounter a mystery—something basic that we cannot get further behind to explain—it is helpful, I think, to follow the lead of the ancient theologians. At a certain point, they ceased in their efforts to explain the mystery further, but set boundaries to mark the space within which we may fruitfully contemplate such wonders. Here are some boundaries that may help us as we consider the problem of God's will, eternal judgment, humankind, and salvation. We cannot pick and choose which boundaries we like best: they must all be considered together to achieve a balanced perspective and to remain faithful to the complex scriptural tradition. Holding all these boundaries as simultaneously true proves difficult, of course, as we must rest in paradox and mystery:

- We cannot say that God's will may ultimately be thwarted.

- We cannot deny that God "desires all men to be saved and to come to the knowledge of the truth" (1 Tim 2.4).

- We cannot view the salvation accomplished by Christ as automatic in such a way that it violates human integrity or choice, or that it does not require a human response.

- We cannot say that salvation depends upon us in a foundational sense.

- We cannot say that human acceptance of God's loving offer is unnecessary.

- We cannot claim to know that someone is damned.

- We cannot say that the effect of Christ's righteousness on humanity is less powerful than Adam's sin.[36]

---

[36]Some Christian theologians, for example, have described Adam's sin as inescapably conferring guilt upon all humanity, without regard to the participation of each person; however, few theologians who hold this position describe Christ's righteousness as having a balancing universal effect. From the Orthodox perspective, both inherited guilt and the prospect of salvation without human assent miss the mark. In any case, Jesus' work is infinitely more potent than the ancient transgression.

- We cannot assert that the doctrine of hell is only "heuristic"—
  that it is *only* a warning.

All of these negative boundaries are drawn from the Scriptures that we
have considered in this section. They are the markers retained by the
Fathers as they consider these deep questions, and they are not transgressed by Lewis, even in his most imaginative moments. They remind
us of the God who has made Himself known to us, His creation of us in
His own image, and His desire for our rescue and transformation—that
each of us should experience the glory of Sarah and the other saints.

We must, after all, remember that we are still in "the Shadowlands,"
looking through a glass darkly. And indeed, that is where Lewis leaves
us. We hear his Teacher inform him that he has not *actually* been transported to the shining land, but is simply having a dream—and, "Mac-
Donald" warns, he must make this clear to anyone who reads his book.
He should not claim to know more than anyone can know. There is
One who has ascended and descended—and it is not Lewis. "God has
forbidden" that we engage in such pretense.[37] We are called to reality,
and the purpose of the "dream" he has narrated is to help us to see better. So that we are absolutely clear that Lewis is not playing the role of
a predictive mystic, he closes with three more scenes.

The first is a kind of a parable, a vision in which he sees people like
little chessmen playing out their lives on a silver plate, raptly watched
by their larger eternal souls. The drama is intense, but the relationship
between the actors and the shining spectators, their true selves, remains
unclear. "Lewis" wonders, then, if the drama he has seen in the shining country was all a farce—was everything already decided *before* the
visitors came there? Should he interpret the decisive actions as taking
place in the here and now, as fateful actions that prejudge the eternal
outcome? Or should he rather see what is decided by humans on earth
as *anticipations* of a choice that will finally come at the end? His Teacher

[37] *Divorce*, 117.

will not give him an answer about this—what he has seen are two different ways of looking at the importance of choices. The "visitors" who
have been whisked off to see the Bright Land are told at several points
that they must not delay, because the time to choose is now; indeed,
they have been choosing every day of their lives.

And then he has another final vision. "MacDonald" and he are back
in the shining woods, but "Lewis" has his back to the sunrise that is
steadily coming. Though he is not looking at the sun, he sees its glow,
lighting up his Mentor, and the greenery, and the trees, calling everything into life as the birds and other animals begin to herald the dawn
with their waking music. But *he* is not prepared: he is still a ghost! Terrified, the all-too-solid light breaks upon his softer head. And then, he
finds himself in a third scene: back in his study, knocked not by light
but by books falling from his desk. He has fallen asleep, but wakes in the
middle of an air raid warning. We are warned clearly: these are images,
and the reality is yet to come. Be prepared.

Surprised by Sarah

I want to finish, though, not with Lewis's rude awakening, but with
the image of that splendid mother of *The Great Divorce*, who lingers in
my imagination. I have in my mind's eye the final glimpse of Sarah, as
the bright spirits sing of her bliss in a celebratory hymn reminiscent
of Psalm 91/90. Like David, she dwells "in the help of the Most High,
in the shadow of the Almighty." And even that shadow is brilliant! The
language is updated, with reference to "bogies" in the dark, "dinosaurs,"
and "invisible germs";[38] it is Christianized, with reference to "the happy
Trinity" as her dwelling place; it is also rationalized for the theologian, or those who are dealing with intellectual questions of the faith.
For example, instead of "a thousand fall at his right hand," we hear "a
thousand fail to solve the problem." But it is unmistakably a reworking

---

[38]*Divorce*, 118–19. All the references come from Lewis's "psalm" on these pages.

of this comforting psalm of David, in which the faithful pass through danger unscathed, just as Sarah has. She has been filled "brim-full with immensity of life" and so is eternally blessed. "Nothing can trouble her joy." In the end, when we contemplate heaven and hell, blessings and curses, we may be left with questions. But alongside the questions, because of the tour to hell and the triumph to heaven accomplished by our Lord Jesus, we can retain a settled confidence in a world that is *real*. As we sing at the conclusion of the Orthodox Divine Liturgy: "We have seen the true light; we have received the heavenly Spirit!" Lewis does not shrink back from the difficult, even the tortuous matters of our faith. But he broaches these, knowing that we are, in all of our journeying, defended by the one who is Light and Love. Of all the characters in *The Great Divorce,* we may be surprised to find that it is Sarah who stays most vividly in our imaginations. She is this strange novel's living embodiment of the hope that the Apostle Paul celebrated, as he joyfully interrupted his intricate discussion of faith, works, the fall, salvation, and warning: "For I am sure that neither death, nor life, nor angels, nor principalities, nor things present, nor things to come, nor powers, nor height, nor depth, nor anything else in all creation, will be able to separate us from the love of God in Christ Jesus our Lord" (Rom 8.38–39). At the sight of splendid Sarah, we are similarly moved to rejoice.

It is the images that stick. In the end, we are left with Sarah's immensity of life lingering in our hopeful minds. This may help us as we turn in our final chapter to what will be for many Lewis's most bracing (and contentious) topic—his treatment of the relation between male and female, and his notion of masculine and feminine within a sacramental universe.

CHAPTER 9

Sacrament and Essence, Masculine and Feminine

(That Hideous Strength and Evdokimov's
Woman and the Salvation of the World)

I approach our final topics with wonder, but also in fear and trembling. We are returning to the depths of *That Hideous Strength,* with the assumption that by going further into this complex narrative, we can also reach further up. Fortunately, in this chapter, we will not be dwelling upon the depths of depravity. Nevertheless, our topics and the related Scriptural texts that illumine them are just as demanding. For we will be considering the disputed matter of sacramentalism and "real being." (I am hopeful that some readers of this study will be Protestant friends, many of whom are usually content to talk more practically about the faith than about mystery.) Before us lies also uncharted territory in the area of what scholars call "theological anthropology"—that is, the theological study of the human being. This study includes the contentious topic of gender, which we must probe in our own twenty-first-century context, where such discussions are dismissed, avoided, or shallowly regarded as already settled.

Since so much of this terrain is very deep or very high, we must rely more on what others have said than on personal experience. Indeed, I myself have fewer answers than questions to share as we track with Lewis (or perhaps resist his ideas) on these matters. And some of the questions that I am compelled to ask will sound a discordant note in our gender-neutral climate. We will be helped in our investigation by searching the Scriptures, by touching on Evdokimov's exploratory work, *Woman and the Salvation of the World,* by recalling our earlier reading of Schmemann's *For the Life of the World,* and by reflecting upon the implications of McFague's celebrated books on metaphorical theology. After these explorations, we will follow the same procedure as the last chapter. That is, we shall attempt to construct some boundaries for our continued thought about the mystery of the human gendered condition, just as the ancient theologians did when they were approaching the mystery of God. Some have said that this question of sexuality is a major one for Christians of our day, alongside the nature of the Church. Our hope, then, is to make a modest start in what may occupy many brothers and sisters during this century. And so, we follow Lewis where even angels fear to tread . . .

Sacraments and Sacramentality

> Let all mortal flesh keep silence,
> And with fear and trembling stand;
> Ponder nothing earthly minded,
> For with blessing in His hand,
> Christ our God to earth descending
> Comes our homage to demand.
>
> King of kings, yet born of Mary,
> As of old on earth He stood,
> Lord of lords, in human vesture,
> In the body and the blood;
> He will give to all the faithful
> His own self for heavenly food.
>
> Rank on rank the host of heaven
> Spreads its vanguard on the way,
> As the Light of light descendeth

> From the realms of endless day,
> Comes the powers of hell to vanquish
> As the darkness clears away.
>
> At His feet the six-winged seraph,
> Cherubim with sleepless eye,
> Veil their faces to the presence,
> As with ceaseless voice they cry:
> Alleluia, Alleluia,
> Alleluia, Lord Most High!

I was not exaggerating about us entering upon holy ground. Gerard Moultrie, the Victorian hymnist, rendered in English poetry this hymn that leads into the eucharistic portion of the Liturgy of St James. (It is also sung in place of the Cherubic Hymn on Great and Holy Saturday.) The prayer depicts the angels *amazed* at the descent of the solid and real Lord of heaven and earth into the earth, into flesh, into hell, and into bread and wine. His condescension serves as another reason for their adoration—that One so great should stoop so low, for love of His earthbound creatures. The angels veil their faces to "the Presence"; it is therefore meet and right for human beings to receive Him with reverence. This is true when we are actually *receiving* the sacrament, and praying (as Orthodox do) that we may be healed, and not harmed, by such divine power. It is also true when we *contemplate* the wonder of His sacramental presence. This is no place for idle curiosity, but for careful thought and reasonable worship (Rom 12.1).

The idea of sacramentality is, of course, larger than a discussion of the sacraments themselves. For example, one Christian poet, who worshipped in a community that did not actually practice the sacraments, luminously described the Christian life in this way: "My life must be Christ's broken bread, my love his outpoured wine."[1] However,

---

[1]Albert Orsborn, officer and poet of the Salvation Army. Song 512 in *The Song Book of the Salvation Army* (Verona, NJ: The Salvation Army National Headquarters, 1987), 142.

when we are dealing with an author's understanding of sacramentality in general, an obvious beginning point would be to discover what he or she thinks about the holy mysteries (the Eucharist). Leanne Payne, an analyst of Lewis and his work, has this to say:

> C. S. Lewis knew and experienced Christianity in its sacramental context. The sacraments of Baptism and Holy Communion were for him not mere symbols of union, but the means by which the Real Presence and the very life of Christ are channeled to believing man. Speaking of the mystery of Holy Communion he said, "Here a hand from the hidden country touches not only my soul but my body. Here the prig, the don, the modern in me have no privilege over the savage or the child. Here is big medicine and strong magic."[2]

Though Lewis was nurtured as a boy in what we might call a "low Anglican" parish, one that would not stress the *mystery*, but only the symbolic *meaning* of the sacraments, it is clear that as an adult he went beyond this approach. His phrase about "big medicine and strong magic," though distasteful to some, clinches the matter. No, he considered baptism and the Eucharist as mysteries—the main means by which God makes an impact upon body as well as soul, the locale where a person's intelligence does not give him or her any deeper insight. Elsewhere, Lewis registers our surprise that God uses created elements such as bread and wine "to put the new life into us."[3] At the Eucharist, he was level with every other participant—at the brink of eternity, with all its joy and all its terror. In speaking to his friends about why he had not written a good deal on the Eucharist, he explained that it was wholly mysterious to him: that neither Western Catholic explanations using

---

[2] *Real Presence: The Holy Spirit in the Works of C. S. Lewis* (Westchester, IL: Cornerstone Books, 1979), 30. Payne is quoting Lewis's *Letters to Malcolm: Chiefly on Prayer* (London: Geoffrey Bles, 1964; London: Collins / Fontana, 1966), 115.

[3] *Mere Christianity*, 62.

Aristotle (that the "accidents," or outward properties, remain bread and wine, while the "substance" or "essence" changes) *nor* Protestant denials of miracle satisfied him. He wished that in the debates of the Church no one had felt it necessary to offer such theories, for at God's presence, we should rather *keep silence*.[4] There is an impermeable nature to the Holy Mysteries, an inexplicability to the way that they work among us, that Lewis says is akin to "magic." He does not mean the magic that attempts to co-opt or manipulate nature, but "magic" that simply presents itself as an inexplicable "brute fact" that has an effect. This is the way God has chosen to work among us. There is a "givenness" to the sacraments that cannot be probed, in his view.[5] His reverent reluctance to either minimize or theorize is utterly congenial to Orthodoxy and the eastern fathers.

Payne describes Lewis's conviction in typical Anglican terms, as "Real Presence," and envisages a downward movement of God "channeling" into our world. Lewis himself avoided such denominational jargon. About the phrase "real presence" I can imagine him quipping, "When we are speaking of God, what other kind of Presence is there?" Further, he spoke as often of humanity being caught up in the divine life as he did of having it infused into us. In *That Hideous Strength,* for example, human beings are *both* visited by Maleldil and his superhuman messengers, *and* they can be assumed into the Presence. At the climax of the story, Ransom is finally transported by divine mystery, like an Enoch or an Elijah. So, then, Lewis himself does not seem to be confined to the lens that Payne uses in trying to describe his views. These criticisms aside, though, she is quite correct in her major point: Lewis refused to speak of the sacraments as "mere symbols" of union. He believed that the bread and wine, and other elements of our created world—for example, human existence as male and female—do not

---

[4]In *Malcolm,* 105, he uses the Latin expression "*Favete linguis*"—"Hold your tongue!"

[5]*Malcolm,* 105–106.

only *point to* mystery, but *participate in and make present* solid realities not normally seen. This, then, is how we can tentatively define the word "sacramental." (Though how does one define something so very mysterious?) Sacramentality is the God-given ability of the physical world to participate in God's life and make it present to us.

Protestants with a "high" view of the sacraments (that is, those who think that they are not merely teaching symbols) tend to limit this sacramental ability to the ordinances that Jesus himself commanded: the Lord's Supper and baptism. Catholics typically enumerate five more (that is, confirmation or chrismation, confession and penance, anointing of the sick, holy orders, and matrimony). However, they also use the term "a sacramental" to designate when God mysteriously acts in material beyond these seven rites. Orthodox stress the two, and sometimes speak specifically of the seven, but they also do not limit or enumerate in a formal way. Instead, they follow the fathers who taught that many things in the world (including bread, wine, water, oil, icons, music, natural beauty, married couples, priests, and humans in general) have been created *for the very purpose of* showing God's glory. As St Irenaeus put it: "For the glory of God is a living man; and the life of man consists in beholding God. For if the manifestation of God which is made by means of the creation, affords life to all living in the earth, much more does that revelation of the Father which comes through the Word, give life to those who see God."[6] The saint follows this logic: even the created order reveals God, and brings life; the truest revelation is seen in the One who is the Word, the very Image of God. One might reverse this and say that for those whose eyes have been opened by the One who shows God's glory (2 Cor 4.6), the whole creation speaks even more eloquently. For those whose eyes have been made whole, the ability of God's creation to glorify God is made even more apparent. With the eyes of Christ, we may therefore extend to other physical objects what St Basil said about the elements of bread and wine in his

[6] *Against Heresies* 4.20.7 (*ANF* 1:489–490).

Divine Liturgy.[7] As well as praying, as we do in St John Chrysostom's Divine Liturgy, that the elements would be *transformed*, we may be informed by the wording of St Basil: "*show these to be* your body and blood. . . ." It is the delight of the Holy Spirit, who indwells all things, to "show these to be" what they were created to be—signposts to his glory, places at which heaven and earth are conjoined.

This the Holy Spirit is free to do, and our eyes are able to see, because the Son has assumed the created nature, and has plunged deep into the matter of this world, going even into its depths. We recall Fr Schmemann's insight that "[t]he world . . . becomes an epiphany of God, a source of his revelation, presence, and power."[8] With regard to the actual sacraments, there is, as Lewis put it, "nowhere else as thin and permeable to divine operation."[9] But, in the hands of the Creator, other places admit of the "veil between the worlds" being removed before our eyes: for God the Son is reconciling heaven and earth.

Some who are practically minded may be concerned at Lewis's use of the term "magic," even qualified, and at what may seem a romantic or sentimental extension of mystery into the created order. I must confess to an immediate connection with Lewis here: it must be the Scots-Irish in us, for we are, as they say, "fay"—prone to see fairies everywhere! I immediately worry about those readers who, like my husband, will snort, and say, like the Mad Hatter in Wonderland: "Don't let's be silly now!" And Lewis himself took pains to bring to his side those who had a more prosaic mind than his own. For example, in the first part of his book *Miracles,* he presents a careful argument pleading that human rationality and morality may be seen as miracles, in the technical sense, because they are observable places where the supernatural has

---

[7]The most common Divine Liturgy used by the Orthodox is that associated with St John Chrysostom. However, the Liturgy of St Basil takes an important part in Orthodox worship, particularly during Great Lent. Besides this, there is also the Liturgy of St James, whose glorious hymn we noticed as we began this discussion of mystery.

[8]*For the Life,* 120.

[9]*Malcolm,* 105.

exceptionally indwelt the created order. But he knows the rhetorical danger of trying to make such an argument: he may lose readers who are not prone to see miracles in common places like the human mind. At the moment that he makes this conclusion, he begs the practical reader not to fling the book away, exasperated that *if this* is what Lewis thinks is a miracle, he or she will not find any answers concerning what we normally call miracles.[10] After all, rationality and morality are a *regular* thing, and miracles are normally considered to be irregular.

Lewis is, of course, especially concerned about the "Grand Miracle," in which God became man, defeated death, and brought the created order to glory. This is the *great* exception. But, once we admit to this great reversal in our world, he goes on to suggest, "We might later find that it was the very nature of Nature to suffer Miracles."[11] It would appear that he wants to have his cake here and eat it, too. We wonder at the resurrection because it is so exceptional. Yet, it is by this exceptional act of God that we can see a deeper relationship between God and the creation—the creation is *made* to show God's grandeur. There is a deep distinction between God and nature: Christians are not pantheists, calling *everything* God. Yet it is not a category error for God to "put on" humanity, since He made us after His image. Indeed, we may suspect that the incarnation, the joining of God with man, was always in the plan, and not simply a response to the ancestral sin. Both, then, are true: God is utterly distinct from His creation; God has joined intimately in the creation through the incarnation, and will never leave it again. The Holy Spirit abides. The Great Union has undone the Great Divorce!

Some may well be irritated by Lewis's enchanted world, or the way in which I have spoken about his Christian pan-sacramentalism ("everything created may take on a sacramental role"). For such readers, I have the following plea. We are *not* letting down our guard against silly sentimentality, like the sixties evangelical hit tune, "Everything's

[10] *Miracles*, 47.
[11] *Miracles*, 47.

a miracle, in its own way. . . ." We are also not devolving into a sub-Christian world of paganism, which sees spirits in every tree, rock, and river, and which domesticates God, tying the divine nature down to the created order. No, neither sentimentality nor paganism is the goal. Rather, we acknowledge that since the Great Miracle (the assumption of humanity by God), everything has changed. And now, without fear of shallow make-believe, and without fear of paganism, we can truly say that "He is everywhere and fills all things." He is not contained by matter; but He does not disdain it, for He did not "disdain the Virgin's womb!"[12] If we are still afraid of sentimentality or magical thinking, let us add to our discussion by quoting Karl Barth: "God may speak to us through Russian Communism, a flute concerto, a blossoming shrub, or a *dead dog.*"[13] The Protestant Barth, of course, was focusing upon God's *speech.* Orthodox (in concert with C. S. Lewis) would respond, "and He can and *does* use the matter of this world to *show Himself* and to *commune* with us." So what about the human gendered condition? Does it speak in any way of who God is? Does it show forth something of His communion with us?

The Sacramental Cosmos and Gender

We have read *That Hideous Strength* for what it can tell us about the demonic attack on human society, and about humanity's participation in the schemes of the enemy. Lewis's most serious task in that novel was to warn us against being complicit with, or subjecting ourselves to an ideology crafted in hell. So he raised his voice against the danger with which human beings are toying when they yield to the pervasive philosophy of subjectivism. They could easily become enslaved to

[12]The Ambrosian hymn *Te Deum* speaks of whole cosmos blessing God, and highlights the humble descent of the Mighty One into our world: "Thou art the King of glory, O Christ. Thou art the everlasting Son of the Father. Thou, having taken upon thee to deliver man, didst not disdain the Virgin's womb. When Thou hadst overcome the sting of death, Thou didst open the kingdom of heaven to all believers."

[13]*Church Dogmatics* I.I, trans. G. W. Bromiley (Edinburgh: T & T Clark, 1975), 55.

themselves, and thus to nature—or, worse than nature, to the demonic. But alongside this clear and present danger we can also see in *That Hideous Strength* (indeed, in all three of these "cosmic" novels) that there is a consistent pattern to Reality. Lewis offers his fictional world as a compelling cosmos where his characters, and unseen beings, live. But clearly he means also to show us the world in which *we* live. As we hear the humans and creatures in this universe speak, and as we overhear Ransom thinking, here is the pattern: the Higher descends to communion with the lower. Those beings who are high have the ability to indwell those things or beings which are lower: that supernatural ability gives the lesser things what we could call, borrowing a Thomistic (and Aristotelian) term, their sacramental "potency," or potential. As Lewis explained in *Miracles*, "We might later find that it was the very nature of Nature to suffer Miracles." Where the supernatural has visited our world, where the traces of God—or even of His angels—remain, the created order "tells the glory of God." Indeed, the whole of reality is, as Lewis describes it in *Perelandra* (*Voyage to Venus*), like a grand dance, or "ball," with its intricate rhythms, beauties, and relations.[14] Some of these interconnections are visible to us, and others are not normally seen. But those mysteries that we can perceive are connected with the unseen realms in deep ways that we can only glimpse.

His protagonist, Ransom, catches a glimpse of these wonders in the first novel, *Out of the Silent Planet*. There, he meets not only different kinds of creatures who are similar in their limitations to human beings, but also *eldila*, creatures surrounded by light, and their head *Oyarsa*. His insight into these wonders is amplified in *Perelandra,* where he hears a description of, and puts before our mind's eye, the cosmic dance. There he converses with the *eldila,* whose speech was "like parts of a music into which [they] had entered as instruments or like a wind blowing through . . . trees that stand together on a hilltop."[15] Their conversation

---

[14] *Perelandra,* 343.
[15] *Perelandra,* 340.

with Ransom and the first parents of Venus takes on the quality of a litany or song of praise, punctuated with the refrain "Blessed be He!" Ransom (and the reader) are drawn into praise by this hymn about the Three-in-One for whom each thing was made, who is at the center and who is with each one of us. For Him and from Him and through Him is this great dance. Participation of the dancers occurs not by equality, but by "giving place . . . receiving it, the small things by their smallness and the great by their greatness, and all the patterns linked and looped together by the unions of a kneeling with a sceptred love."[16] As they chant in joy, we hear about mutuality, the exchange of positions, the importance of each dancer, willing submission, and utter insignificance next to the true Center. Headship and mutuality come together in an unspeakable manner, with the give and take, the structure and flexibility, of a courtly dance.

Alongside the ineffable song of the *eldila*, Ransom also is illumined (and instructs the reader) concerning the great mystery of physical male and female, as an echo or reflection of Masculine and Feminine. In the presence of the perfect King and Queen of Perelandra, he grasps that he has lived his whole life "among shadows and broken images," with an understanding of the male and female that is terribly skewed. He is overwhelmed with the beauty and apt harmony of these two in the flesh, who command respect even from the more powerful *eldila*:

> All was pure daylight. . . . For as the light reached its perfection and settled itself . . . like a lord upon his throne or like wine in a bowl . . . the holy thing, Paradise itself in its two persons, Paradise walking hand in hand, its two bodies shining in the light like emeralds yet not themselves too bright to look at, came in sight. . . . And the gods kneeled and bowed their huge bodies before the small forms of that young King and Queen.[17]

[16] *Perelandra*, 343.
[17] *Perelandra*, 331.

The King and Queen are male and female, both in body and in spirit. Their glory has its origin in the fact that they are reflecting God's image. But it also comes from their perfect echoing, each and together, of masculinity and femininity—a unified wonder not normally seen by the fallen human eye.

Lewis describes bodily and psychic gender as a reflection of something greater. He argues against the idea that the principles of masculinity and femininity are simply a projection of our physically gendered state. It is the opposite. Beyond the human gendered condition, there is something even more solid to which our sexual natures point, and in which we participate—realities of which we can hardly conceive. In this unseen relation of Masculine and Feminine, there is One who is dominant, the Other reflexive and responsive; yet there is also a matching, or a mutuality. We glimpse at Lewis's meaning as we look beyond the Lord and Lady of Perelandra, to the head *eldila* (*Oyéru*). Perelandra, for example, shows the Feminine, and Malacandra the Masculine:

> Malacandra was like rhythm and Perelandra like melody.... [T]he first held in his hand something like a spear, but the hands of the other were open, with the palms towards him.... Gender is a reality, and a more fundamental reality than sex.... Female sex is simply one of the things that have feminine gender; there are many others, and Masculine and Feminine meet us on planes of reality where male and female would simply be meaningless.... [T]he male and female of organic creatures are ... faint and blurred reflections of masculine and feminine.[18]

He does not have in view vague Platonic forms. Rather, he is using the capitalized adjectives (Masculine and Feminine) to gesture at unseen angelic wonders. More than that, he is hinting at the Christian *mystery* unveiled by the apostle in Ephesians 5.32, where Christian marriage is

---

[18] *Perelandra*, 327.

said to be linked to Christ's love for the Church. In another of his writings, Lewis offers this explanation:

> One of the ends for which sex was created was to symbolize to us the hidden things of God. One of the functions of human marriage is to express the nature of the union between Christ and the Church. . . . With the Church, we are farther in: for there we are dealing with male and female not merely as facts of nature but as the live and awful shadows of realities utterly beyond our control and largely beyond our direct knowledge.[19]

Further in! Some who are reading may fear that Lewis is over his head in deep water. For the essay from which I am quoting was written specifically as an argument against ordaining women to the priesthood in the Anglican Church. It is helpful, in reading the whole of this essay, to know that Lewis was in ongoing conversation with Dorothy Sayers about the nature of male and female. She warned him, apparently, that his Bridegroom archetypes may border on Platonist or pagan imagery, and will make no sense to contemporary women. In writing back to her, he hopes that he was able to avoid such dangers in this editorial (which he had already submitted), which calls female ordination into question.[20] We never hear Sayers's response to the actual article.

Certainly there was a difference between Sayers and Lewis on this matter, though Sayers did concede that "it is obviously more dramatically appropriate that a man should be, so to speak, cast for the part [of representing Christ in the Eucharist]."[21] Even those intrigued with Lewis's notion of Masculine and Feminine are discomfited, with Sayers,

---

[19]"Priestesses in the Church?," in *God in the Dock: Essays on Theology and Ethics* (Grand Rapids, MI: Eerdmans, 1970), 238–39. This essay was originally an editorial called "Notes on the Way," in *Tide and Time* 29 (August 14, 1948): 830–31.

[20]We see his side of the correspondence in *Collected Letters*, vol. 2, on pages 860 and 863, and part of hers on page 861.

[21]Dorothy Sayers's July 13, 1948 letter to C. S. Lewis, cited in Barbara Reynolds, *Dorothy L. Sayers: Her Life and Soul* (New York: St. Martin's Press, 1993), 359.

that in *The Cosmic Trilogy* Lewis expresses a somewhat circumscribed notion of the proper domain of men and women. Jane is stalled in her writing of a thesis. The novel finds its resolution in the hope that she will have children, as women are called to do. One wishes that he had affirmed the one calling without denying her the other. However, the richness with which Lewis portrays her character somewhat cuts across the stereotype—clearly, she is anything but subhuman to him, and is a far more complex character than her childish and egotistical husband.

We might also add that, in practical terms, he moved further from a stereotypical notion of male and female by the time that he penned his Narnian *Chronicles* in the fifties, with its young heroes and heroines who all play active roles in the drama. (Even if Susan is not to fight in the battle, except in extreme need.) And his portrayal of Psyche and Orual, also from this later period, is iconoclastic, as we have seen. That development is hardly surprising considering his romance and marriage with Joy.[22] (But I can imagine Lewis shaking his head as I verge upon the personal fallacy.) Perhaps his personal life did not make an impact on his writing in this direct way. Could it have been the reverse: that his growing understanding paved the way for his appreciation of this fine woman?

Yet, in watching Lewis through the decades, it would seem that we are talking about development, not repudiation, or even evolution of his position. In his mature study of Eros in *The Four Loves,* he is indeed very careful to say that though we play specific roles of dominion and yielding in the marriage bed, we are doing so in *play*—*only* God is

[22]Mary Stewart Van Leeuwen probes this development, and makes a good case that Lewis's view on these matters became more nuanced, as he moved from his mother-less adolescence, through his difficult relationship with his adopted mother, Mrs. Janie Moore, to his platonic, then intimate relations with the sparky Joy Davidman. See *A Sword Between the Sexes? C. S. Lewis and the Gender Debate* (Grand Rapids, MI: Brazos, 2010). She also suggests that Lewis's foundational appeal to Masculine and Feminine is limited to his earlier and less enlightened period. However, the presence of these arche-types in one of his last written books, *The Four Loves,* suggests she has played her hand too boldly. In his section on Eros, Lewis speaks both of a "Pagan sacrament" that mar-

worthy to receive complete subjection, or to assert sovereign rule. And, at any rate, God gave His life for the Church: a daunting action for any husband to try to imitate![23] But I believe that the seeds of this mature reflection are to be found also in his pictures of the Perelandran Lady or Jane, who emerge as characters in their own right.

There *are* points, however, in his early stories and in the interchange between characters where Lewis pictures the universe as a *continuous* hierarchy, rather than a more complicated state of affairs, with order and mutuality both in play. This is confirmed in his discussion of 1 Corinthians 11, included in his 1939 essay "Christianity and Literature." There he describes Pauline theology as "a whole series of Head relations running from God to woman . . . and I suppose that of which one is the image and glory is that which one glorifies by copying and imitating."[24] Here, it appears that Lewis partially (and, I would say, unfortunately) agrees with the poet John Milton in his reading of St Paul. The *apostle* does *not* say that woman is created "in the image" of man! Rather, she is the "glory" of man. It is the slipping of the little word "image" (rather than "glory") into the hierarchy that hardens the picture. For if every member is made in the image of the one higher up, as Lewis suggests, then it is indeed a "hierarchical ladder" from "rung to rung"[25]—Father to Son to Man to Woman, etc. Here, he verges on the same error as Milton, who wrote thus about Adam and Eve:

> For contemplation he and valor formed,
> For softness she and sweet attractive grace;
> He for God only, *she for God in him.*[26]

ried couples enact, playing "Sky-Father" and "Earth-Mother," and of the correlation with Christ and the Church. See *The Four Loves* (London: G. Bles, 1960), 106–132.

[23] *The Four Loves,* 119.

[24] "Christianity and Literature," pages 1–11, in *Christian Reflections* (Grand Rapids, MI: Eerdmans 1967), 4–5.

[25] Ibid.

[26] *Paradise Lost,* 4.296–98. My emphasis.

Milton had not noticed that both "male and female" are ascribed God's image in Genesis 1, and that Paul speaks of there being no distinction, "no male and female" in Christ (Galatians 4.6). Women, no less than men, are created directly for God, though the two are, in creation, made to complete each other. It is as though woman has a *double* (and contrasting) iconic function—with all human beings to reflect Christ, but in her relationship with her husband to portray the Church.

Unlike Milton, however, Lewis does not wholly subordinate the Son to the Father, nor rob women of their God-given role as Christ-bearers. Even in this early essay, he attempts to preserve the mysterious tension of hierarchy-*with-mutuality*. There is an *asymmetry* in the relationship (the Father is not the Son, Woman is not the Man) even while each is of equal dignity. This tension is found, also, in his early novels, where there are surprising reversals of the norm: Jane aids in the protection of Mark, rather than vice versa. What saved Lewis from what we may call hierarchal*ism* was his creedal Trinitarian faith—which the poet John Milton did not retain. So, even in the early essay about the "ladder," he also speaks, with astonishment, of the "apparent equivalence of the woman-man . . . relations with the relation between . . . the First and Second Persons of the Trinity."[27] Lewis, despite criticism from some quarters,[28] truly perceived the mystery of the Holy Trinity, and so held

[27]"Christianity and Literature," 5.

[28]See Van Leeuwen, *A Sword,* 72–81, who mistakenly agrees with Kevin Giles and others that the idea of eternal ordering in the relationship of the Son to the Father must always be considered heretical. (Of course, there *is* a heretical subordinationism, seen in Arius and others, which the Church rejected). In her estimation, it was flirtation with this that led Lewis astray in the early years. Rather, I see an orthodox and courageous attempt in Lewis to hold in tension truths about the Trinity not easily resolved by reason—both the headship of the Father (from whom the Son is eternally begotten, and the Spirit eternally proceeds) *and* full worship of the God-Man, equally to be adored with the Father and the Spirit. Van Leeuwen, for her part, seems too enamoured of the so-called Athanasian Creed, which *may* be read as asserting an unqualified "equality" between Father and Son. In the case of both Van Leeuwen and Kevin Giles (*The Trinity and Subordination: The Doctrine of God and the Contemporary Gender Debate* [Downers Grove, IL : IVP, 2002] and *Jesus and the Father: Modern Evangelicals Reinvent the Doctrine*

together the Divine Persons' ordering with their mutuality.[29] And he also embraced St Paul's analogy in 1 Corinthians, that woman is to man as Son is to Father (at least in terms of headship). These two factors— a fully Orthodox grasp of the Holy Trinity, and the recognition that the male-female communion was, in part, a reflection of this—served him well. Eventually, this combination issued in a nuanced and careful understanding of the relation between husband and wife.

So Lewis, from the beginning to the end, insisted that "equality" does not mean "interchangeability":[30] the Father is not the Son, and male is not female. But he was able to create a strong woman such as Orual, the seeds of whose strong character are to be seen in his awestruck representation of the Perelandran Lady, and his tender depiction of Jane Studdock. Though he became more careful in the articulation of this, he retained, right until the end of his life, a view of Masculine and Feminine mysteries in which the human gendered condition participates.[31] For this reason,

of the Trinity [Grand Rapids, MI: Zondervan, 2006]), the controlling issue appears to be women's ordination rather than the full Trinitarian mystery. Reaction does not make for careful theology, or history. If order in the Trinity is decried as heretical, what is to be done with the patristic insistence upon the Father's *monarchy*—his ultimate headship?

[29]Van Leeuwen (*A Sword*, 78) asserts that in a later piece Lewis reversed his position with regard to hierarchy in the Trinity. She does not read him carefully enough. In *The Discarded Image* (Cambridge: Cambridge University Press, 1964), Lewis says that there is a difference between "begetting" and the ancient neo-Platonic philosophers who saw mind and soul as emanating from God, in a kind of "trinity." He does *not* reverse his view of the relation between the Father and the Son—both are God, yet not symmetrical in relations. Nor should he have, if he is to follow in the mainstream of both Orthodox and Catholic thought. As a 2003 statement reminds us: "Both traditions [i.e., the Orthodox Church and the Catholic Church] also clearly affirm that the Father is the primordial source (*archē*) and ultimate cause (*aitia*) of the divine being, and thus of all God's operations: the 'spring' from which both the Son and Spirit flow, the 'root' of their being and fruitfulness, the 'sun' from which their existence and their activity radiates." (North American Orthodox-Catholic Theological Consultation, "The Filioque: A Church-Dividing Issue?: An Agreed Statement" (statement, Washington, DC, October 25, 2003), http://www.usccb.org/beliefs-and-teachings/ecumenical-and-interreligious/ecumenical/orthodox/filioque-church-dividing-issue-english.cfm).

[30]"Priestesses?," 238.

[31]See pages 106–132 of *The Four Loves*.

he insisted that the progressivist (whom he calls the "innovator") should not tamper with these human images: the living metaphors reflect something given, something real, something hidden from human eyes.

These wonders are dramatized for us in *That Hideous Strength,* if sometimes clumsily. The story begins by talking of marriage, and by Jane meditating upon the topic of her thesis, Donne's *Love's Alchymie,* from which Jane ironically quotes, "hope not for minde in women."[32] It is, after all, Jane's mind that will lead her to Ransom's company and help to save Mark. The double trek of Jane and Mark through the troubled landscape of their little part of England also underscores a complex interweaving of roles and gifts. She is seeking by means of her vision; he is hampered by his blindness. Jane's own conversion begins as she uncannily remembers a quotation from a book immediately *before* she finds that very passage lying upon a table in the parlor at St Anne's: "The beauty of the female is the root of joy to the female as well as to the male."[33] Jane's view of female (and human) autonomy is being undone—she is being led to see her responsiveness to Mark as a primary good, as a surprise of creation. And the spiritual operation continues, as she and the Director Ransom talk about obedience and love: equality, though necessary for a just society in the fallen world, is not "the deepest thing."[34] Even with this talk of obedience and headship, there is a thickness, or complexity, and not a rigidity in the suggested picture. With regard to the interchange between male and female, she hears this: "But you see that obedience and rule are more like a dance than a drill—specially between man and woman where the rules are always changing."[35] And finally, the utter Sovereignty of God is invoked. God's authority is a matter of infinitely more importance than the difference between human beings, male and female: "But the masculine

[32] *Hideous,* 358.
[33] *Hideous,* 409. (The precept appears to be Lewis's own making.)
[34] *Hideous,* 501.
[35] *Hideous,* 503.

none of us can escape. What is above and beyond all things is so masculine that we are all feminine in relation to it."[36] Jane (with all of us, including men) must acknowledge that we are, as creatures, *adjectives* and not *nouns* in our own right. Yet God, with our cooperation, will give us faces and solid personhood in the end.[37]

That Hideous Strength, then, moves from setting up the rift between the couple, to tracing their different paths in the action, to questioning Jane's modernist assumptions about her marriage, to envisaging questions and mysteries *beyond* that of marriage. Lewis's ability to include a contemporary dilemma within a larger theological arena is masterful. Here, too, he follows the path of the apostle in 1 Corinthians 11.1–16. There St Paul is tackling the problem of women's attire in the Church when they prophesy or pray. He makes a distinction between male and female, appealing to the created order: woman came from man. He adds complexity to this, though, by saying that they are also interdependent, (verse 11), since all men have come from women since that primordial time. He suggests that there are mysteries beyond the human realm to which this issue is related ("because of the angels"). And he closes by putting everything under the authority of God, since the vertical relationship is most important: "And all things are from God" (verse 12). Lewis matches his insight. Obedience and headship in the human arena are not like a military drill, a hierarchy all the way up and down. Instead, there is a general headship and responsiveness, joined to surprising give and take, dance and steps, dwelling with and making room. One image dominates all of this: that One, who is properly the Head, was content to become low, for our sake.

---

[36] *Hideous,* 680.

[37] *The Problem of Pain* (1940; repr., New York: HarperOne, 2015), 76. In this discussion, Lewis says that we must be "eternally" adjectives. In terms of the distinction between creature and Creator, this is an understandable analogy. I think, though, that he overstates the case here, and elsewhere contradicts himself by describing the theosis of the human being. What else is this but the transformation of an "adjective" into a "noun?"

Place for God

It is Jane, and not Mark, who takes the reader on the adventure of conversion. Chapter fourteen, entitled "Real Life is Meeting," ends with her first direct encounter with God. It is interesting to notice that Lewis here nods at Martin Buber's celebrated book *I and Thou*. Besides telling us that "real life" is "a full and complete meeting,"[38] the Jewish theologian also says things that are reflected in Jane's meeting in the garden with the *Christian* God. He asserts that the *Thou* meets me through grace rather than by seeking.[39] It is God who seeks. He also writes that at this meeting, because of human limitations, there will be "some semblance of suffering." Further, even "the primary word *I-Thou* can be spoken only with the whole being," because I become who I am in relation to God, the Thou. "As I become *I*, I say *Thou*." All this is illustrated in Jane's mysterious encounter,[40] where she learns who she is in relation to God, and comes to accept her place as a treasured creation. The meeting is a beginning for her, but is immediately followed by temptations to draw back, or to idolize the experience rather than have gratitude towards God. Her transformation will not be automatic, though it is provided for by God. Seeing her creaturely "femininity" in relation to the God, the Existing One, is a first step. Readers come to understand the ongoing nature of human transformation as we come to the penultimate scene of the novel, when the *Oyérsu* descend upon St Anne's, transfiguring it with their presence. Lewis's description of these head *eldila* adds texture to the theme of Masculine and Feminine. (I cannot reproduce these here, for such poetic passages must be read and savored in their fullness.) Almost, in the presence of such greatness, we are tempted to worship the *Oyarsa* of Jupiter. But we are warned

[38]Martin Buber, *I and Thou*, trans. Ronald Gregor Smith, First Scribner Classics ed. (1958; New York: Sribner, 2000), 102.
[39]*I and Thou*, 26. This and all the precepts that I repeat here are outlined on p. 26, and the book amplifies them.
[40]*Hideous*, 682–84.

against such idolatry, much as the seer John is told not to bow before the interpreting angel in the book of Revelation. Finally the conclusion comes, with its satisfying pairing of animals and husband-and-wife teams. The exception to the blissful harmony of partners is Ransom, who returns to Deep Heaven: his goal is God alone, rather than mere communion with the *eldila*, or with another human being.

All this is, of course, not intended as strict "theology": we are not intended to supplement the Christian creeds with lore about the *Oyérsu* any more than we are to replace the New Jerusalem with Lewis's bright City in *The Great Divorce,* or accept as dogma the relations between devils in *The Screwtape Letters.* But his main point is utterly serious. He pleads with us to see that gender may well be far more than a matter of animal sexuality. This material world, including our gender, is interconnected with *deeper* realities, in ways that we cannot yet fathom. We will sometimes find him constrained in envisaging roles for men and women—especially in the earlier novels. Yet the caution that he offers regarding the givenness and significance of human sexuality remains timely. For the gender-inclusive "innovators" among us may be meddling with things that we do not understand: Masculinity and Femininity are not, in the end, concepts constructed by the human imagination or by society. The pervasiveness of such symbolism in Scriptures and the Christian tradition is instructive. To a generation brought up on children's books like *The Paper-Bag Princess,* where the heroine does the rescuing of the prince, Lewis poses this question: "Suppose . . . that the mystical marriage were reversed, that the Church were the Bridegroom and Christ the Bride."[41] Well, if we suppose that, Lewis cautions, we have formed a different religion, not kept the Christian faith.

---

[41]"Priestesses?," 237.

About Metaphors

Is metaphor window dressing for an ineffable concept? Or are some metaphors real, living things that partake of the reality? The one who has a sacramental view of the universe would say, yes, they do. Not all metaphors are artistic fancy. For Lewis to take male and female in humanity seriously is similar to insisting that wine and bread become the presence of the Lord in the Eucharist. The creatures are part and parcel of a bigger picture of reality, and may be caught up explicitly into this real world. Paul Evdokimov, in *Woman and Salvation of the World,* is one of the few contemporary theologians who have tried to go beyond the frontier in exploring the deeper meaning of male and female. He types woman as the *stronger* spiritual being in the pair, and suggests a special connection between woman and the Holy Spirit, while man mirrors the Word, or the Son.[42] But both stand in relation to the Father. Going further, because the Father is Himself the ultimate mystery, he insists that "a man does not possess the paternal instinct in the same way as a woman possesses the maternal instinct."[43] His understanding is that the female charism is prophetic, while the male charism is priestly— and both are to give glory to God together. Their life together is also redemptive: "As the Glory of man . . . woman is, in her luminous purity, like a mirror that reflects the man's countenance, reveals it to himself, and thereby corrects it. . . . The prophetic function of woman that is directed toward his being changes him."[44] And he points to the icon screen at the front of the nave, where Mary appears on Christ's right and John the Baptist on Christ's left. Moreover, the female and male are meant to show forth Christ's love for the Church. Thus, human sexuality has multiple functions beyond the biological. Masculinity and

---

[42]Paul Evdokimov, *Woman and the Salvation of the World: A Christian Anthropology on the Charisms of Women,* trans. Anthony P. Gythiel (Yonkers, NY: St. Vladimir's Seminary Press, 1994), 157.

[43]*Woman,* 152.

[44]*Woman,* 258–59.

Femininity are not insignificant features of our human transitory lives, but partake of greater realities than we can hardly imagine.

All this is very different from the way many are teaching and have been taught in the contemporary world. Lewis and Evdokimov may not have everything right. They may sometimes confuse cultural observations with theology, and mix in human imagination with Holy Tradition. But I think they are worth hearing. For they stand against the flat rendering of gender today, and are at least *thinking* about the mystery of who we are as male and female, as human beings. Moreover, who we are, and how we talk about it, are related to our understanding and talk about God Himself.

As Christian people, we claim that something new has happened in the human understanding of God. We have been told, and believe, that God Himself came to dwell among us, and taught us truly if not exhaustively about His own nature, and about how He should be named. Our knowledge about the Father comes not simply from what we know of human fathers, by our own understanding, but by God Himself taking up our human language and teaching us the best way to use it. As the Reformers said, "God 'lisps' His word to us like the parent to an infant." And so, God gives us back our own words about Him, showing the name that is best suited to His nature, and filling in what that name means. It is very instructive that one of the entries in the revised Canadian Anglican hymnbook neutralizes the idea that Jesus has revealed something essential about God in the way that He calls God "Father." Hymn 283, in its optional verse for St Joseph's day is alarming:

All praise, O God, for Joseph, the guardian of your Son.
Who saved him from King Herod, when safety there was none.
He taught the trade of builder, when they to Nazareth came,
And Joseph's love made "Father" to be, for Christ, God's name.[45]

---

[45] *Common Praise* (Toronto: Anglican Book Center, 1998), Hymn 283.

This is, it seems, a nice, domestic picture of Jesus and His father. Yet, look at the assumptions here: Jesus could only understand about God being *like* a father because He had a positive experience of father at home. It was His human experience of father, and that alone, that opened the door to this way of picturing God. What audacity is here! First, there is no indication in Scripture or the Tradition about Jesus' theological development, and how He owed it to His human parents. It is of course most probably true that Jesus' human environment played some part in his thinking: but the self-consciousness of the One who was truly human, but also the Word of God and truly divine, is a mystery far beyond our comprehension. Who are we to assume that Jesus' name for God was born of His own human understanding, and that we can do better, or use richer terminology? When Jesus taught us boldly to say, without condemnation, "Our Father," was this the simple fruit of His environment and upbringing, or was He revealing to us, in fact, opening to us, as His redeemed brothers and sisters, a new way, a true way, of addressing God? Was St Paul simply incorrect when he continued in this tradition, telling us to bow our knees to the Father, because He is the Father of our Lord Jesus Christ?

But role-model theology, made popular by authors such as Sallie McFague, in her influential *Metaphorical Theology* (1982) and *Models of God* (1987), puts a large question mark beside the "Abba" ("my father") language of our Lord. A whole generation of priests and pastors has been brought up intent to repudiate any talk of hierarchy and patriarchy. They have been taught, and pass on by means of sermon and contemporary hymnody, that our talk about God is simply made up of human images. Thus, we are at liberty to change the symbols. Today, our picture of God should avoid gender terms like Father, or use both equally (Father and "Mother"). What Lewis envisaged as a ridiculous extreme in his early essay on priestesses has come to pass, because metaphor is now understood simply as our way of seeking to name the unnameable, mysterious God. As with the subjectivist menace, so with this teaching:

it has become all about how *we* feel. The first threat leads to the abolition of man; the second leads to the abolition of the Christian God—at
least in our memories, for God cannot really be banished. In all this
talk about gendered language, we reach back behind a squabble about
names to root issues. Metaphorical or role-model theology urges us to
"try out new pictures."[46] If we do not, these innovators exclaim, we are
not putting forward descriptions of God most suited for our own day.
The language of God as Father may devolve into idolatry, they caution, because we are mistaking the *language* for the mystery: when we
use language to speak about God, it also communicates what we think
about people.

It is indeed true that language about God is connected with our
language about people. And there are many titles, biblical and traditional, that help us to fill out the picture of our ineffable God, who will
always be greater than we can describe Him. But we also must remember the grand story of the incarnation, in which God moves into our
arena, assuming human language with human nature and showing us
about Himself, as well as about our true human nature. It is primarily a
movement down into our midst, not a human grasping up as we try to
imagine God by mustering as many images as we can find.

How, anyway, does the Bible treat this? We have imagery in the Bible
that speaks of God's Wisdom as feminine, and God's Word as masculine.
But never does the New Testament call the Holy Spirit "She," and the
Christ is always called "He." There is a normative pattern, such as Lewis
has discerned, in the Great Tradition of the Church, beginning with the
Bible. It is within this symbolic sphere that the mystery of marriage (as
we see in Ephesians 5) plays its part. Yet, from time to time there are
surprising reversals. It is helpful to consider the "virtue" (literally, the
"manliness," from the Latin, "*vir*") of the *mother* of the Maccabean mar-
tyrs, so celebrated in Scripture (2 Macc 7; 4 Macc; cf. Heb 11.35) and in

---

[46]Sallie McFague, *Models of God: Theology for an Ecological, Nuclear Age* (Philadelphia:
Fortress Press, 1987), xii.

later hymns. It is helpful to remember that the asymmetrical picture of husband (to love) and wife (to respect) is headed in Ephesians 5.21 by a call to *mutual* submission. Lewis was well aware of this when he spoke of absolute submission as due only to God Himself. Our human headships are nothing in comparison to our common service, our "bowing of the head and subjection of the neck"[47] to Christ, our God. In the end, St Paul's balancing words prove to be a rudder that helps us to sail straight in uncharted territory: "In the Lord, woman is not independent of man nor man of woman; for as woman was made from man, so man is now born of woman. And all things are from God" (1 Cor 11.12). It is not, after all, mainly about us and our positions, but about God, who calls each one of us, and who is Himself the center. He it is who gives each of us our significance.

Further than this I dare not go. I have no full answers. Indeed, I am not sure about the answers suggested by Evdokimov, though I do find it intriguing to consider whether Woman, in her femininity, shows forth the Holy Spirit, and Man shows forth God the Word in his masculinity. If this be so, then I hasten to add that the Holy Spirit is not, in essence, feminine—at least, not in terms of the "theological grammar" suggested by Lewis or the Scriptures. That would be to subordinate the third person of the Trinity, and to import actual gender into God. But certainly the "energies" of the Spirit, the way in which the Spirit works, are frequently described in terms that we consider to be feminine—bringing to birth (cf. Rom 8.26), indwelling, comforting, and the like. Moreover, if the male specifically shows forth Christ, so too does the female, by virtue of her baptism and chrismation. This is a complex state of affairs, with common, distinct, and overlapping iconic functions of male, female, male and female together, and the particular person. We are interconnected with God and the unseen world in mul-

---

[47]These words come from the "Prayer of Inclination" in the vespers service, when Orthodox worshippers everywhere physically bow their heads before Christ, and entreat Him for protection.

tiple personal and corporate ways, much as an interval takes its various places in a musical piece, showing different aspects of the melody or the harmony by its placement.

It is not a good idea, I think, to plead "mystery!" too quickly, as a means of halting a discussion. Sandals must be removed when we are on holy ground, but God does welcome us, and sometimes invites us to come closer. Because of the current crisis in understanding human identity, more dispassionate thought on gender and our common humanity is required. We must not allow political and social pressures to control our forays into this mystery, but they may be an important catalyst. Consider how the Church articulated its teachings with greater precision when it was forced to think about the nature of the God–Man because of the heresies of the past. My hope is that we will similarly come to more clarity about this wonderful mystery of human nature because of the challenges of feminist and sociological gender studies.

Contemporary Catholics like Dorothy Sayers, as well as Metropolitan Kallistos Ware, who in other respects cleave to the Tradition, have said that they see no *theological* reasons for retaining the tradition of ordaining males only to the priesthood. This may be true, if we take "theological" in the very narrow definition as "talk about God." But why is it that the Bible, while it sometimes uses the feminine imagery for a God who transcends human sexuality, never *addresses* God in feminine terms? (God is compared to a mother bear, a mother eagle, a nursing mother, a midwife helping a woman in childbirth, but is never actually *called* these. He *is* called "Father.") And does this clue lead us to wonder if there are reasons for the tradition that we can glean from theological *anthropology*—a careful study of who we are as human beings? Sayers herself gestured, as we saw, at the particular iconic suitability of a male at the altar. Susanne Heine astutely amplifies this. She comments that if it is a man serving at table, this shows the great humility of the Christ who became least for us:

A woman could not represent the humiliated because she herself is already where these people are. It makes a difference whether we are already with others in the same boat or whether we voluntarily get into the boat out of love. Therefore, God, who does not sit with us in the boat, comes to us in the boat. Jesus the man turns things upside down. Jesa the woman would always have been at the bottom.[48]

Heine's argument is, of course, practical. But what if there is reason to think, as do Lewis and Evdokimov, that the asymmetry of male-female relations is not simply a cultural matter, but something given? What if Jesus' appearance as a male who gave up prerogative is the human echo of something far more profound about God? What if the sociological reasons to which Ware and Sayers allude might in this way be enriched by theological ones? After all, human beings, male and female, together and singly *speak of* or *show forth* God simply by who they are. This is the challenge that Lewis poses to us, independently of the question concerning which specific roles or actions women and men may or may not live lawfully live out in the Church.

My own impression is that it is not a particular understanding of male priesthood, but lay apathy and the clericalism of the Church that has done the most damage to women (and lay men). And it is not simply a matter of clergy seeking power, but of laypeople happily relegating *so large* a domain (beyond service at the altar) to the already overburdened clergy. Women and lay men, too, are called to ministry, and given numerous gifts for that purpose. The current restriction of *service* in many quarters can be remedied without a new theology of ordination that would admit women to serve at the altar as "priests." Even if this delegation of tasks were to happen, however, the questions being asked by our feminist friends compel us to think more deeply. I pray that the

[48]Susanne Heine, *Matriarchs, Goddesses, and Images of God: A Critique of Feminist Theology*, trans John Bowden. (Minneapolis, MN: Augsburg, 1989), 139–41.

debates of the day over this issue result in deeper thinking, just as they did in the patristic eras. Before us is this question: is the tradition concerning ordination arbitrary, or has Lewis, however roughly, sketched something of ultimate importance that concerns each of us, and all of us together, when he speaks about gendered language and the relation between male and female, masculinity and femininity?

Boundaries in the Wilds

Let us close our particular study—though not the debate—with some boundaries that I have found helpful, and that I hope may guide future discussion that we must pursue together as the Church. I hope that I am simply illumining boundaries that may be found clearly in Scripture or the Tradition, and not erecting jerry-rigged fences by myself. These are meant to mark off the danger points for further sane excursions, showing where some have stepped off a cliff or disappeared in the quicksand.

- We cannot say that all symbols are merely human expressions, and that language and action are detachable from the reality to which they point.

- We cannot say that gendered language is expendable in talking about God or humanity.

- We cannot say that there is an absolutely confined role for each gender—reversals are part of our story.

- We cannot say that the relations of Father, Son, and Spirit are symmetrical, nor can we say that they are not mutual and equal.

- We cannot say that the relations of husband and wife are totally symmetrical, nor ought we say that there is no mutuality or equality.

- We cannot say that there are no "higher" gifts and no "lesser" gifts—but all are necessary, and the higher need the lower, so that sometimes it is impossible to discern which is more important.

- In God-talk, we cannot forbid the use of feminine imagery, for the Bible uses it.

- In God-talk, we cannot ignore the usual or normative use of masculine language, even it it is uncomfortable to us.

These, I think, give us some parameters, both guarding us from danger and recognizing the mystery. They recognize that God is disclosing to us, at least partially, a mystery about Himself and us, as we live in our families, in the Church, and in Christ. I believe that, though he sometimes irritates with stereotypes, we are indebted to our leader Lewis for venturing into this quagmire. He fastens our eyes upon the contemporary debate concerning gender and spirituality by his astonishing use of symbol, and does not let us rest with easy answers. If we follow him, we will not think mistakenly that gendered symbols are arbitrary and infinitely malleable. Instead, he opens up Scripture's world of metaphors, showing how they may be inextricably intertwined with reality. These mysteries we must guard, but also probe, for we want both to remain in Christ and also to learn more and more of Him.

Full Circle at Journey's "End"

In our study, it appears that we have come full circle, but with our return at a higher level of the spiral. We began by adopting Lewis as our very own Reepicheep, and listening to the serious things that he has to say about the magic of reading and writing, and how these are related to a deeper and higher Reality than we can even imagine. In the first part, we followed him as, with children, he explored the possibility of "sub-creation," an activity in which we engage because we bear the image of the Creator, and because creation itself shows forth the glory of God. This led us to consider his "worldview"—a word he surely would have detested, because it may be taken to suggest that all knowledge is perspectival *only*. There we saw why the Great Miracle is so central to our grasp of this world, and to our understanding of God. And there we had our customary self-centered questions about reality redirected, so that we gaze upon the One Who Is, the Holy One. God has given Himself to us, as well as the creation.

Our second exploration into arduous places led us into a difficult analysis concerning how we think and how we should live. In his allegorical writing and his essays on subjectivism, Lewis suggests to us what he thinks he has already learned about the path before us. But in his mythological writing, he tries to render for us what he does not yet fully know. So we moved from the hard work put forward by *The Abolition of Man* and *The Pilgrim's Regress* to the wonder and challenge of *Till We Have Faces.* The problem of God's justice, the challenges of ascesis, the deep truths of the atonement, and the hope of theosis sweep us away. It is as though Lewis becomes the interpreter of a vision for us. Yet the interpretation leaves us with questions as well as supplying satisfying and surprising answers. We find ourselves trying to "sort the seeds" with Psyche, but filled with hope for a meeting with the One who is Love.

In the third section, we pursued Lewis, sometimes panting, by means of *That Hideous Strength* and *The Great Divorce,* to places that are manifestly not safe. Yet, God is there with us in the heights and the depths. There is nothing He has not plumbed, and nowhere higher than the heavens where He, having ascended, pleads on our behalf. Depravity and possession, final blessings and curses, and the sacramental nature of the universe are seemingly beyond our theological and human pay grade. But they are topics broached by God himself, in communion with His people. Where He has gone, we must follow, warned by Lewis that we may well not go *very* far in these lands, for our feet are not yet solid enough to get a solid purchase there. Rather than simply rehearsing and taking a side in the culture wars, we deeply reflected upon the nature of male and female. And we found ourselves back at Lewis's starting point—how symbols and images can say best what's to be said of mystery. By means of Sarah and Jane, Ike and Mark, he *shows* (rather than tells of) how our life's decisions are momentous. He also reminds us of the tenderness and insistence of God's reach to us when we would rather not follow. If we make our bed in hell, or fly to the highest heights, there is He, both rescuing us and encouraging us. Our fall can be low, but God is deeper. The stakes are high, but God is higher.

As is sometimes the case with human beings created in the image of God, we frequently find Lewis to be like an open window, allowing a means of conversation not only with himself, but with the Creator. Lewis's sub-creative verve, faithfulness, and subtlety are, in the end, self-effacing. It is the images, rather than his own prowess, that remain in our imaginations. These images point us to the Holy One, the One who plumbed heights and depths for love of us. It is not because Lewis's words and images are luminous in their own right, but because their light is a borrowed one, that he makes an exemplary guide. And all the while he gives us reason to give thanks for the divine Pioneer, whose heavenly calling we have been enabled to hear better by heeding the advice of Lewis, a more seasoned explorer.

> With the drawing of this Love and the voice of this Calling
> We shall not cease from exploration
> And the end of all our exploring
> Will be to arrive where we started
> And know the place for the first time.[49]

If Lewis's luminous writings can, in the end, part like clouds, becoming a frame by which we can glimpse, perhaps for just a moment, the

[49] T. S. Eliot, "Little Gidding," in *Four Quartets* (1943; repr. Orlando, FL: Harcourt, 1971), 59. This is the fourth of his *Four Quartets*.

Son (who has always been with us!) then he would be content. The journey has been long, and yet the travelling has just begun. For our joyful yearning for this Holy One grows, nourished by fellow pilgrims like C. S. Lewis.

Come down, O love divine,
seek thou this soul of mine,
and visit it with thine own ardor glowing;
O Comforter, draw near,
within my heart appear,
and kindle it, thy holy flame bestowing.

O let it freely burn,
till earthly passions turn
to dust and ashes in its heat consuming;
and let thy glorious light
shine ever on my sight,
and clothe me round, the while my path illuming.

Let holy charity
mine outward vesture be,
and lowliness become mine inner clothing;
true lowliness of heart,
which takes the humbler part,
and o'er its own shortcomings weeps with loathing.

And so the yearning strong,
with which the soul will long,
shall far outpass the power of human telling;
for none can guess its grace,
till Love create a place
wherein the Holy Spirit makes a dwelling.[50]

[50]This fifteenth century hymn, originally written in Latin by Bianco da Siena, was translated by Richard Frederick Littledale, Jr. in 1867.

Pentecost, the descent of the Holy Spirit
(Kirillo-Belozersk Monastery, c. 1497)

Bibliography

Abbreviations used in the text (for patristic works)

ANF   *The Ante-Nicene Fathers.* Edited by Alexander Roberts and James Donaldson. 10 vols. Buffalo, 1885–1896. Reprint, Peabody, MA: Hendrickson, 1994.

NPNF[1]   *The Nicene and Post-Nicene Fathers, Series 1.* Edited by Philip Schaff. 14 vols. New York, 1886–1889. Reprint, Peabody, MA: Hendrickson, 1994.

NPNF[2]   *The Nicene and Post-Nicene Fathers, Series 2.* Edited by Philip Schaff and Henry Wace. 14 vols. New York, 1890. Reprint, Peabody, MA: Hendrickson, 1994.

PG   Patrologia Graeca [= Patrologiae cursus completes: Series graeca]. Edited by J.-P. Migne. 162 vols. Paris, 1857–1866.

Bibliography of modern works

Anglican Church of Canada. *Common Praise.* Toronto: Anglican Book Center, 1998.

Auerbach, Erich. *Mimesis: The Representation of Reality in Western Literature.* Translated by Willard R. Trask. Princeton, NJ: Princeton University Press, 1953. First published 1946 by A. Francke Verlag.

Aulén, Gustav. *Christus Victor: An Historical Study of the Three Main Types of the Atonement.* New York, NY: Macmillan, 1969.

Balthasar, Hans Urs von. *Dare We Hope "That All Men Be Saved"? With a Short Discourse on Hell.* Translated by David Kipp and Lothar Krauth. San Francisco, CA: Ignatius Press, 1988. First published in German in 1986 and 1987, respectively.

Barth, Karl. *Church Dogmatics* 1.1. Translated by G. W. Bromiley. Edinburgh: T & T Clark, 1975. First English translation by G. T. Thompson in 1936.

Baynes, Leslie. "C. S. Lewis's Use of Scripture in the Liar, Lunatic, or Lord Argument." *Journal for Inklings Studies* 4, no. 2 (2014): 27–66.

Bell, Rob. *Love Wins: A Book about Heaven, Hell, and The Fate of Every Person Who Ever Existed.* New York, NY: HarperOne, 2011.

Buber, Martin. *I and Thou.* Translated by Ronald Gregor Smith. First Scribner Classics edition. New York, NY: Scribner, 2000. First published 1958 by Scribner.

Bultmann, Rudolf. *The New Testament and Mythology and Other Basic Writings.* Translated and edited by Schubert M. Ogden. Philadelphia, PA: Fortress, 1984.

Caird, G. B. *The Language and Imagery of the Bible.* London: Duckworth and Co., 1980.

Caland, Fabienne Claire. "Le mythos spermatikos." In *Horizons du mythe*, edited by Denise Brassard and Fabienne Claire Caland, 7–32. Montreal: Cahiers du CELAT, 2007.

Calvin, John. *Institutes of the Christian Religion.* Translated by Elsie Anne McKee. Grand Rapids, MI: Eerdmans, 2009. First published in Latin in 1536 and in French in 1541.

Conn, Marie A. *C. S. Lewis and Human Suffering: Light Among the Shadows.* Mahwah, NJ: Hidden Spring, 2008.

Craigie, Peter. *The Problem of War in the Old Testament.* Grand Rapids, MI: Eerdmans, 1978.

Edwards, Jonathan. *Sinners in the Hands of an Angry God: A Sermon Preached at Enfield, July 8th 1741, at a Time of Great Awakenings; and Attended with Remarkable Impressions on many of the Hearers.* Boston, MA: S. Kneeland and T. Green, 1741.

Eliot, T. S. "Little Gidding." In *Four Quartets*, 49–59. 1943. Reprint, Orlando, FL: Harcourt, 1971.

———. "Tradition and the Individual Talent." *The Egoist* 6, no. 4 (September 1919): 54–55.

Evdokimov, Paul. *Woman and the Salvation of the World: A Christian Anthropology on the Charisms of Women.* Translated by Anthony P. Gythiel. Yonkers, NY: St. Vladimir's Seminary Press, 1994.

Giles, Kevin. *Jesus and the Father: Modern Evangelicals Reinvent the Doctrine of the Trinity.* Grand Rapids, MI: Zondervan, 2006.

———. *The Trinity and Subordination: the Doctrine of God and the Contemporary Gender Debate.* Downers Grove, IL : IVP, 2002.

Goethe, Johann Wolfgang von. "Food in Travel" [1807]. In *The Poems of Goethe, Translated in the Original Metres*, translated by E. A. Bowring, 281. London: Parker and Sons, 1853.

Goggins, Phillip. "The Abolition of Man: C. S. Lewis' Defense of Objective Morality." *Response* (web magazine). Seattle Pacific University, Fall 2000. Accessed July 15, 2016. https://spu.edu/depts/uc/response/fall2k/abolition.html.

Green, Roger Lancelyn. *The Land of the Lord High Tiger*. London: G. Bell & Sons, 1958.

Gregory of Nazianzus. *Festal Orations*. Translated by Nonna Verna Harrison. Popular Patristics Series 36. Crestwood, NY: St Vladimir's Seminary Press, 2008.

Heine, Susanne. *Matriarchs, Goddesses, and Images of God: A Critique of Feminist Theology*. Translated by John Bowden. Minneapolis, MN: Augsburg, 1989.

Himmelfarb, Martha. *Tours of Hell: An Apocalyptic Form in Jewish and Christian Literature*. Philadelphia, PA: University of Pennsylvania Press, 1983.

Hooker, Morna. "On Using the Wrong Tool." *Theology* 75 (1972): 570–81.

Hopko, Thomas. "The Abolition of Man." *Speaking the Truth in Love* (podcast). Ancient Faith Radio, August 2, 2011. http://www.ancientfaith.com/podcasts/hopko/recommended_reading_from_fr._ tom_hopko.

––––––. "Recommended Reading from Fr. Tom Hopko." *Speaking the Truth in Love* (podcast). Ancient Faith Radio, April 4, 2011. http://www.ancientfaith.com/podcasts/hopko/recommended_reading_from_fr._ tom_hopko.

Kilby, Clyde S. *The Christian World of C. S. Lewis*. Grand Rapids, MI: Eerdmans, 1964.

Kreeft, Peter. *C. S. Lewis for the Third Millennium*. San Francisco, CA: Ignatius Press, 1994.

Leeuwen, Mary Stewart Van. *A Sword Between the Sexes? C. S. Lewis and the Gender Debate*. Grand Rapids, MI: Brazos, 2010.

Lewis, C. S. *The Abolition of Man: Or, Reflections on Education with Special Reference to the Teaching of English in the Upper Forms of Schools*. New York: HarperOne, 2001. First published 1944 by Oxford University Press.

––––––. "Christianity and Culture." In *Christian Reflections*, edited by Walter Hooper, 12–36. Grand Rapids, MI: Eerdmans, 1967.

––––––. "Christianity and Literature." In *Christian Reflections*, edited by Walter Hooper, 1–11. Grand Rapids, MI: Eerdmans, 1967.

––––––. *The Discarded Image: An Introduction to Medieval and Renaissance Literature*. 1964. Reprint, Cambridge: Cambridge University Press, 2002.

––––––. *An Experiment in Criticism*. 1961. Reprint, Cambridge: Cambridge University Press, 1988.

_____."The Fall of Man." Chapter 5 in *The Problem of Pain*, 63–85. New York, NY: HarperCollins, 2001. First published 1940 by Centenary Press.

_____. "Footnote to All Prayers." In *Poems*, edited by Walter Hooper, 129. New York, NY: Harcourt Brace Jovanovich, 1977. First published 1964 by Geoffrey Bles.

_____. *The Four Loves*. London: Geoffrey Bles, 1960.

_____. *The Great Divorce*. Glasgow: Collins / Fontana, 1972. First published 1946 by Geoffrey Bles.

_____."It All Began With A Picture ... " In *Of This and Other Worlds*, edited by Walter Hooper, 78–79. London: Collins, 1982.

_____. *The Last Battle*. In *The Chronicles of Narnia*. New York, NY: HarperEntertainment, 2005. First published 1956 by Bodley Head.

_____. *Letters To Malcolm: Chiefly on Prayer*. London: Collins / Fontana, 1966. First published 1964 by Geoffrey Bles.

_____. *The Lion, the Witch and the Wardrobe*. In *The Chronicles of Narnia*. New York, NY: HarperEntertainment, 2005. First published 1950 by Geoffrey Bles.

_____. *The Magician's Nephew*. In *The Chronicles of Narnia*. New York, NY: HarperEntertainment, 2005. First published 1955 by Bodley Head.

_____. *Mere Christianity*. Glasgow: Collins Fount Paperbacks, 1984. *Mere Christianity* was first published by Macmillan as three books: *The Case for Christianity* (aka *Broadcast Talks*), 1942; *Christian Behavior*, 1943; *Beyond Personality*, 1944.

_____. *Miracles: A Preliminary Study*. London: Collins / Fontana, 1974; New York, NY: HarperOne, 1974. First published 1947 by Macmillan.Lewis, C. S. "Modern Theology and Biblical Criticism." In *Christian Reflections*, edited by Walter Hooper, 152–66. Grand Rapids, MI: Eerdmans, 1967.

_____. *Narnia, Cambridge and Joy, 1950–1963*. Vol. 3 of *The Collected Letters of C. S. Lewis*, edited by Walter Hooper. San Francisco, CA: HarperSanFrancisco, 2007.

_____. Preface to *On the Incarnation*, by Athanasius of Alexandria, 11–18. Translated by John Behr. Popular Patristics Series 44a. Yonkers, NY: St Vladimir's Seminary Press, 2011. The preface was first published in *The Incarnation of the Word of God*, by Athanasius of Alexandria, trans. Sr Penelope (London: Geoffrey Bles, 1944).

_____. "On Three Ways of Writing For Children." In *On Stories: And Other Essays On Literature*, edited by Walter Hooper, 31–43. Orlando, FL: Harcourt, 1982.

_____. *Out of the Silent Planet.* In *The Cosmic Trilogy.* London: Bodley Head, 1990. First published separately in 1938 by Bodley Head.

_____. *Perelandra.* In *The Cosmic Trilogy.* London: Bodley Head, 1999. First published separately in 1943 by Bodley Head.

_____. "The Personal Heresy in Criticism." *Essays and Studies by Members of the English Association* 19 (1934): 7–28.

_____. *Pilgrim's Regress.* Edited by David C. Downing. Wade Annotated edition. Grand Rapids, MI: Eerdmans, 2014.

_____. *The Pilgrim's Regress.* Glasgow: Collins, 1977. First published 1933 by J. M. Dent & Sons.

_____. *A Preface to Paradise Lost.* New York, NY: Oxford University Press / Galaxy Books, 1961. First published 1942 by Oxford University Press.

_____. "Priestesses in the Church?" In *God in the Dock: Essays on Theology and Ethics*, edited by Walter Hooper, 238–9. Grand Rapids, MI: Eerdmans, 1970. Originally published as "Notes on the Way," in *Time and Tide* 29 (August 14, 1948): 830–31.

_____. *The Problem of Pain.* New York: HarperOne, 2015. First published 1940 by Centenary Press.

_____. *Reflections on the Psalms.* 1958. Reprint, San Diego, CA: Harcourt, 1986.

_____. "Religion: Reality or Substitute." In *Christian Reflections*, edited by Walter Hooper, 37–43. Grand Rapids, MI: Eerdmans, 1967.

_____. *The Silver Chair.* In *The Chronicles of Narnia.* New York, NY: Harper-Entertainment, 2005. First published 1953 by Geoffrey Bles.

_____. "Sometimes Fairy Stories May Say Best What's to be Said," pages 45–48 in *On Stories: And Other Essays On Literature*, edited by Walter Hooper, 45–48. Orlando, FL: Harcourt, 1982. First published November 18, 1956 in the *New York Times.*

_____. *That Hideous Strength.* In *The Cosmic Trilogy.* London: Bodley Head, 1990. First published separately in 1945 by Bodley Head.

_____. *Till We Have Faces: A Myth Retold.* Grand Rapids, MI: Eerdmans, 1966. First published 1956 by Geoffrey Bles.

_____. *The Voyage of the Dawn Treader.* In *The Chronicles of Narnia.* New York, NY: HarperEntertainment, 2005. First published 1952 by Geoffrey Bles.

_____. "The Weight of Glory." In *The Weight of Glory and Other Addresses*, 1–19. 1949. Reprint, New York, NY: Macmillan, 1980.

Lindskoog, Kathryn Ann. *Surprised by C. S. Lewis, George MacDonald and Dante.* Macon, GA: Mercer University Press, 2001.

_____. *Finding the Landlord: A Guidebook to C. S. Lewis's Pilgrim's Regress*. Chicago, IL: Cornerstone Press, 1995.

Macaulay, Rose. *Letters to a Sister*. Edited by Constance Babington Smith. London: Collins, 1946.

McFague, Sallie. *Metaphorical Theology: Models of God in Religious Language*. Philadelphia, PA: Fortress Press, 1984

_____. *Models of God: Theology for an Ecological, Nuclear Age*. Philadelphia, PA: Fortress Press, 1987.

Middleton, J. Richard and Walsh, Brian J. *Truth Is Stranger Than It Used to Be*. Downer's Grove, IL, InterVarsity Press, 1995.

Milton, John. *Paradise Lost*. 2nd edition. London: S. Simmons.

North American Orthodox-Catholic Theological Consultation. "The Filioque: A Church-Dividing Issue?: An Agreed Statement" Statement. Washington, DC, October 25, 2003. http://www.usccb.org/beliefs-and-teachings/ ecumenical-and-interreligious/ecumenical/orthodox/filioque-church-dividing-issue-english.cfm.

O'Brien, Michael D. *The Island of the World: A Novel*. San Francisco, CA: Ignatius Press, 2007.

Payne, Leanne. *Real Presence: The Holy Spirit in the Works of C. S. Lewis*. Westchester, IL: Cornerstone Books, 1979.

Reynolds, Barbara. *Dorothy L. Sayers: Her Life and Soul*. New York, NY: St. Martin's Press, 1993.

Salvation Army. *The Song Book of the Salvation Army*. Verona, NJ: The Salvation Army National Headquarters, 1987.

Schmemann, Alexander. *For the Life of the World*. 2nd revised edition. Crestwood, NY: St. Vladimir's Press, 1973.

Schüssler Fiorenza, Elisabeth. *Rhetoric and Ethic: The Politics of Biblical Studies*. Minneapolis, MN: Fortress Press, 1999.

"Sinners in the Hands of an Angry God (1741): Introduction." Jonathan Edwards Center at Yale University. Accessed May 21, 2017. http://edwards. yale.edu/research/major-works/sinners-in-the-hands-of-an-angry-god.

Smilde, Arend. "What Lewis Really Did to Miracles." *Journal of Inklings Studies* 1, no. 2 (October 2011): 9–24. http://www.lewisiana.nl/anscombe/

Thiede, Carsten Peter. "'By Prayer and Fasting.'" *Tyndale Society Journal* 13 (August 1999): 17–23. http://www.tyndale.org/tsj13/thiede.html.

Tolkien, J. R. R. *The Lord of the Rings*. 3 vols. London: Allen & Unwin, 1954–5.

Vanauken, Sheldon. *A Severe Mercy*. San Francisco, CA: Harper & Row, 1977.

Minor Indices

2. Index of liturgical texts and hymns

3. Index of names

Subject Index

Abolition of Man, The, 99–111, 120, 273
    and *Hideous,* 188–189, 201, 212
    and *Regress,* 111–113
    and *Sinners,* 206
    (as phrase) and subjectivism, 267
Adam
    creation of, 48, 52
    death through, 160, 162, 236
    first and second, 59, 160–162, 239,
        239n36
    humans as sons of, 53–54, 59, 67, 95
Adam and Eve
    God with, 90
    humans as sons and daughters of, 95
    Milton on, 257
    redemption of, 91, 166 (illust.)
    represented in Narnia, 49
"An Experiment in Criticism," 35–38
ancestral sin, 236, 250
    as "original guilt," 124
    mortality due to Adam's, 54, 160, 239
Andrew (*Chronicles*). *See* Uncle Andrew
        (*Chronicles*)
angel
    in Daniel, 44, 222
    in Revelation, 263
angels
    fallen, 188
    glorifying God, 26, 42, 44, 154, 245
    in *Hideous,* 191
    reason shared with, 105
    See also *eldila*
anger. *See* wrath
Anglican Church
    ecclesiology of, 23n9

Lewis as layman in, 16, 19, 20, 247, 255
Lewis on issues in, 76–78, 255
liturgical texts of, 41, 49, 265
Anscombe, Elizabeth, 73, 83–84
Apocalypse
    of John, 211, 216, 228
    of Peter, 216–7
    See also eschatology
Aravis (*Chronicles*), 62
ascension
    after descending, 91, 96, 235, 240
    and *Chronicles,* 60
    Jesus', 81–82, 95–96
ascesis
    benefits and dangers of, 139–146
    Christian, 115, 135–7, 138–9, 180n44
    in *Faces,* 139, 142, 144–5, 149
    personhood and, 132–7
asceticism. *See* ascesis
Aslan (*Chronicles*), 13, 80, 94
    in *Dawn,* 15
    in *Last,* 15
    in *Lion,* 28–30, 39
    in *Magician's,* 46, 48, 50–56, 58–60
    in *Silver,* 61, 64–67, 69–70;
assumption of humanity by God, 153,
        251. *See also* incarnation, the
Athanasius of Alexandria, Saint, 157,
        213n1
    as influence on Lewis, 19, 89, 92n29
    The Life of Antony, 138–39
    On the Incarnation, 176–79
atonement
    and divine justice, 171, 173
    by victory, 165–171, 173, 177, 181, 236

289

of St James, 245, 249n7
of St John Chrysostom, 249
dragon(s)
    in *Chronicles*, 61
    in *Regress*, 114–15
    in Revelation, 210–11
    spiritual, 188

Eastern Christianity. *See* Orthodox
        Church
ecclesiology, 22–23n9. *See also* Church,
        the; Mother Kirk (*Regress*)
Edmund Pevensie. *See* Pevensie, Edmund
        (*Chronicles*)
Edwards, Jonathan, 185–87, 206
eldila, 190, 208, 252–54, 262–63. *See also*
        angels
Elijah (prophet), 94, 225, 247
Eliot, T. S., 21–22, 274
Emmaus, 64
energies of the Spirit, 268
England
    in *Chronicles*, 53, 65, 66, 67
    in *Hideous*, 200, 260
    like Narnia, 50
Epicureanism, 113, 125, 131
epiphany of God, 69, 249
eros, 256. See also *Four Loves, The*
eschatology, 210, 213–4. *See also*
        Apocalypse
essence, 247
ethics
    acting ethically, 120–21, 179
    Christian, 100, 102, 110
    objective truth in, 188
    power over, 109
    relativistic, 112
    "Situation," 108
    as "supernature," 86
Eucharist, 96n32, 160, 168, 245–46, 255,
        264
Eustace (*Chronicles*), 61–63, 70, 142
Evagrius, Saint, 57

evangelicalism, 107, 250, 258–59n28
Evdokimov, Paul, 243–44, 264–65, 268,
        270
evil, 54, 56–58, 60
    from outside, 210–12
    in *Cosmic*, 187–91
    in *Hideous*, 187, 194, 201–213
    introduced to creation, 49, 50, 55
    as privation of good, 213, 218
    response to, 123–25
    within, 212–21
    See also depravity; theodicy

faith
    Lewis on, 30
    and faithfulness, 117–19
    and justification, 162, 180n44
    importance of, 99, 119
    and theodicy, 124
    in *Regress*, 113
faithfulness
    Nietzsche on, 116
    of God, 123–24
    See also faith: and faithfulness
Fall, the, 50, 90, 124, 229–230n22, 242
Fantasia (Disney film), 39–40
fantasy
    in Lewis's writing, 20, 100, 220
    in *The Matrix*, 27
    in myth, 36
    popularity of, 104
    Puritan disapproval of, 31–32
Father, the
    and atonement, 162, 167n20
    and gendered language, 265–67, 269
    headship of, 257–59, 264, 271
    image of, 86
    as person of the Trinity, 128, 180, 194
    revealed in the Son, 34, 48, 178, 248,
        265–67
    working through the Son, 96, 177, 207
fear (before the Divine)
    in *Faces*, 129, 163–164

in *Regress*, 114
of God, 67, 94, 154, 185, 244
See also awe
female, the. *See* woman. *See also*
      Feminine, the; male and female
Feminine, the, 253–255, 256n22, 259,
      261–62 , 265, 271
and imagery for God, 267–69
See also gender
"Fern-seed and Elephants." *See* "Modern
      Theology and Biblical Criticism"
form criticism, 80
Four Loves, The, 256–57, 259n31
freedom
  enslavement and, 212–13, 227–31, 233,
      234
  as keyword in modern criticism, 33
  in relation to God's sovereignty, 52,
      238
  self-determining, 75
  and submission, 53, 58, 218
  through self-sacrifice, 149, 229
Freud, Sigmund, 113
  Freudian projections, 22

gender, 243–44
  in language for God, 17n3, 266–69,
      271–72
  as reflection of greater reality, 254, 263,
      265, 271–72
  the sacramental cosmos and, 251–61
  See also Feminine, the; male and
      female; male-female relations;
      man; Masculine, the; woman
Glome (*Faces*), 126, 132, 145, 168
glory
  beholding God's, 130, 225
  the cross as God's, 93
  future, 94, 228
  humans called to, 49, 120, 147, 177, 187,
      213, 221
  in creation, 53, 69, 111, 248–49, 252,
      254, 272–73

of the saints, 240
sharing God's, 160–61
woman as man's, 257, 264
veiled, 128, 153
Goethe, Johann Wolfgang von, 40, 97
Great Divorce, The, 18, 19, 178, 209–42,
      263, 273
Gresham, Joy. *See* Davidman, Joy
      (Gresham)
Grief Observed, A, 21, 22
guide(s)
  Lewis as, 16, 19–20, 38
  and pilgrim characters, 18
    in *Chronicles*, 64
    in *Divorce*, 222–23, 230
    in *Faces*, 170, 172
    in *Hideous*, 290, 194
    in *Regress*, 114
  See also Beatrice (*Divine Comedy*)

hades
  Jesus' descent to, 117, 163, 170, 235, 245
  Psyche's descent to, 137
  rescue from, 43
  See also hell
Haldane, J. B. S., 83
headship. *See* hierarchy. *See also* Father,
      the: headship of
heaven
  Blake on, 217–18
  and earth, 220, 237, 249
  and hell, 209–11, 219, 226, 234, 242
  reality of, 209, 220
Hegelianism, 113
hell
  in *Apocalypse of Peter*, 216–17
  Blake on, 217–18
  as choice, 188, 209, 212, 226, 233
  in *Divorce*, 233–35
  and heaven (*see* heaven: and hell)
  Jesus' descent to (*see* hades: Jesus'
      descent to)
  and judgment, 185–89